FLIGHT RISK

FLIGHT RISK

Memoirs of a New Orleans Bad Boy

JAMES NOLAN

University Press of Mississippi • Jackson

WILLIE MORRIS BOOKS IN MEMOIR AND BIOGRAPHY

www.upress.state.ms.us

Designed by Peter D. Halverson

Title page illustration from cover painting, *Perch III,* by Steven Kenny
www.stevenkenny.com

The University Press of Mississippi is a member of the Association
of American University Presses.

Along with the details, the events narrated in these pages are accurate to the best of the author's memory or true to the memories of the family members who first related these stories to him. The first names of two people portrayed here have been changed to protect their privacy. Others have been referred to by first names only or are not named at all.

All photographs courtesy of the author

First printing 2017

∞

Library of Congress Cataloging-in-Publication Data available

CLOTH	978-1-4968-1127-1
EPUB SINGLE	978-1-4968-1128-8
EPUB INST.	978-1-4968-1129-5
PDF SINGLE	978-1-4968-1130-1
PDF INST.	978-1-4968-1131-8

British Library Cataloging-in-Publication Data available

For my lifelong friend Father Ulysses,
who has seen the first and the last

My life has been incredible. I don't believe a word of it.

—Madame Du Barry

Time: He's waiting in the wings
He speaks of senseless things
His script is you and me, boy

—David Bowie, "Time"

(New Orleans, 1973)

CONTENTS

I. RUNNING EVER SINCE

I was born by the river in a little tent
Oh, and just like that river running I've been running ever since . . .
—Sam Cooke, "A Change Is Gonna Come"

SIXTY-EIGHT

It didn't look like I would be going to New York City that winter after all. Neither would I be heading back to college in St. Petersburg, Florida. The Greyhound bus fare that my girlfriend Joylynn had wired me to escape over the Louisiana state line was waiting at American Express, but I wouldn't be claiming it anytime soon. As I lay on the bed in the darkened ward, on the other side of barred windows the night sky over Uptown New Orleans crackled with fireworks. It was New Year's Eve 1967, and bombs were exploding in Viet Nam. Both in Southeast Asia and within my own family, we were at war.

The world was on fire.

At that moment, I should have been on my way to a poetry reading by Allen Ginsberg, walking down St. Mark's Place dressed in an Afghani sheepskin coat, huddled arm-in-arm with Joylynn like Bob Dylan on his *Freewheelin'* album cover. Joylynn's Buffy Sainte-Marie–like mane of straight Indian hair would be whipping in a gust of winter wind, and smelling of patchouli, we would be sharing hot fish-and-chips wrapped in a cone of newspaper. Or perhaps I should have been with the other angry *soisant-huitards*—the student generation of '68, as they later became known—as they made love in the corridors of the Sorbonne and prepared to take over the university that May. Or with Dr. King in Memphis, singing "We Shall Not Be Moved." Or back in San Francisco, where I'd visited last July during the Summer of Love, climbing Union Street through a chill fog, on the way from the basement of City Lights Bookstore to the literary discussion group at Gavin Arthur's house. Or, at the very least, I should have been with my friends in the French Quarter, dancing in the raucous third bar of La Casa de los Marinos on Decatur Street, raising a Dixie beer to toast in the year that would tear the globe apart.

Instead, on the eve of the revolution, I was on Rosary Three, the "acutely disturbed" ward of St. Vincent DePaul, a mental hospital run by the Daughters of Charity. Originally founded as the Louisiana Retreat for the Insane, it was a forbiddingly gothic brick building straight out of a Dickens novel. That evening, as far as I could tell, I wasn't disturbed, acutely or otherwise, or not until the old man in the bed next to mine tried to commit suicide by ramming a sharpened pencil up his nose. After the orderlies cleaned up the blood and buckled him down with leather restraints, he spent the rest of the evening bucking in his harness, whimpering like a wounded hound. Inside, I was also bucking in harness, but my drained pallor probably read more as shell-shocked. I felt betrayed by the very people who had brought me into the world.

How could my parents do this to me?

On the other side of the window, passersby on Henry Clay Avenue shouted "Happy New Year!" to each other as firecrackers popped in the distance like the approaching Tet Offensive. My teeth clenched every time I thought about the war, to which thousands of young men my age were being shipped off every month to slaughter people they didn't know, and to be killed by them. I would have moved to Canada or shot off my little toe or become a conscientious objector before letting that happen to me. The night before, in the basement room where I slept at my grandparents' house on South Clark Street, I'd been writing a fiery poem denouncing the war. The smudged page was now packed among other papers, along with a few pairs of jeans and army surplus shirts, in the vinyl valise I rescued from the basement before the cops nabbed me. That had been my fatal flaw: the poetry manuscripts for which I returned home. Otherwise, I would have made it to American Express, picked up Joylynn's ticket money, and snuck out of the state on a bus.

I would be free.

I berated myself: what a dumb decision. All for a few poems. But maybe I wanted to be caught, caged like Ezra Pound in Pisa after the war. Perhaps being committed to a mental hospital validated me as a poet like Robert Lowell and Sylvia Plath and Anne Sexton and Allen Ginsberg, all of the tortured souls that I was reading. No, I decided, it would have proven my mettle more to go to New York and read my poetry to the audiences at St. Mark's-on-the-Bowery. That was where I'd been heading, to the bohemian literary life I yearned for with every fiber of my pale, skinny body.

The deal had been this: I was to audit classes at New York University while I expanded my term paper on radical new fiction—the French *nouveau roman*, Beckett, Burroughs, Pynchon and other American post-modernists, although that term had yet to be invented—into a book. My mind was percolating with ideas. This was a semester of independent study I'd cooked up on my own, one that I called "Junior-Year-Abroad-at-Home," because I hadn't been able to afford to study at a European university that year. My professors at Florida Presbyterian College, whose innovative program was inspired by Antioch College, had approved my project enthusiastically. As a minor, all I needed was for my mother to sign the papers authorizing me to receive my scholarship money in New York.

But she would do so only on one condition: that I talked to her psychiatrist. Dr. Kyle Hamm taught experimental psychiatry at Tulane University and was an expert on adolescent schizophrenia. He would make the decision, although I'm sure that he had already made up his mind long before I showed up at his office.

"I know what you're really going up there for," my mother told me the day after an unusually tense Christmas. "To take drugs and hobnob with Communists. That beatnik college has destroyed your values."

The previous morning, while my father had been driving us to the lavish Christmas spread that his sister put on every year in Metairie, he warned me that I shouldn't talk to anyone.

"Not talk to anyone at Christmas?" Here we go, I thought. My hand grabbed the inside handle of the car door. I had put on a tie and plastered down my unruly hair. What more did they want?

"About your crazy ideas. What you said last year about napalming babies really upset your Aunt Genie."

I told him to stop the car, then jumped out in the middle of traffic on Jefferson Highway and caught the pokey Kenner Local bus back to my grandparents' house. I had Christmas dinner with them at my aunts' run-down Creole plantation house on Bayou Road. The Chauffe sisters were still recovering from World War I, and there nobody cared a hoot what I said about Vietnam. All over seventy, they barely spoke English, and were too busy yakking about food and people who had died long before I was born.

At the time, my long blond hair curled over my back collar—later it would creep down to the middle of my back—and according to my starched-shirt father, I dressed like a "hick." My parents found out that I had been arrested at a civil rights demonstration during a garbage strike in St. Petersburg, after which I spent the night in jail with several of my professors and the striking black garbagemen, and that I had organized a college march against the war. The dean called them to report that I had attended an off-campus "pot party." An older poet—John Foret must have been thirty-five at the time—was hanging around the campus, turning us on to LSD. John, an on-the-road friend of Jerry Jeff Walker and Gypsy Lou Webb from the Golden Triangle of the New York/San Francisco/New Orleans circuit, was a devotee of Aleister Crowley, and told me he was a Satanist. That, of course, thrilled me.

On the other hand, I was a straight-honors student on full scholarship, one who had begun to publish his writing, and figured that my mind was my own to blow. I was following Arthur Rimbaud's invitation for the young poet to "*dérégler tous les sens*," Aldous Huxley's advice to "cleanse the doors of perception." I'm not sure how my mother found out about the protest marches or the Satanist poet or the LSD, but I really didn't understand what she was so worked up about. After all, every other nineteen-year-old in the country was busy doing "our thing." From Davy Crockett coonskin caps to acid trips to 401(k)s, that has been the synchronistic curse of our massive generation.

Once in New York, my mother envisioned me running the streets wild on dope, protesting everything she held sacred like those long-haired kids on the TV news. I entertained quite a different fantasy, and saw myself having an intense conversation about the new aesthetics with Susan Sontag, smoking cigarettes over espressos in her West Village kitchen. Why couldn't Susan Sontag have been my mother? Why did I have to be born into the most ignorant backwater in the country, with its racial turmoil and police brutality and corrupt politics and nineteenth-century manners? I intended to split this jailhouse as soon as I could, to "shun that house in New Orleans they call the Rising Sun."

So on the afternoon of New Year's Eve, after lunch at my grandparents' house on South Clark Street, where I had lived since I was sixteen, my mother and I took the streetcar to Dr. Hamm's office on Napoleon Avenue near St. Charles. My mother conferred with him for an hour while I waited in the reception area, engrossed by the centipede crawling across the wall in Alain Robbe-Grillet's novel *Jealousy*. Finally I was called in.

I intended to dispense with this hassle pronto.

Dr. Hamm didn't rise to greet me when I entered the office. I reached down to shake his hand as he was lifting his prosthetic right leg to cross it over the left knee. He winced as the metal joint squeaked and I plopped down into a chair, seething with resentment. The one-legged psychiatrist was square-jawed and Germanic, with a snub nose and beady eyes, the face of an Alabama farm boy. Because of his name, Dr. Hamm reminded me of a pink piglet, that is, when he wasn't calling to mind Samuel Beckett's protagonist Hamm from *Endgame*.

He asked me what the heck I planned to do up there in New York City, shaking his head and leaning forward with a smirk, as if I were expected to tell him a dirty joke. He probably assumed that I was going to spill my boyish guts about crash pads and balling chicks and dropping tabs, but instead, knowing he was a college professor, I laid it on thick, real thick. That was the one thing I knew how to do, impress college professors. While he sat observing me through steepled fingers, I rattled on breathlessly about how the medium was the message that had reconfigured our consciousness in this McLuhanesque age; how contemporary fiction was reflecting this new phenomenological mode of fragmented perception with the boundaries between characters dissolving; how chronology was warping to fit the time bends of an Einsteinian universe; and how our loss of faith in the objective authority of a supreme narrator reflected the death of God.

Take that, I thought. Maybe this professor would be so impressed by my radical theories that he'd invite me to deliver a paper at Tulane. Then my mother would have to eat crow.

"I see," he said, once again lifting the creaking prosthetic ankle over his good knee. "Are you ever afraid *you* are dissolving?"

"The whole cosmos is a 'Heraclitean fire,'" I said, quoting the poet Gerard Manley Hopkins. "Everything is in flux." I assumed that would end the conversation. I'd demonstrated that I was smart. Smart people weren't crazy, were they?

"Tell you what, I think you need to stay here in New Orleans and see me three times a week."

"You've got to be kidding," I snorted. Who did this crippled piglet think he was?

"Your mother and I wouldn't want you to go to New York and have a breakdown."

"Neither is going to happen," I said, leaping up, "me staying in New Orleans or having a breakdown in New York." Unlike most nineteen-year-olds, I knew exactly what I was doing, or thought so at the time.

"Then we'll have to put you in the hospital."

I laughed out loud. "Who do you think I am, Ezra Pound?" That was the most absurd thing I'd ever heard, like the plot of some gothic novel. Wait till they heard about this in New York.

At that point my mother walked back into the room, and Dr. Hamm shot her a complicit look of concern. "The doctor thinks," she said, "that in your condition you need—"

"What the hell is going on here?" I demanded.

I was surrounded.

Dr. Hamm picked up the telephone to call the coroner's office. I listened just long enough to understand that he was arranging my commitment. I bolted from the office, ran down the stairs and onto Napoleon Avenue. At the corner of St. Charles I spotted a phone booth. I dug into the pocket of my jeans, where all I could come up with was a handful of change and a few crumpled dollar bills. My mind was racing. I knew that in New Orleans the coroner could commit people without a court appearance, but figured that the police jurisdiction to enact the commitment ended at the state line. I dropped a nickel, collect, to Joylynn in Ft. Lauderdale, who was home with her parents for the holidays.

"What a horror show!" I gasped, shaking my shaggy head in disbelief. "My mother's creepy doctor is going to commit me to the loony bin. I need to get out of the state fast. Please wire me twenty-five dollars care of the downtown office of American Express so I can take the bus back to St. Pete. And meet me on campus tomorrow night, if you can."

It would take several hours for the wire to go through, so I decided to stop by my grandparents' house on South Clark Street to collect my manuscripts and a change of clothes. When I arrived, Mémère, my mother's mother, was sitting in her cane-backed rocking chair in the parlor reading the *Times-Picayune*.

"What are your plans for New Year's Eve?" she asked. "Do you want an artichoke?"

"*Pas parler maintenant*," I shot back in the kitchen French she was teaching me. Adrenaline pumping, I sped downstairs into the cold, dank basement, threw my papers into the vinyl valise with which I'd traveled home, and then raced out of the side door into the narrow alley between the raised shotgun houses.

Hands resting on their holstered guns, two policemen were walking up the alley as I was scurrying down it, clutching to my stomach the valise filled with poems.

"You must be Jimmy," one of the cops drawled in syrupy tones. "Come with us, young fellah, and everything will be all right."

"Where are you taking me?" In a panic I glanced up and down the alley.

"They say you been sick and need to go to the hospital." The cop grabbed me by the elbow and yanked.

They dragged me out of the alley and toward the squad car parked in front of the house. Mémère was standing on the front porch, wringing her hands around a dish towel, tears streaming down her face. She caught my eye as they were shoving me into the back seat of the car. I felt so sorry for her, having to witness this. After his death, her teenage son Jimmy's mangled bicycle had been delivered home in a police car. Now she must think his namesake was a common criminal.

"Hear you a college boy now," said one of the cops, turning around to face me, a smarmy smile pasted on his luncheon-meat face. "Where you go to high school, son?"

"Ben Franklin," I said, bracing for the response. Franklin was the nerdy college-preparatory public high school popularly associated with Jews, sissies, and civil rights activists.

"Figures," the cop said, swinging his big belly back around.

We rode without speaking until we reached the looming iron gates of St. Vincent DePaul Hospital, where orderlies rushed out to escort me to the third floor, the acute ward called Rosary Three, still clutching the vinyl valise of poems to my stomach. In some memories of this moment—one that sliced my life like no other into a clear *before* and *after*—the cops turned on their siren and flashing red lights as we sped through the violet twilight of the last day of 1967. During those final moments of childhood, I studied the menacing city of my birth through the grimy squad-car window, saying goodbye to the boy I was leaving behind.

W hack her ball," barked Miss Hinds, the head psychiatric nurse. "Knock Gretchen out of the way."

We were playing croquet on the hospital lawn, part of the recreational therapy that would turn us into well-adjusted human beings. When I found out that Miss Hinds was a Unitarian, I loaned her the copy of Ken Kesey's *One Flew over the Cuckoo's Nest* that my professor Dr. Carter had sent me in a care package. "A good read," she told me later, returning the book, "but you've got to admit Randle McMurphy is crazy." Now she was trying to teach us what was sane.

"But I can just as easily go around Gretchen's ball," I protested, angling my mallet to take a slant shot through the wicket. "Why would I want to hit her?"

"So she won't win," Miss Hinds said, "and you will!"

"But if I can get where I'm going without bothering somebody else—"

"That's not how you play the game," our Nurse Ratchet insisted.

"We're playing *love* croquet," Gretchen explained to her. "Nonconfron-tational, harmonious. . . ."

"You'll never win that way," Miss Hinds said.

"We don't want to win," Gretchen said, shaking her untamed mane of hair and stomping her foot.

"Then why are you playing the game?"

"Because you're making us," Gretchen said. "I'd just as soon be reading T. S. Eliot."

I had met Gretchen Hirt during my first few days on the ward. She was my age and had been reading *The Waste Land and Other Poems*, so we hit it off right away. The musician Al Hirt's daughter had been a rising starlet in Hollywood, but something happened—she never told me what—and her family had shipped her home directly to Rosary Three. We read "The Love Song of J. Alfred Prufrock" aloud to each other. Gretchen didn't want to play their stupid reindeer games any more than I did, and seemed no loonier than I was. Both budding artists, together we tried to figure out what we were doing among the manic screamers, saucer-eyed catatonics, schizoid babblers, drug-addicted nurses, society-dame alcoholics, and failed suicides.

This was what we came up with: *We're here because we're crazy and we're crazy because we're here.* To stay sane, we would skip up and down the corridor, holding hands and singing our *Alice-in-Wonderland* jingle. Which in itself must have seemed pretty nuts, although we thought it was hilarious. What most disturbed us was the possibility that our sanity was a delusion and we were, in fact, as bonkers as they claimed.

And that we'd never get out of there.

Whenever I tried to convince the Unitarian Miss Hinds that I wasn't mentally ill but that my family had committed me for my ideas, I would get a knowing look: *they all say that.* Evidently the most telling symptom of being crazy was insisting that you weren't. The only person who didn't believe I was mad was the patient down the hall who accused me of being an undercover psychiatrist planted on the ward to spy on her thoughts.

Gretchen dreamed of returning to her acting career at the Gallery Circle Theater in the French Quarter. Now that the Junior-Year-Abroad-at-Home plan was squashed, I wanted nothing more than to get back to my classes. Gretchen's plan was to sweet-talk her daddy, who was paying for the private room in which she sat on a satin-quilted peach bedspread in a matching satin-quilted robe. My own plan was hatched when Joylynn took the bus from Florida to New Orleans, checked into a cheap motel on Tulane Avenue, and I snuck her in as my cousin.

"I spoke to the American Civil Liberties Union," she told me, smoothing the wrinkles out of her paisley mini-dress after the long bus trip. "They've been looking for a test case for these coroner commitments, and think you could be it. I can't believe how crooked Louisiana is. I brought the lawyer some letters our professors wrote about what a stable, hard-working student you are. The only other idea is that Dr. Carter said he would adopt you. But the lawyer said you can't just adopt somebody else's kid out from under them. Bummer."

While I waited for the A.C.L.U. lawyer's visit, I was kicked out of the ward dorm. The other patients, including the old man who tried to kill himself by ramming the pencil up his nose, didn't want to share it with a hippie. I was considered a hippie because I fashioned a mobile out of multi-colored tissue paper that I hung from the lamp next to my bed. I

also read and wrote all day, and sometimes stared into the trippy kalei-
doscope that Joylynn had brought me, muttering *wow*.

Much to my relief, I was transferred to a padded cell.

In my own windowless tile cell stripped of its padding, I could read
and write well into the night, pretending that I was back at college. Every
evening I fell asleep clutching the patchwork pillow that the artist Jeanne
Meinke had stitched together and mailed to me from St. Petersburg.
Jeanne's husband, the poet Peter Meinke, was one of my professors, and
she had covered the pillow with squares of leftover fabric from shirts
she'd made for other faculty. She even enclosed a guide identifying the
swatches: this square was from Peter's shirt, that one from Eliot scholar
Dr. Carter's, another one from theater director James Carlson's, another
from literary critic Robert Detweiler's, another from artist Margaret
Rigg's. These weren't people who pitied or even just liked me, but those
teachers I admired who actually *believed* in me, as if I were some imaginary creature like Tinkerbell. Whenever I put my head to the pillow, I
could hear their distant clapping, better than any sleeping pill.

Yet Jeanne's patchwork pillow wasn't what Dr. Hamm had prescribed.
Twice a day patients had to line up at the nurses' station for their meds.
Mine was Thorazine, a powerful antipsychotic sedative that caused tics.
Rather than allow myself to be turned into another twitching ward vegetable drooling in the corridor, I stuck the Thorazines under my tongue
before I took a gulp of water and swallowed. I should have flushed the
pills down the toilet, but frugal hippie that I was, I stuffed them into a
sock in my clothes drawer, hoping that I could trade them on the street
for some pot or hash when I got out. Miss Hinds discovered my stash,
and assumed that I was saving them up to do myself in.

I was put on suicide watch, called Constant Visual Contact. The door
to my isolation cell was propped open, and chain-smoking black orderlies
were stationed outside to observe me. I found out they weren't being paid
much, and encouraged them to form a union and strike like the garbage
collectors in St. Petersburg with whom I'd spent the night in jail. That
bit of rabble-rousing got reported, and I was prohibited from speaking
to the only normal people on the ward.

Everything I did to preserve my humanity made me appear crazier.

Three days a week I braced myself. I could hear Dr. Hamm's aluminum crutch creaking down the corridor long before his Alabama farmboy face appeared grinning at my door. Sitting in my isolation cell, he accused me of withdrawing. I wasn't playing croquet right. I always had my nose in a book. I didn't "share inner feelings" during the screaming matches of group therapy. I was refusing medication and provoking the staff. Didn't I want to get better? The crippled piglet shook his head, at a loss about what to do with me.

Unless I improved, there was always shock therapy. Or he might have to transfer me to Seton, the ward for disturbed adolescents where the average stay was two to three years. I'd heard that life on Seton involved 24-hour-a-day group therapy, and that every time patients there used the toilet, they were required to invite someone of the same sex to accompany them. That would have cured my withdrawal. And Seton's buddy-up trips to the bathroom certainly would have discouraged me from exploring any homosexual proclivity, which I sometimes suspected was the real reason I was locked up. Dr. Hamm never broached this indelicate subject with me—and years later I would find out why.

My accountant father had a more down-to-earth idea. "Look, you've been perverted by *The Communist Manifesto*," he told me, "and if you don't come back to reality before the college's insurance runs out, we'll have to send you to Mandeville." The state-run mental hospital across Lake Pontchartrain at Mandeville was a notorious snake-pit from which few ever returned. But that gave me a clearer idea of why I was locked up in St. Vincent DePaul, which had less to do with *The Communist Manifesto* than with easy insurance money. The doctor and hospital were making out like capitalist bandits.

For people with good insurance, getting rid of a troublesome relative was a mere phone call away. Another convenient part of this system was that on Rosary Three, only relatives were allowed to visit patients, who were usually committed by their families. So one day my Seminole heroine Joylynn appeared holding hands with an A.C.L.U. lawyer, who was posing as my so-called cousin's husband. Together the three of us huddled inside my isolation cell, conspiring in whispers. The young lawyer's brow creased, studying me. To my relief, he finally observed that I didn't belong there. So he would file a writ of habeas corpus, which meant that I would be scheduled to appear before a magistrate. Then if the judge didn't release me on the spot, the lawyer would lodge a suit for involuntary detainment against the hospital, the doctor, and my parents. He explained that this would be a test case to challenge arbitrary coroner commitments in the state of Louisiana, and warned me not to get my hopes up. The outcome was dicey.

One evening later that week, I was sitting with Joylynn in the recreational therapy room as rain lashed the wall of barred windowpanes and a January storm blew outside. Suddenly my mother and great-aunt Marguerite filled the doorway, their hair spiked straight up in rigid wind-whipped peaks like the demons in a Chinese opera. Joylynn cowered, and I grabbed her hand. She was my first real girlfriend, and in spite of the surroundings, I was beaming as I introduced her.

"What's she doing here?" my mother asked, ignoring the introduction.

I let her have it. "Joylynn quit college during the second semester of her senior year, just before graduating, to stay in a motel on Tulane Avenue at her own expense to help me get through this. She loves and understands me and I'd be completely freaked out now if it weren't for her." I squeezed Joylynn's hand, hanging on for dear life. "That's what she's doing here."

My mother yanked a wad of photostats out of her purse. "Then I suppose this habeas corpus business is her doing."

My great-aunt Marguerite, obviously along for moral support, stared at the floor. This was not how her generation did things. Nobody in Reete's Creole family was ever put into what they called a "home," and children did not sue their parents. Pepère decided these matters at the kitchen table over bowls of gumbo.

"Those papers," I shouted, standing up to face my mother, "mean I'll finally get to appear before a judge before I can be plucked off the street and locked up in your wintry tower."

"Oh honey," my mother said with a grimace, "we were trying to spare you that. Do you have any idea what a *luuunacy* hearing is like?"

I shot her a determined look. "Guess I'll find out."

After they left, Joylynn's eyes widened in disbelief. "Does their hair always look like that?"

The next day I graduated downstairs, to Rosary Two.

My first visitor on the less restricted ward on the second floor was the Satanist poet, John Foret. He tagged along with my friend Lynn

Bultman, who came to see me as soon as she heard I'd been promoted from Acute. Dressed in flowing robes and draped with amulets, John, one of the most charming con men I've ever met, must have imagined himself a suitor like the French poet Verlaine. He brought the mad young Rimbaud a single red rose, which I never received. Lynn said that John traded my red rose for a dose of speed with a psych tech whom he chatted up along the way. As nuns floated along the breezeway in their sailboat wimples, John, Lynn, and I sat on the steps next to the building's cornerstone ("Louisiana Retreat for the Insane, Founded by the Daughters of Charity in 1862"), talking about what was going down in the French Quarter and concocting an elaborate escape scenario that involved a fake laundry truck, stolen uniforms, and me being smuggled out in a cart of soiled linens.

I couldn't wipe the smile off my face. If only for a moment, I was back in the life.

The real world was still out there, difficult as it was to imagine, and my first week on Rosary Two brought one piece of cheering news. As soon as I was committed, I'd dropped a line to my local draft board, which I was required to keep apprised of my whereabouts. On a sheet ripped from my poetry notebook, I scrawled this request: "Please change my permanent address from 421 South Clark St., New Orleans 19, La., to St. Vincent DePaul INSANE ASYLUM !!!, 602 Henry Clay Avenue, New Orleans 18, La. Thank you for your attention to this matter."

One month later, on Thursday, February 1, I received a new Selective Service System card in the mail. I was reclassified as 4-F, unfit for military duty. Standing at the nurses' station with my new draft card in hand, proudly incapable of invasion and slaughter, I flipped through the *Times-Picayune*. The newspaper reported that two days earlier, the bloody Tet Offensive had been launched, and yesterday Viet Cong soldiers attacked the U.S. Embassy in Saigon. American losses were heavy. Anybody in his right mind—and I still counted myself in this number—could see that Lyndon Johnson's demented game of dominos in Asia would end tragically. I cringed at the grisly photograph plastered across the front page of a Viet Cong officer being shot in the head by a South Vietnamese policeman, a photo that would become iconic to the antiwar movement. My heart sank wondering how many draftees had been blown to pieces in a Southeast Asian jungle on the same day that I got my 4-F reclassification.

I needed to get back to St. Petersburg, where I'd been counseling pro-
spective draftees to register as conscientious objectors to war, mostly by
reminding them that "girls say yes to boys who say no." But at least now
I wouldn't have to become a Jehovah's Witness or, almost as bad, shoot
off my little toe.

Even if I dropped out of college, my next stop would not be Vietnam.

My next stop, during this tricky new Year of the Monkey, turned out
to be the Audubon Park Zoo, where that week we patients were taken on
a field trip. For the first time in what felt like forever, I inhaled the deliri-
ously free air circulating on the street as guards marched us double-file
toward the zoo along sidewalks buckled by the thick roots of the stately
live oaks overhead. My exhilaration crashed as we stood in front of the
first cage. I wondered whose brilliant therapeutic ploy it had been to bring
incarcerated humans to stare through bars at caged animals. Zoo-goers
kept a wider berth from us than they did from the tigers and alligators,
holding their kids close as our ragtag column of inmates shuffled past. In
front of a mangy, depressed-looking lion's cage, a schizophrenic doubled
over the guard rail and puked up her popcorn. This seemed to set off
other patients, who began to act out, babbling, crying, and screaming.

Nurse Hinds took control as onlookers backed away from our bedlam.

As a chameleon of impressionable adolescence, unsure about who or
what I was, this was the first time I was trying on my new lunatic identity
in public. It occurred to me that at least half of being crazy was playing
crazy, meeting social expectations of what the mentally ill looked and
acted like. Shifting my gaze back and forth between the ratty caged lion
and my pallid fellow inmates, I also started to act out. I was overwhelmed
to the point of tears by what I saw.

I thought of a patient whom I knew only as Teacher-of-the-Year, one
who hadn't come with us to the zoo because it was her time of month. She
was a crisply suited professional woman who marched up and down the
corridor of Rosary Two every day carrying a briefcase, as if on her way to
an important meeting. Last year, they said, she had been voted "Teacher
of the Year" for the whole country, and she appeared undoubtedly sane.
Except when she had her period. Then, with alarming howls of pain, she
set fire to her pubic hair. During these savage episodes, she let everybody
within earshot know that her stepfather had raped her during childhood,
and that she intended to burn his seed out of her so she wouldn't have

his baby. The hospital was the only opt-out card she could play to escape from what I imagined were the impossible circumstances of her life. The shocker for me was that, committed or not, like most patients on the ward, *she wanted to be there*. Once I asked Teacher-of-the-Year if she would leave the hospital if she could, and curling her upper lip, she sneered that my question was "pseudo-intellectual."

Or even more disturbing: one evening I heard the familiar strains of "*Milord*" soaring from the recreational therapy room. A new patient, a balding man with stooped shoulders, was chain-smoking cigarettes and listening to my favorite Edith Piaf album on the portable phonograph. Here was somebody I could talk to, I decided, dropping into a nearby chair. It turned out that he was a psychiatric nurse at another hospital, one who checked himself into DePaul as a patient whenever he had a vacation. My mouth fell open in disbelief.

The most difficult aspect of the hospital for me to accept, even more than my own involuntary confinement, was that older people had been so maimed by life that they actually *wanted* to be there. They couldn't hack the jungle so they chose the zoo. If these were the casualties, what kind of upside-down world awaited me? For a variety of reasons I couldn't understand at the time, everyone on that ward needed to be there, the doctors and nurses as much as the inmates, to sustain their own gated subdivision of alternate reality. Despondent beyond words at my first experience in the outside world as a newly minted mental patient, I trudged back from our field trip to the zoo and called Joylynn at the motel on Tulane Avenue.

"I need to get out soon," I told her, "before I start thinking that I really need to be here."

"Any day now," she said. "The A.C.L.U. is still working on it. The lawyer says he has Dr. Hamm and your mother on the run."

As Mardi Gras approached and the first parades passed along St. Charles Avenue, a new patient appeared on Rosary Two, a heavily rouged elderly lady who called herself Eustacia Beauchaud. For the first week, she thought she was on a cruise ship and, red wig askew, would leave her private room dressed to the nines to strut up and down the corridor, waving to her glassy-eyed public like a debutante maid on a Carnival float. We soon found out the source of her high spirits. Every

few days a friend would send her an enormous flower arrangement or
fruit basket with bottles of Gordon's gin tucked into the bottoms. She
spoke with a refined country drawl, lived on a plantation in New Roads,
Louisiana, and was the former mayor Chep Morrison's aunt. Her real
name, I discovered years later, was Eustacia Doumanchaud, but we called
her Miss Beauchaud, which in French, she reminded us with a naughty
wink, meant "good and hot."

"I was at a family dinner at a long, long table," she told me, gesturing
the entire length of the ward corridor, "having one too many cocktails,
and my face fell smack down into a bowl of turtle soup. I almost drowned.
The next thing I knew, I woke up here. Someone had even packed me a
suitcase with all of my loveliest frocks. It took me a while to figure out
this wasn't the Caribbean cruise I'd signed up for," she said with a rueful
chuckle. "Face it, honey, the food here just isn't up to par."

It turned out that Eustacia Beauchaud not only sang but played bar-
relhouse piano. After dinner she would sashay into the recreational
therapy room trailing her motley retinue of inmates, where she would
entertain us at the old upright with her repertoire until the orderlies
jangled their key rings at Individual Lock Up Time. She wrote her own
lyrics, and my seasonal favorite, despite the circumstances, was one that
began: "We're just twenty-five minutes from Canal Street / Let's go see
the parade!" Most of her songs were preceded by a story, like the one
about the origins of "Lady Levee," the levee's answer to Old Man River.
Those lyrics had been commissioned by the novelist Frances Parkinson
Keyes for her novel *Dinner at Antoine's*. But before Miss Beauchaud
would launch into her famous song, she always informed us that Miss
Keyes was a real bitch.

"She came up to stay in New Roads to write some book or another,"
Miss Beauchaud would say, batting her false eyelashes, "and invited us
ladies to lunch. You know how we are, so I asked, 'Miss Keyes, is there
anything I can bring?' And she told me sandwiches. I said, 'Sandwiches?
How many do you mean, my dear?' She said, 'You know these ladies' dress
boxes from Maison Blanche? Fill up one of those.' Well, I never!"

As far as I was concerned, the hospital should have put this old dame,
deposited here periodically by her family to dry out, on payroll. She was
kick-ass alive, and did more for my spirits than the tense sessions with
Dr. Hamm, the hours of croquet, pottery, and group therapy, and certainly

more than the distressing field trip to the zoo. The other inmates and I applauded, joked, and even laughed. Occasionally Miss Beauchaud's audience became so rowdy that the night nurse on duty would stomp down the corridor to stand at the doorway, arms folded, frowning in disapproval. Just before we were locked up for the evening, Eustacia Beauchaud would end the performance with "Dixie." During the finale she raised her spindly, varicose-blue leg to the keyboard to pick out the notes with the spiked heel of her shoe. Then, strolling arm-in-arm, a black orderly would escort the old white lady to her room, high heels clicking down the empty corridor.

Finally Joylynn brought me an encouraging message from the A.C.L.U. Apparently the time limit was running out on the writ of habeas corpus, and my parents and Dr. Hamm were hesitant to involve themselves in an expensive court case. They were ready to negotiate. The deal they offered was this: I would be released into a halfway house for mental patients and juvenile offenders, which would provide me with limited mobility, if I agreed to sessions with the psychiatrist twice a week at his office until he felt that I was "making progress." My own condition, I countered, was that I would have to be out of the halfway house and into my own apartment within a week. We went back and forth on this. A month. Three weeks. Finally, when two weeks were agreed on, I felt victorious.

"Of course," I promised Joylynn, "any minute we can hop on a Greyhound bus and escape the state, back to college in St. Petersburg." But now it was the middle of the semester, I was no longer a registered student, and she had withdrawn two days after the drop deadline. Even though she had paid a full semester's tuition, she wouldn't be graduating. We could leave, but to where? "Now that it's time / Now that the hour hand has landed at the end," rasped the mournful voice of Nico on *Chelsea Girl*, a record I wore out on the hospital phonograph. "I want to know do I stay or do I go / And do I have to do just one. . . ."

"If I had my d'rathers," answered Eustacia Beauchaud, pounding her red-hot piano, "I'd d'rather be down in old Louisiana." For Fat Tuesday, the nurses were planning a Carnival ball on the ward. Miss Beauchaud had been elected queen, and we were supposed to costume.

"Who," Nurse Hinds asked me, "are you going to be?"

Good question. Who exactly was I going to be? A mental patient? A poet? A college student? A hippie?

On the Sunday afternoon before Mardi Gras, I stood staring out of the barred windows of the recreational therapy room at a pewter-gray February sky that hung over the gabled rooftops of the Victorian hospital compound. Most of the schools and churches in New Orleans were still segregated, and it was only within the past few years that whites and blacks could sit next to each other on streetcars or use the same restrooms. The city struck me as brutally backward, nowhere I wanted to call home. But from the window I could hear a crowd cheering and a band playing as Thoth, one of the day parades, came marching down Henry Clay Avenue, right in front of DePaul. Childhood instincts intact, I longed to be down there, my foot tapping on the curb, yelling "Throw me something, mister."

As the din from the parade trailed off down the street, I glanced around the hushed ward. Battered ping-pong paddles were piled with worn leather restraints on a chair next to the upright piano. The scuffed linoleum floor, littered with paper med cups, smelled of Pine-Sol and vomit, and beyond the pale amber light of the glassed-in nurses' station, somebody was crying her heart out.

Look at what this town has done to me, I told myself.

Just look.

I was released from St. Vincent DePaul on Mardi Gras morning, February 27, 1968. I stashed my vinyl valise filled with poems, books, and the patchwork pillow in my locker at the halfway house, signed out, and hightailed it with Joylynn to the French Quarter. Costumed as the lost waif that I was, I stood back from the madcap revelry, observing the supposedly sane world at a cautious distance from behind my John Lennon sunglasses, like Alan Bates in *King of Hearts*. I reconnected with my tribe of older bohemian friends and visited my high-school haunts: drinking at the Napoleon House, eating at Victor's, and dancing among the foreign sailors at La Casa de los Marinos and the Acropolis. Joylynn and I borrowed somebody's bed for an hour. Neither of us could stop crying, except when we burst out laughing. "We're here because we're crazy," I kept saying between hungry kisses, "and we're crazy because we're here."

Amid the drunken anarchy of the day, I learned that the city was in another kind of uproar. After a lengthy headline-grabbing investigation, Jim Garrison, the district attorney, finally had indicted a prominent businessman named Clay Shaw, along with a slew of local crackpots, for plotting the assassination of President Kennedy in Dallas five years earlier. The trial was set for that summer. Garrison maintained that every day "the involvement of high officials in the U.S. government becomes more apparent. The key to the whole case is through the looking glass. Black is white, white is black." These words, spoken by the man in charge of the civic order of the city, were there to welcome me back to reality as I stepped through the looking glass of the loony bin and out onto the street.

Somehow I survived two weeks in the halfway house, dutifully signing myself in and out, sitting tight-lipped in the corner during boisterous group therapy sessions. I'd never before known any real drug addicts or juvenile delinquents, and I was all ears for any useful tips on how to be a more spectacular fuck-up. Joylynn and I then rented a one-room attic apartment with a skylight and Juliet balcony at 929 Dumaine Street. The chipped woodwork was painted lavender, the kitchenette red, and the sloping floor black. The sink was backed up, the walls crawled with cockroaches, and I'd never felt so free in my life. In my first home as an adult, we made love on top of clothes hot from the dryer and cooked spaghetti whenever we felt hungry. In the distance the cathedral bells chimed from Jackson Square, and at sunset we would sit hand-in-hand in front of the dwarf balcony under the slanted ceiling decorated with a Theda Bara poster, watching the moon rise over the slate rooftops of the French Quarter. The lustrous tress of Joylynn's hair would be draped like a silky shawl around her bare shoulders, and one of our four scratchy records would be playing on the portable phonograph, usually Bob Dylan: "Tolling for the searching ones, on their speechless, seeking trail . . . / And for each unharmful, gentle soul misplaced inside a jail / And we gazed upon the chimes of freedom flashing."

I got a job pasting due-date flaps into the backs of books at the public library, and Joylynn worked at Lerner Dress Shop on Canal Street. John Foret, the Satanist poet, had moved on to the Haight-Ashbury to stay at the writer Irving Rosenthal's commune, but I did manage to reconnect with Gretchen Hirt, just released from the hospital, who was performing in the antiwar play *Viet Rock* at the Gallery Circle Theater. At the cast party, I found out that almost everyone else in the production had passed at one time or another through DePaul. Laughing, somebody told me that being committed to DePaul was a New Orleans rite of passage. I didn't want to belong to his exclusive Uptown club, and almost slugged the supercilious brat.

Often after work Joylynn and I hung out at Brocato's on Ursulines Street, a tiled Italian café where a blaring TV was mounted on the wall. It was there that, squinting up at the tiny screen from our ice-cream parlor chairs, we first heard of the My Lai massacre and the May student revolution in Paris. That was also where we witnessed the assassinations of both Martin Luther King and Robert Kennedy. We sat hunched over at our wobbly café table, trying to digest the numbing footage. Our government was unleashing unimaginable violence in Southeast Asia, and as Malcolm X said at the time, the "chickens are coming home to roost." That spring even Andy Warhol was shot, by an ex–mental patient from a feminist organization called S.C.U.M., the Society to Cut Up Men. It wasn't easy to make plans on such a treacherous battlefield. I wanted to publish the book of poems I was typing up; Joylynn dreamed of going to New York to audition for the new musical *Hair*. We settled for another cappuccino or a lemon ice. I still had to see Dr. Hamm twice a week, and was afraid that if I skipped a session, he'd have the cops pick me up and take me back to DePaul. The Greyhound bus station was only two blocks from the library on Tulane Avenue where I worked, but for some reason it took me months to get there.

Everywhere I looked, the world was in flames. My heart was a Molotov cocktail, and my mind a kerosene factory ready to pour every last drop that it distilled onto the towering conflagration around me. As far as I was concerned, everything couldn't burn quickly enough, including flags, Selective Service Centers, draft cards, university administration buildings, police cars on Parisian streets, ghettos, and bras. No matter how many times I blinked, wherever I looked I saw only charred ruins. I didn't have a shred of faith left in any form of authority, whether the government, military, law, education, church, family, or the worlds of medicine, science, or even letters, for that matter. Anyone in charge of anything struck me as a pathetic buffoon, not to be trusted. If what we were by then calling the counterculture hadn't already existed, I would have dreamed it up on the spot. I took as dead serious Bob Dylan's lyric "to live outside the law you must be honest," and identified myself as an outlaw, an underground gypsy ready to rob, scheme, scam, and sabotage a dishonorable society in which I wanted to play no part. I vowed to live a just life among children, poets, lovers, artists, clowns, revolutionaries, and my fellow madmen.

I tore up my draft card and the hospital release papers, then threw them in the trash.

Before I'd ever had a chance to join the world, I quit.

It wasn't until mid-June that I finally made it to the Greyhound bus station lugging my vinyl valise. My professors had gotten me a summer job teaching writing in the Upward Bound program at the college, and Joylynn would join me in St. Petersburg within the month. Dr. Hamm had finally sent me off with the less than mollifying words: "I've never treated anyone quite like you. Your head is more connected to your gut than I thought." As the bus swerved out of the station on Tulane Avenue, I studied the city through a lime-tinted window, trying to envision the future.

At the time I didn't know it, but the A.C.L.U. test case about coroner commitments would eventually be won—eight years later. I never could have conceived that within a few years I'd stumble upon Gretchen Hirt's name carved onto a marble plaque a few crypts down from my own family's tomb in St. Louis Cemetery Number Three. I had no idea that both my mother and sister would continue as Dr. Hamm's patients until he died of a heart attack in the late eighties. After my father's death, they'd quarrel over which one would schedule the first available appointment with their psychiatrist, whom by then I was calling "Dr. Rent-a-Dad." And never could I have imagined the drunken conversation that I'd have one evening far in the future with a radiologist named Russell Albright at his antebellum home on Royal Street, a mansion where slaves chained in the attic had been ritually tortured by their mistress, the sadistic Madame LaLaurie.

There Dr. Albright would confess to me that the great love of his life had been a married family man named Kyle Hamm, with whom he had an ongoing affair until the psychiatrist's death. As I spoke with the radiologist, my mind swarmed with the popular legends associated with his house, of Madame LaLaurie's "medical experiments" in the attic, during which she supposedly sliced off the top of a slave's head and stirred his brains with a spoon, or severed the arms and legs of another slave and reattached his limbs backwards, so that he resembled a crab. Was that what Dr. Hamm's "experimental psychiatry" had done to me, make me into a crab person, cut up and sewed back together all wrong? Did every New Orleans memory, if you waited long enough, turn into a macabre haunting? After talking with Dr. Albright, I ran out of the LaLaurie Mansion to sit on the curb in front, head between my legs, revisiting the horror of what had happened thirty years earlier.

You're here because you're crazy and you're crazy because you're here.

But now, on that bright June morning in 1968 when I finally made it out of the city in a Greyhound bus, it was the future that beckoned, not the past. At the moment I didn't know that I was also bisexual, or that in six years Wesleyan University Press would publish my first collection containing the DePaul poems, or that I would spend much of my life abroad, or that I would ever tell this story, one which for decades I tried to forget. I was nineteen years old, trembling with the newness of myself, and the violent year that would brand my generation for a lifetime was opening before me through a bus windshield with all of its hidden promise and unforeseen consequences. As the Greyhound wheezed along Tulane Avenue, I shoved the vinyl valise containing my jeans, patchwork pillow, and manuscripts under the seat, leaned back my head in relief, and yanked down the window shade, vowing never again to set foot inside the city of New Orleans. If only for a moment, barreling toward the future in a cloud of diesel exhaust, I thought I heard the chimes of freedom flashing.

THE UNSPOKEN

My life actually began eleven years before I was born, with an accident involving a hearse one Thanksgiving afternoon.

It was November 25, 1936, and after dinner at 2:00 p.m., a skinny, dark-complexioned teenager named James Lenow Partee burst through the rusty screen door onto the back gallery at 1454 North Galvez Street in the Faubourg Tremé. Late for his paper route, he grabbed the sturdy black bicycle with a deep wire basket and shouted goodbye to the family still seated around the dining room table sipping demitasses of coffee and chicory. Jimmy was a bright and sensitive sixteen-year-old, a senior who studied Latin, French, and Dramatic Arts at the all-boys Warren Easton High School on Canal Street. Like those plucky street-corner newspaper boys in Depression-era movies, he was ambitious and alert to any opportunity to get ahead. For him and his family, every penny counted. He had just joined The 23 Club—"Skidoo to Small Sales" was their motto—which fostered "Character, Service, Courtesy, and Manliness" among the young salesmen of *Liberty* magazine. In addition to peddling *Liberty*, he delivered door-to-door copies of the city's afternoon newspaper, the New Orleans *States*.

That was the same newspaper in which his obituary would appear the next day.

The sky was enameled a cobalt blue yet a winter chill already hung in the autumn air. Still hungry, Jimmy was looking forward to the free hot dogs at the Christian Endeavor weenie roast that evening near the Mississippi River Bridge. He was something of a rebel, and couldn't imagine what his life would be like without the Presbyterian church on Esplanade

Avenue that he and his kid sister Helen Alice had joined. Most of his family remained devout Catholics, but what could they say in protest against the Presbyterians? The church fed and chaperoned its young members, organizing a social life and summer camp for them, which was more than his family's austere churches, St. Augustine and St. Rose de Lima, had ever done. All of the kids in the neighborhood went to Third Presbyterian Church, even the Italian, Jewish, and Chinese ones. Catholic, Presbyterian, Jewish: Jimmy's family was all mixed up, but at home he never heard anyone breathe a cross word about anybody else's religion. Intolerance was an unaffordable luxury during the Depression, when it was in everyone's best interest to get along.

Although it was Thanksgiving, Jimmy hadn't had enough to eat at dinner, which was what his Creole family called the midday meal. This year there wasn't the traditional turkey stuffed with oyster dressing that he remembered from better times, before the crash in 1929, when they dined in style at his grandparents' grand house on Ursulines Avenue. Today his mother had roasted a chicken, which she served with rice and gravy. But the scrawny bird had to feed the nine people crammed into the five-room shotgun-double house: his mother and father, Olga and Lenow; his grandparents, whom he called Mémère and Pepère; his maiden aunt Marguerite; his twelve-year-old sister Helen Alice; the baby Doris Mae, who had turned three this month; and his four-year-old cousin Marie Terese Levis, whose mother had just died. Today he had only gotten a wing and thigh and, as usual, filled up on rice. But better days were around the corner. He could just feel it. His fifty-six-year-old father now had a part-time accounting job with the W.P.A., so they didn't have to scrape by only on his aunt Marguerite's measly paycheck as a parochial school teacher. For several years now, after Pepère lost Glaudot & Lévy, his tobacco shop in the French Quarter, his aunt's salary and his paper route had kept the family alive.

In looks, Jimmy took after his mother's side of the family with whom he lived, the Glaudots and Landrys, who were latté-hued, French-speaking Creoles with dark hair, Mediterranean eyes, and pronounced Alsatian chins. His sister Helen Alice was pale and sickly, with stringy brown hair and blue eyes magnified behind wire-rimmed glasses. She took after his father's side, the Partees and Lenows (originally Lenowitz), a prominent Memphis family of French and German-Polish-Jewish origins. Jimmy never saw much of the Partees, but when the family did visit New Orleans, they stayed in the luxurious Roosevelt Hotel and brought suitcases stuffed with gifts for everyone. Jimmy's father Lenow Partee had also been well off, living on investments until 1929. The sky had come tumbling down on Jimmy's head the year he turned ten, and now a shroud of hardscrabble poverty had descended upon the once prosperous family.

Jimmy had spent the morning pasting newly acquired first editions into his stamp album and reading the latest cover story in *Time* magazine, one celebrating Big Tony Grzebyk. He was amazed that the 300-pound Polish night-shift worker earned almost a dollar an hour making Plymouth automobiles in Detroit. That was where Mr. Levis, his orphaned baby cousin's father, came from, and maybe he would get there himself one day. There was real money in that town, and Jimmy wished some of it would find its way down to New Orleans. But now he was off to work, glad to be out of the stuffy house packed with finicky old people and whining kids.

He could feel the breeze through his hair as he pedaled his bicycle under the canopy of live oaks along Esplanade Avenue toward the Fair Grounds. The first day of horse-racing season was under way, and although he'd never been to a horse race—his mother didn't approve one bit of her husband's gaming habits—he knew that the annual Thanksgiving kick-off at the race track was a wild, boozy event. Now that Prohibition was over, the grandstand would be filled with tipsy ladies in cloche hats and gentlemen in double-breasted suits with pocket flasks. His paper route was toward the rear of the track, along Gentilly Avenue. Freshly printed copies of the *States* bounced in the wire basket as his bike tires bumped through weedy potholes along the side streets paved with crushed oyster shells.

After he finished his delivery, he could meet up with his friends Leon Trice and Putt-Putt and then the three pals would head to the Christian Endeavor weenie roast on the levee. Taped to the armoire mirror in his parents' room was a photo of the three of them that Leon's father, a society portrait photographer, had taken on a French Quarter balcony last Mardi Gras. All three boys were dressed up as women in their mothers' clothes, the only costumes they could scrounge up. Jimmy was wearing a ruffled silk flapper dress from the twenties, with white stockings and clunky boy's shoes. One hand was on his hip, the other thrown over Leon's shoulder.

Every time Jimmy looked at the photo, he chuckled, wondering what in the dickens he could dig up to wear this Mardi Gras, now that he'd grown too big to fit in his mother's dresses.

Jimmy brushed a swath of hair from his forehead and stuffed the tie he had worn during Thanksgiving dinner into the back pocket of his corduroys. Peeling a newspaper off the stack in the basket, he rolled it up and tossed it toward the stoop of a Creole cottage. *Whack!* Direct hit. Then another newspaper. *Whack!* Five more blocks and he'd be home free. He wondered what Leon and Putt-Putt were doing now, and could already smell the campfire smoke on the levee and taste those roasted hot dogs.

From out of nowhere, a long black hearse swayed around the corner on Aubrey Street. With squealing tires, the vehicle swerved from one side of the road to the other. Gerard Schoen, the fair-haired, thirty-year-old son of a local mortuary family, had had too much to drink at Thanksgiving dinner, and was now trying to make it to the Fair Grounds for the third race, on which he'd bet heavily. The hearse was the only car available, so he'd hopped into it in front of the funeral home on Canal Street. Now if he just stepped on the gas, he could make it to the racetrack entrance before the starting gun. He shifted into third, and just at that moment, the white shirt of a dark boy on a bicycle flashed to the right. As he sped past, a dull thud sounded along the side of the car, just under the gold lettering that spelled out "Schoen Funeral Home." He slammed on the brakes but it was too late. The bicycle was crumpled under the rear wheel, and next to it, still gripping a rolled up copy of the *States*, the teenager lay twisted on his side, blood oozing from his head through the oyster shells paving Gentilly Avenue.

Dazed and hiccupping, Gerard Schoen picked up the boy, placed him on the front seat of the hearse, and delivered him to Hôtel Dieu Hospital. The next day, another name would be inserted at the last minute into the funeral roster at Schoen Funeral Home on Canal Street: *James Lenow Partee.*

From what my mother told me years later, her brother's funeral was free.

That was the fateful day I was conceived in the mind of Helen Alice Partee, although it would take her eleven years to produce another

Jimmy. The memory of that Thanksgiving afternoon would plague her with self-recriminations, even when her son Jimmy sat at his own desk, pasting first editions into her brother's stamp album. It was as if a magician had snapped his fingers and—*poof*—her protector and hero, her older brother, had disappeared into thin air. And it was somehow her fault. The last time she saw him alive was over chicken and rice at the dining room table. Then he jumped up and raced through the rusty screen door in the kitchen that led onto the back gallery.

"So long," he yelled. The rusty chain of his bicycle creaked down the narrow alley that separated their peeling shotgun house from the one next door.

She wasn't able to speak with him before. . . . My mother never had the chance to tell her brother goodbye.

She picked up his plate at the table along with the others. Then she collected his rose-colored tumbler made of cheap rippled glass—years later they would call it Depression glass—and stacked it with the other dishes in the sink. Every plate was gobbled clean, so they wouldn't be hard to wash, but her mother never let her do that.

"Out of my kitchen," said her mother, Olga, drying her hands on a flowered apron. "Where are you off to?"

"To the show," Helen Alice said. "At the Loew's State."

"And where did you get the money?"

"Pepère gave it to me." At seventy-two, Auguste Glaudot doted on his first granddaughter, even though she refused to learn French and had run off to join the Presbyterians.

Helen Alice had already put on one of her two good dresses, and now was fastening her hair back with a lavender barrette. She and her best friend from McDonogh, Wanda Siegel, were going to see the new Busby Berkeley movie on Canal Street. It was a double feature—she forgot what the other movie was, but hoped it was one with Lauren Bacall or Bette Davis. The girls didn't have the money for the Desire streetcar, so they would walk the ten blocks, as they usually did, in the shade of the massive live oaks lining North Claiborne Avenue, the leisurely route everybody took from Esplanade to Canal Street. Both she and Wanda went to the Third Presbyterian Church, although Wanda's family was Jewish. Wanda was in love with the Chinese boy, Jackie Wong, whose family had the laundry on Esplanade. Helen Alice didn't understand what being in love was about, and wondered if it was like what she felt for her brother. Or for Jesus. Or for Pepère, who gave her the money to go to the movie palaces on Canal Street anytime she wanted.

It was in the middle of the first feature—a tap dance number—when Helen Alice spotted her aunt Marguerite walking up and down the aisle, scanning the faces in each row. Marguerite was wrapped in a black cloth coat, and with her tawny features and jerky movements, looked like a raven, scuttling up and down the dimly lit aisle. Helen Alice stood up, and her aunt strode over to her, scowling.

"Get your coat," she hissed. "We're going home."

"But the show's just getting started and—"

"There's been an accident. Tell your little friend goodbye."

Marguerite said nothing as she marched Helen Alice down murky Canal Street at dusk toward the Desire streetcar stop. She held her head high, and didn't look the girl in the eye. Her aunt was a strict third-grade teacher, and Helen Alice felt as if she were in detention. She must have done something terribly wrong to be punished so, yanked out of the show at the tap dance number.

Finally, when they were settled into the rattling streetcar, Marguerite stared into Helen Alice's face, brushing back a lank strand of hair hanging in front of her glasses. The lavender barrette had come undone in the hurried exit from the movie theater.

"Jimmy has gone home to God," her aunt said, choking back a sob.

"Why?" Helen Alice had no idea what that meant. Wasn't he supposed to go to the weenie roast?

"Because God loves him more than we do."

Then her aunt turned to face her own stony reflection in the darkened glass of the streetcar window. *Not more than me*, Helen Alice wanted to scream. *Didn't I love him enough?* But nothing more was said until they reached North Galvez Street. The police had tossed the crumpled bicycle onto the front gallery from their squad car, and none of the lights were on. The vanity and armoire mirrors were covered with sheets, and a single candle was lit on the dining room table, where only a few hours before Jimmy had sat gnawing on a chicken wing.

The next day, the *States* ran a two-column account of the accident, the sixty-first traffic fatality to be recorded in New Orleans that year. According to the article, "Schoen told police investigators that the youth

. . . rode his bicycle into his vehicle from behind a row of palm trees. The driver was released from custody after questioning by Rudolf F. Becker, Jr., an assistant district attorney . . . and further investigation of the fatal accident is to be made today to determine the feasibility of bringing charges in the criminal court." As the owners of one of the largest funeral homes in city, the Schoens were a wealthy and influential family. And at the height of the Depression, Jimmy's family could barely afford the next sack of rice, much less a funeral. Criminal charges were never brought against Gerard Schoen, and the next day James Partee's funeral took place at Schoen Funeral Home, after which he was buried in the Glaudot family tomb in St. Louis Cemetery Number Three on Esplanade Avenue, right next to the Fair Grounds, a few blocks from where he was killed.

They say that a deceased child dies twice when nobody speaks his name. Such was the family's shock that a steely reserve then buried Jimmy a second time, in the realm of the unspoken—the unspeakable— which is where I, the poet and writer, come in.

On the rare occasions that my family ever mentioned my uncle Jimmy, they always maintained that, in spite of what the police said, he was run over on his bicycle by a drunk driver. Yet the criminal's identity was never mentioned. I only learned who the driver was, and that the vehicle was a hearse, at my father's funeral in 1987. I was speaking with Jimmy's childhood friend from his church, a blind banker named Joe White.

"Did they ever catch the guy who killed my uncle?" I asked, staring into his round dark glasses.

"Catch him?" Joe White lifted his white cane and stepped back in disbelief. "His family runs this funeral home."

We were standing in the parlor at Schoen Funeral Home on Canal Street, where all of the family funerals I can remember have taken place.

When my mother was making the arrangements for my father's funeral, she had reminded the funeral director, Derrick Schoen, who she was.

"James Partee?" he said. "Of course I remember. Gerard didn't enter the business with us as he'd planned to, and, frankly, my brother has never gotten over what happened that Thanksgiving day."

Fifty years later, Helen Alice, dragged as a child from a Busby Berkeley film into a life of guilt and mourning, adjusted her glasses and looked the funeral director in the eye. "Neither have I, Mr. Schoen," my mother said, standing, "neither have I."

As garrulous as they may be about the weather, politics, Mardi Gras, food, or any other subject you care to bring up, Creoles are remarkably tight-lipped about family tragedies. My family always prized those who "had conversation"—what they called *répartie*—but there were certain subjects upon which a curtain of utter silence would drop, as final as after the last act of one of their beloved operas.

My mother told me that the day after Jimmy's funeral, as soon as his possessions were boxed up and stored in the wash shed, his name was never spoken again inside the house. It was as if he had never existed. It was as if there had always been only two kids, Helen Alice and Doris Mae, especially after Mr. Levis came to collect their cousin Marie Terese, who was then raised by her father's Jewish family in Detroit. If my mother mentioned her brother's name, the room froze and she was stared down, as if she'd just spoken a curse word.

Over the years, the boxes in the wash shed were never opened, even as they were hauled from one shotgun rental to another in downtown New Orleans. These sacks of inexpressible grief were lugged from wash shed to attic to closet, where they stayed buried, turning the whole house into a mausoleum. My mother was only able to acknowledge her brother's memory during the many visits the family made every year to the tomb in St. Louis Cemetery. She would stand there with gladiola blooms in hand and read what was plainly carved into the marble plaque that covered the mouth of the tomb: *James Lenow Partee, décédé le 25 novembre 1936 à l'age de 16 ans.* She read these words with a degree of relief: no, she wasn't going crazy. Her imaginary playmate was real, or had been real, confirming the power of the unspoken to mesmerize and take possession. The spectral boy with the mournful eyes whom she spotted in cobwebby corners, or seated at an unset place at the dining room table, or riding a bicycle through her dreams, continued to exist, if only for her alone.

The boxes stored in the wash sheds, attics, and closets were finally opened after I was born, when once again my mother was able to pronounce her brother's name. Blond and blue-eyed in his new incarnation, a flesh-and-blood boy named Jimmy stepped back into the room. The toys from the boxes may have been my dead uncle's, but he let me play. The silver baby cup that said "James." The arrowheads. The tattered red stamp album. The Boy Scout jackknife. The sketch books filled with decals of birds and angels. The musty volumes of Oz with the art nouveau illustrations. Somebody else was reading over my shoulder whenever I curled up with Frank Baum's *Tick Tock of Oz*.

My dark doppelgänger. My invisible twin. My phantasmal brother.

In the summers, I swam at the Lee Circle Y.M.C.A. because Jimmy had. I joined the Scouts because he did. I drew my loopy drawings because he was good at art, and later on, studied Latin because it was his best subject. Like Athena springing from the brow of Zeus, I wasn't so much born as I stepped fully formed from a stack of dusty boxes stored in the wash shed. As Freud said, "all things are tragic when the mother watches," and as my mother saw it, I would unconsciously mirror her brother's fate.

Exactly at age sixteen, she lost Jimmy again.

I left home.

That was the age when I moved in with my grandparents and great-aunt Marguerite on South Clark Street. I did this ostensibly so that I could continue attending Ben Franklin, a college-preparatory public high school in Orleans Parish, after my parents moved during white flight to Jefferson Parish. Actually, stuck in a circle of squat brick tract houses with no transportation except for a torpid suburban bus, I couldn't wait to return to the city, and lasted in River Ridge only an agonizing two months. Soon after I left, my mother started to see Dr. Hamm, the psychiatrist.

I, on the other hand, was in heaven. I felt like the young Rudolfo in *La Bohème* while typing up my first poems on Pepère's 1920s Royal typewriter in the student *garçonnière* that I fashioned in my grandparents' damp Mid-City basement. Although lying in my rollaway cot I stared up at a ceiling of exposed pipes, and at night had to lob shoes at the beaverboard paneling to quiet the rats scurrying around inside the walls, I had my own entrance and telephone extension. To my grandparents and aunt Marguerite, Jimmy returned home at age sixteen, as if he'd never left to deliver newspapers that fateful November afternoon. They must have considered it a miracle that one day I should appear at the kitchen table—a serious, artistic high school student—at the same age at which the first Jimmy was killed. Needless to say, nobody ever suggested I acquire a bicycle or a paper route.

"The first time something terrible happens," my mother told me while I was in high school, "you think what rotten luck. The second time the same thing happens, you think you're going crazy." Years later, this comment would put much of my early life in perspective, although at the time I had little idea what she was talking about.

In September of 1947, I had been delivered by a hurricane into grateful arms deformed by grief, born already haunted into a city filled with lingering spirits somehow more alive than the people they moved among. As best I could, I played my inherited role as the replacement son of tragedy, but my childhood wasn't an unhappy one. Yet at age sixteen, when I left my mother's house and began to explore who I—the other Jimmy—might be, all hell broke loose. That operatic conflict, during which a grieving little girl named Helen Alice finally came face to face with what she lost on that Thanksgiving afternoon in 1936, lasted until after I left St. Vincent DePaul Hospital, when for many years my footprints disappeared over the horizon.

Jimmy, as I was soon to discover, was born to leave, and never doubting this calling for a moment, I approached my destiny, vinyl valise in hand.

- 3 -

THE OLD COUNTRY

To this day, whenever a tropical storm approaches, I'm exhilarated as the sky darkens, the wind picks up, the pressure lowers, and a foreboding front of clouds rolls overhead, sinister as a line of Sherman tanks. It's as if the fat lady, the pregnant-looking one, is finally about to sing, and some aria of great consequence will soon unfold. Tree tops sway, claps of thunder reverberate in the distance, preliminary drops of rain patter against window panes, and the story—the one we've been waiting to hear—is about to begin.

Or, in any case, that was how mine began.

When the devastating hurricane of 1947 hit New Orleans, my parents were living in a second-floor apartment in the Tremé at 1202 North Galvez, corner of Governor Nicholls, a mere two blocks from Mémère, Pepère, and the rest of my mother's extended family. That was the village proximity at which newlywed Creole couples located at the time, around the corner from their parents, if not next door. Although in this era storms weren't given names, I had just received mine, not a brand-new one but my own, nonetheless. The hurricane and I were hatched at the same moment, September 3, the day when the storm developed off the west coast of Africa and I was delivered at a hospital called Hôtel Dieu, the same one in which the first Jimmy had died. The storm and I were both two weeks old when its eye crossed New Orleans on September 19. My mother always referred to the storm that brought me into the world as Hurricane James, and told me that I was born in the middle of it, an exaggeration on her part. Yet it must have seemed that way to her as she pronounced her brother's name for the first time in eleven years. James was no longer *décédé* on a marble slab in St. Louis Cemetery, but was now in the next room, howling in a crib.

My mother said that it was the most destructive storm that anyone in the city could remember. And here people only remember three things: storms, recipes, and family stories.

Mayor Chep Morrison claimed that the unannounced storm caused "the most serious flooding ever to hit New Orleans," unmatched until Hurricane Katrina in 2005. Higgins shallow-draft boats, manufactured locally for the war effort, rescued people from the lakefront, Gentilly, and the eastern part of the city. Three thousand people were crowded into the Municipal Auditorium, a few blocks from the Tremé apartment where I was having my first dreams. The wind howled at 112 mph, leaving downtown streets impassable, heaped with tree limbs and housing debris. The hurricane caused $100 million in damages, and was the twentieth deadliest storm to land in the United States during the century. In its aftermath, for the first time the federal government undertook the construction of hurricane protection levees along the south shore of Lake Pontchartrain to prevent future catastrophes. Almost sixty years later, many of these same levees would be the cause of the flooding that engulfed the city following Katrina.

What my mother called Hurricane James formed my initial impression of the world.

How exciting life must have seemed during those first few weeks: everyone shouting through open windows; people paddling down the inundated streets in boats; piles of splintered wood crashing down stairs; the incessant din of saws and hammers repairing the damage; the smells of waterlogged rot and mold-killing bleach; the soft glow of candles and kerosene lanterns illuminating the impenetrable darkness of the Tremé, as gumbo pots filled with drinking water boiled on the stove and fat flood mosquitoes buzzed over my crib. Years later, when I would arrive in the most forlorn villages in Asia or Latin America, I often recovered what seemed like some primordial memory: the sounds and smells of an impoverished community in survival mode. I immediately understood how this, too, could feel like home.

In the first photograph ever taken of me, shot by my father with his war-souvenir Leica, I'm sitting on my great-grandfather's knee on the side gallery of his shotgun house on North Galvez Street. We are seated before a background of peeling clapboards and rusty water pipes in the post-hurricane city. In the sharp black-and-white tones of the German camera, Auguste Glaudot's deeply lined face emerges Rembrandt-like from a shadow, studying the robust little creature in his lap. Alice Marie Landry, my great-grandmother, is hovering over us in her eternal flowered housedress, long white mane twisted up into a Gibson topknot, fussing with my jacket sleeve. Grande Mémère, as usual, is trying to be useful, while I imagine that Pepère is contemplating the future of the Glaudot family in the bobbing head of his male heir.

At the moment, his parents' native countries lie in ruins, invaded twice by the Germans during the past quarter century, and he must be pleased that during the family visit he made to Brussels and Paris in 1890, he reached the right decision. At age twenty-six, in the Creole tradition, his father had sent him on the grand tour to visit family, giving him the choice between settling in Europe or New Orleans. Harboring some misgivings, which he recorded in Franglish in the pocket-sized leather diary that I still have, he came home. But now, even the ruins of New Orleans after a hurricane must have been better than the bombed-out buildings in Brussels where his aunts, uncles, and cousins were living. "Over there," as the song went, the war had finally been won, and here was Pepére, bouncing a blond victory baby on his knee.

After four generations in the United States, there I was, pink-cheeked and blue-eyed, and with an Anglo surname: the first *real* American in the family.

Or so he probably thought.

A lmost every American story begins with exile, and decades later, I wasn't the first in the family to pull up roots and move across oceans.

Our own family story began in the winter of 1862, when Pepère's father, Auguste Glaudot Sr., a military man, slapped his commanding officer in Brussels. Born in 1830 in what was then the Netherlands, one year before Belgium's independence, this French-speaking Walloon was probably retaliating for an ethnic slur by a Flemish-speaker, and so had to get out of town quick. Taking flight, Monsieur Glaudot joined what was then the equivalent of the French Foreign Legion, a mercenary group called the "French Volunteers of the European Brigade of the Confederate Army." On March 1, 1862, he was commissioned as a captain in New

Orleans. "This Corps," his certificate of commission stipulates, is "required to serve only within the limits of the City of New Orleans, as per offer made to the Commander in Chief." In other words, these Francophone mercenaries were not invited to settle in the Confederacy, only to serve in New Orleans, and for more than a century my family kept their part of this bargain. Nobody left. The certificate, framed and hanging on my living room wall, was signed and sealed by Louisiana Governor Thomas O. Moore on March 26, and so my great-great-grandfather did, in fact, serve as a Confederate officer.

For exactly one month: just enough time to polish his new boots and admire the spectacle he made in the mirror dressed in a spiffy grey Confederate uniform. But the battle was lost before he even picked up a rifle.

I've no doubt that it was much to this Belgian gentleman's relief when New Orleans was occupied by the Union army on April 29, and his military duties were over before they began. Yet there he was, a foreign mercenary stranded in a port occupied by an enemy army, living among African slaves and Houma Indians in a steaming swamp, prohibited from regrouping with the Confederate army elsewhere. But at least he must have consoled himself that almost everyone here, no matter what their color, was normal—that is, they spoke French—and nobody would ever address him again in Flemish. A refugee from ethnic strife in Europe, what did he care about this North-South monkey business, which he barely understood? He was an immigrant businessman, and had no use for slaves.

Thus began my family's history in the New World, with a slap to authority over a question of political identity, echoing the same French-Flemish conflict that still rages today in the capital of the European Union.

Soon this disoriented Confederate-for-a-day would meet Marie-Josephe Dieudonné, a steely thirty-three-year-old French woman who had arrived in New Orleans nine years earlier. Newly formed Belgium wasn't the only region being torn apart by ethnic turmoil in mid-nineteenth-century Europe. The French Alsatians were bracing themselves for the encroaching "blood and iron" of Bismark's pan-Germanic unification campaign, and swore that, as they put it, they "would prefer to crawl on their knees to Le Havre rather than live under German rule." On March

1, 1853, Mademoiselle Dieudonné's ship from the port of Le Havre docked in New Orleans, and she was accompanied by her elderly aunt Marie, her cousins Adele and Catherine, with a four-year-old girl in tow. Raised in the Meurthe-et-Moselle province of Lorraine, Mlle. Dieudonné's father had been a farmer in the tiny village of Gogney (present population: sixty-five), and her mother was already forty when she was born, according to the ornate calligraphy on the framed birth certificate that hangs on another of my walls.

What drove a twenty-four-year-old French country girl also to take flight, packing a valise and moving halfway across the world to a tropical swamp? Of course, everyone knew that the Germans were coming, and within twenty years the Franco-Prussian War would subsume her region of France into Bismark's empire. It's possible that her parents died and her brother then inherited the farm, or that the agents pushing American immigration door-to-door in Lorraine during the 1850s convinced her widowed aunt to undertake the voyage with her unmarried daughters, and cousin Marie-Josephe decided to tag along. Perhaps the little girl with whom she was traveling, named Elise after her own mother Elisabeth, was her love child, and like her future husband, she had to get out of town quick. The 1850s also saw a massive migration of French Jews from Alsace-Lorraine to Louisiana, so it's possible that religious persecution had something to do with the family's decision to leave—Dieudonné, or gift of God, translates into Hebrew as the familiar name Natanyahu—and thus began the assimilated Jewish strain in my Southern family.

In 1863, during the middle of the Civil War, the farmer's daughter Marie-Josephe married the suddenly unemployed Confederate mercenary Auguste. This frugal country woman had saved a bit of money during her decade in New Orleans, so together they opened a grocery store. Later Auguste would go into partnership with Leon Lévy on a tobacco shop that imported cigars directly from Cuba. Glaudot & Lévy advertised "Havana and domestic cigars, smoking and chewing tobacco, snuff, Meerschaum pipes, and all kinds of smokers' articles." Perhaps for a while, as Creole merchants did at the time, the Glaudots lived in the apartment over their shop at 440 Chartres Street, corner of St. Louis, in a building known as Maspero's Exchange, a notorious auction house for slaves earlier in the century. In June of 1893, three months before my grandmother was born, they settled in a courtyard double maisonette at

825 Royal Street—the immigrant grandparents on one side, and their only son, his wife, and kids on the other—and also purchased the four shotgun houses facing the noisy street in front. I didn't know this in 2003, when I moved around the corner, no doubt lured to the spot by some ancestral magnetism.

In their portraits, both taken around this time at the Adams photographic studio at 111 Royal Street, Madame Glaudot appears as a severe, bony lady dressed in a ruffled black blouse closed at the throat with a cameo, and her husband as a corpulent businessman with a buzz-cut and bushy goatee, done up for the grand occasion in a bow tie, jacket, and vest. Her stare is penetrating and defiant, and his gaze is dazed and hungover, as if he'd just forgotten where he was or what he was about to say. I wouldn't be surprised if there were a turtle soup stain on his starched white shirt and a flask of cognac tucked into his jacket pocket, or if he'd spent the previous night at Lulu White's Mahogany Hall in Storyville. His expression is contrite; his wife's thin lips are pursed, unforgiving.

Neither ever learned a word of English. There in the Francophone enclave of the French Quarter, no doubt they felt relieved—*enough of that foolishness!*—that they would never be obligated to speak either Flemish or German. Both died in their late seventies, a few years before the Great War would ravage their mother countries, and are the original inhabitants of our family tomb in St. Louis Cemetery Number Three.

Their only child, Auguste, the great-grandfather I called Pepère, was born in 1864, inherited his father's tobacco business, and eventually became a state legislator, representing New Orleans Creoles in Baton Rouge. I'm now writing these words at his desk from the tobacco shop, seated in his favorite cane-backed captain's chair. The picture of Pepère on the North Galvez Street gallery amid the ruins of the 1947 hurricane is the last photograph ever taken of him.

And it's the first one of me.

By that time, the American century was almost half over, and the modern world Pepère both longed for and dreaded was now incarnate in my pudgy cheeks. Holding a first great-grandson in his lap, I imagine he's wondering how this crazy American adventure will eventually turn out.

As a small boy, I loved to play action figures with the plaster figurines from my great-grandparents' nativity scene set up under the Christmas tree: the *crèche*, as they called it. What sparked my imagination about these ornate, painted statues imported from France was that they weren't just the boring Holy Family of Mary, Joseph, and the baby Jesus—that nuclear family that fifties-era manger scenes were reduced to, much like the American family itself—but represented a wide cast of characters worthy of a Hollywood epic, displayed in a panorama around the infant. There were several kneeling shepherds accompanied by dogs and sheep; a donkey and a cow; the three crowned kings, one of them an African, in various stages of genuflection; a camel draped with a scarlet blanket over its hump and, my favorite, a black camel boy wearing a fez; and, of course, an angel with extended wings, which I used to swoop through the air over the beribboned presents. Until an adult yanked me to my feet, I would lie under the fragrant fir tree on my stomach, making up stories about these fascinating characters, introducing the camel boy waiting outside the stable to the Mother of God kneeling next to the crib:

Pleased to meet you, the Queen of Heaven would say. *Y'all like some iced tea?*

Thanks, Miss Mary, sure would appreciate that.

Now don't go waking up the baby Jesus, hear? I had to add a jigger of bourbon to his bottle to get him to sleep.

What rang true to me about the crèche was that it was so much like my own topsy-turvy family, one that included grandparents and great-grandparents, whiskery maiden aunts, tipsy uncles, double-chinned in-laws, cousins, and my mother's teenaged sister Doris, not to mention a black housekeeper who sometimes left *gris-gris* marked in chalk on the front steps. In the tribal Hebrew society of Jesus's day, of course, the nuclear family was unknown, as in most traditional cultures. The nuclear family was a product of the new prosperity and mobility of the postwar era, during a go-getting real-estate expansion that encouraged couples to free themselves from the network of extended families upon whom they previously depended for everything. The current crisis in "family values" doesn't spell the end of the nuclear family. On the contrary, this final phase of disintegration is the inevitable *result* of the nuclear family, the tail end of a generational experiment begun during the fifties that ended the family, as most people in history have known it. I grew up during this transition, in what the writer Wendell Berry calls "the great alteration that followed the war."

Our bustling Seventh Ward household at 2418 Columbus Street, with its slamming screen doors, was connected to another around the corner at 2275 Bayou Road, one consisting of five elderly great-aunts and -uncles who lived in the same house they were born in and who never married. The Chauffes maintained a large Creole plantation house long after they could afford to because Edna, one of the sisters, had gone raving mad and, as Lucille used to say, "back here nobody can hear her scream." They kept chicken and duck coops, drank water from a cistern, and, since they didn't know what a job was, ate their big meal at 1:00 p.m. Family dinners, at a long dining-room table crowded with platters and soup tureens, always involved any number of bachelor uncles and maiden aunts and long-lost cousins. Far from being open, however, the Creoles maintained a fortressed world, much like the Catalans among whom I would live years later in Barcelona. On the losing side of history, both Creoles and Catalans were a besieged class of shopkeepers scraping by behind the latched shutters of a provincial language and heritage, frugal at home but extravagant in public, proud people who spent every penny they pinched on high culture and keeping up appearances.

By Creole, I mean French people and their descendants born in Louisiana, sometimes but not always of mixed race. To narrow the definition, the term more clearly refers to that fast disappearing tribe of New Orleanians who maintained the French language and culture throughout the years. Unlike the men in the family, who needed to communicate in English with the American businessmen on the other side of the Canal Street "neutral ground," my grandmother, a third-generation American educated by French nuns at the Ursulines Convent, didn't learn English until 1909, when she was sixteen and moved away from the courtyard maisonette on Royal Street where she grew up. Years later, I'd occasionally spot Mémère at the living-room secretary squinting over her musty Cassell French-English dictionary (published in 1899), composing a yearly missive to her grandfather's family in Brussels, relatives she'd never met but with whom we continued to exchange wedding and funeral announcements over the past century. This stubborn attachment to origins somehow kept the phantasmal old country more alive than the new one in which we lived. In many ways, I was raised to think of myself as

French, a colonial delusion that disappeared during a first visit to Paris the minute I opened my mouth.

Creoles were incestuous both in friendship and marriage, and it has taken me a lifetime to figure out if and exactly how I might be related to that closed circle of people who passed through our parlor—the Jacquets, Davids, Gelpis, Bagurs, Laurents, Waguesbachs, Landrys, Chauffes, Manuels, Remys, and Abadies, to name a few. In my child's eye, they melded into one: dark ladies with operatic first names in rayon dresses, smelling of lavender sachet, always escorted by amusing gentlemen with Roman first names in rumpled linen, reeking of cigars and bourbon. Much as with the Spanish, who maintain a firewall between their private and public lives, everything I wanted to know about these people was decidedly none of my business. "*En fin,*" as Mémère would say whenever a topic of conversation jumped its prescribed boundaries. As if to make up for the doorless architecture of our shotgun houses, intimate lives were regulated by the sturdy interior walls of custom, manners, and discretion. Children were "to be seen and not heard," brides were unquestionably virgins, spinsters were "unclaimed jewels," disappeared men were "away at sea," Fridays meant fish, and Sunday was for Mass. Divorce was unheard of, what movie stars and rich people did in New York, a word with titillating sexual overtones. Later, when my sister and I were busy becoming the up-to-date kids we intended to be, we'd sometimes "play divorce," dividing her two-story tin dollhouse, the upstairs for me, the downstairs for her. After all, the dolls needed their privacy, that most modern of concepts.

By design, the shotgun houses in which we lived afforded no privacy, and so were well-suited to the expansive life of the extended family, in which a closed door was a rare commodity. Like train cars, each room opened into the next, without a hallway. By maneuvering a system of transoms, ceiling fans, window fans, and shutters, the rooms were easy to ventilate and keep cool during the sweltering summer months before air-conditioning. They say that you can aim the proverbial shotgun from the parlor front door and hit the kitchen back door without the bullet passing through a wall or door. I can only imagine how many drunks have tried this ballistic test, especially today in my old crime-ridden neighborhood, where these days residents are armed with real shotguns.

In those days nobody called it child care, just Mémère's. When I was a boy underfoot in the kitchen on Columbus Street, my great-aunt

Marguerite would say, "Go to the front gallery and see if you're there." I'd run through the dining room with the brand-new Frigidaire, down the short hall between the bathroom and side gallery (where the iceman used to make deliveries), through my great-grandmother's bedroom where the rosary droned on the radio, through my great-aunt's bedroom with a crucifix hanging over the single bed, through my grandparents' bedroom where Pawpaw was taking a nap, through my teenage aunt Doris's bedroom where she was listening to Elvis on the radio, through the parlor's pocket doors, and then swing open the creaky screen door onto the porch with its weathered rockers.

"Quick, come see," I'd shout from the front to the back of the shotgun house, "I'm there."

The values I absorbed from this family—more like a Chekov play than a fifties sitcom—were tolerance, cooperation, and inclusivity. I learned that you could marry or not, believe this or that, listen to Elvis or attend the opera, go crazy if there was a back room, but still you were family, with a permanent place at the table. Later, as the latchkey kid of a nuclear family living in the Broadmoor neighborhood, the values I learned were loneliness, conflict, and exclusivity. The next stage of this transition was my parents' inevitable move to the planetary suburbs during the white flight of the mid-sixties, at which point I dropped out of the nuclear family and moved back downtown with my grandparents and aunt Marguerite. By the time I was in college, everyone in the suburban nuclear family had their own cars, which my mother and sister drove to consult with Dr. Kyle Hamm about how lonely and lost they felt.

Those fifties family sitcoms that programmed this transition by way of our brand-new Motorola TV—*Father Knows Best* and *Leave It to Beaver*—are now reruns that haunt the cultural memory. Watching those black-and-white shows for the first time was when I first suspected there was something fundamentally wrong with the eccentric menagerie of our family. TV families made me feel poor and foreign, as if I were a Haitian eavesdropping on the distant family lives of Swedes or Germans. The perky Anglo-Saxon nests presented in these sitcoms—Mom, Dad, and the kids—were remarkable for those whom they excluded from the picture: in-laws, drunk uncles, crazy aunts, poor relations, the separated, unmarried, elderly, sick, and orphaned.

In the same way, the American nativity scene excludes the three kings and their camels, the shepherds and their flocks, all central as Mediterranean Christmas symbols. The wise men and shepherds, those family members marginalized by nuclear "family values," make up the support system that, in most countries, keeps the traditional family alive and independent of welfare, day care, and nursing homes. The public services necessary to replace the extended family and supplement the nuclear family—even if it were working—would bankrupt any government. Americans have become a nation of lone black sheep, and even in reruns of a fantasy golden age, we've lost the way home.

These days, I live alone in the densely peopled French Quarter, with its flowering balconies and courtyards, around the corner from the Royal Street house where my grandmother grew up, a block from the house at 915 Bourbon where my great-grandmother was raised, and four blocks from Pepére's tobacco shop on Chartres Street. Few families remain in the Quarter now, and even fewer family-run businesses. What my mother referred to as the *real* Tremé—the neighborhood of seventeenth-century Creole cottages surrounding Congo Square—was torn down in the eighties to build Louis Armstrong Park and, irony of ironies, the poured-concrete Mahalia Jackson "cultural center" that looks like an airport. Another monument to progress is the elevated freeway that runs along Claiborne Avenue through the heart of old downtown, blighting the once prosperous neighborhood for two blocks on either side of its looming cement shadow.

Sixties-era urban renewal got a late, halfhearted start in New Orleans, not because of any exaggerated reverence for the past but out of tropical lassitude. When it comes to preservation, sheer laziness has been our saving grace. But the truth remains that city leaders have always been ashamed of the city's charmingly dilapidated, racially hybrid downtown, and have repeatedly sponsored ill-conceived building projects to make the area over into somewhere resembling Dallas. The latest is the sprawling, plate-glass University Medical Center, whose construction leveled thirty-four entire blocks of an historic neighborhood. What little of downtown culture that has managed to survive these bulldozer assaults has now become an international marketing brand, the "authentic New Orleans" we sell to the world: jazz, gumbo, red beans, yat accents, shotgun houses, balconies, cemeteries, voodoo, ghost stories, second lines, and brass bands. We don't take anything local seriously until people from elsewhere are willing to buy it.

A big boy now, I no longer play action figures with the nativity scene, even though every Christmas I still set up my great-grandparents' crèche. As I unwrap each plaster figurine from its tissue paper—the angel and donkey, the shepherds and kings, the Queen of Heaven and the black camel boy (who are by now the best of friends)—I can still hear the tumultuous, bilingual hubbub in which I was raised. Like the Christmas diorama, this childhood now seems as far away as mythical Bethlehem, but the silent night is sometimes broken by a boy's footsteps echoing through the endless rooms of a Seventh Ward shotgun, investigating the difference between here and there.

I'm there, I want to shout from the front gallery to my aunt Marguerite, clanging pots and pans at the the other end of the house on Columbus Street.

Quick, come see. I'm still there.

4

PAPER SPARROWS AND THE BLACK SEXTON

The moment I became an artist was inspired by the chirping sparrows that built a nest in the crepe myrtle outside of our kitchen window. I was four, and we were living temporarily at 6228 Lafaye Street in a termite-ridden house on which my grandfather had just blown the last of his Memphis inheritance. My grandparents lived on the other side of the double, along with their daughter Doris, the first love of my life. I couldn't get enough of my aunt, especially when she lay sprawled on the floor, dressed in an oversized man's dress shirt, rolled up jeans, and saddle oxfords, popping bubble gum, listening to "Rock Around the Clock" on the radio, and trying to concentrate on her high school homework. When not pestering Doris or my little sister, I spent most of the day in my child-sized rocking chair, rocking furiously and singing gibberish along to Brahms records on the Victrola.

One day my mother pointed out that the mama sparrow in the crepe myrtle was sitting on a handful of tiny eggs in her nest, and every day we peeked out the window until the eggs hatched and turned into peeping fledglings. I was enraptured, and wondered how I could be a bird, too.

I came up with a plan, and set to work coloring eggs on construction paper.

Doris helped me cut out the eggs and then fill a shoe box with dried grass in which to nestle them. For several days I sat on my straw nest of eggs, waiting for them to hatch. As anyone could see, I was a sparrow. Although this avant-garde installation exhausted any parental instincts I might harbor for the rest of my life, I was forever hooked on the miraculous act of representation. By drawing eggs on construction paper, I could give birth to a nest of paper sparrows, which would fly fully hatched from my mind until they filled the sky over Gentilly.

I also took flight, and leaving behind the old world bequeathed to me by generations of insular Creoles, I discovered a new one, the borderless country of the imagination, the only one in which I've ever claimed full citizenship. Its gates swung open and I stepped in, bringing only my wildest dreams and a box of waxy Crayolas that smelled better than fudge-ripple ice cream.

That particular Carnival, flocks of paper sparrows covered the sky as a confetti of make-believe showered down, transforming everything. The shrink-wrapped families that intimidated me on the fifties television screen could keep the jingle bells of their alien white Christmas, as long as I could have my purple, green, and gold Mardi Gras. Wherever else in the world I might be living, I've always felt orphaned when, in the depths of winter, Carnival rolled around and I wasn't in New Orleans. It's my favorite season of the year, one in which everyone can be a mother sparrow.

I spent my first Mardi Gras with my wing in a sling. At the time I had to endure wearing Bass orthopedic oxfords because of an in-turned right foot, a genetic defect that plagued the Glaudots. And because my left eye was so much stronger than my astigmatic right, I took in the world cockeyed—a persistent trait, most would agree—head slanted to one side, squinting. I must have looked like a circus pinhead. "Are you retarded?" my sister always teased. To top it off, Mardi Gras was almost upon us, and I'd broken my arm two days earlier. Children can find the most inventive ways to get hurt, and just to see if I could stop it, I'd wedged my right arm under the wooden rocker of a rocking chair in motion, which sent me straight to the emergency room at Charity Hospital. While the broken bone was being set, I woke up from the ether in the middle of the operation, screaming. Then on Mardi Gras morning, the temperature fell below freezing.

But that didn't discourage Mémère.

She yanked three scratchy sweaters over my plaster cast and stuffed me into the sausage casing of a silk clown costume, with a fancy ruffled collar around the neck and a pointy hat topped by a red pompom. Thirty years earlier, her own four-year-old son, the dead Jimmy, had worn an identical clown costume, in which he sat perched on the steps of the

Chauffes' house on Bayou Road. The contrasting photos prove that, over the Buster Brown bangs, his clown hat was bigger, but I look happier.

Dressed up as Mémère's ghost clown, I felt better already. Then we went to the Rex parade on Canal Street.

"Hey, throw me something, mister," I hollered to the float bearing Rex, king of Carnival, waving my one good clown arm. Funny, but the one in the cast didn't hurt anymore.

I had a blast.

That first Mardi Gras evening, after the truck parades rolled along Canal Street, we ventured into the darkening French Quarter, where the mule-drawn Comus floats swayed down Royal Street between looming iron-lace balconies, illuminated by strutting groups of flambeaux torch-bearers. Years later, this image would haunt me when I first witnessed the candlelit Holy Week processions lurch down narrow cobblestone streets in Sevilla and Cádiz. I felt right at home among the Spanish families at midnight, nibbling from newspaper cones heaped with deep-fried shrimp and hoisting children to their shoulders to watch the Macarena float pass by. At that time in segregated New Orleans, the parade music was awful—stiff all-white high-school bands tooting *oompah* military marches—but especially in the French Quarter, the eerily illuminated spell cast by velvet Carnival royalty mounted on prancing steeds was magnetic. Most of the parades then had classical themes, taken from literature and mythology, and as the tinselly Greek gods waving from the floats knew, character is fate.

How fitting that during my first visit to the Quarter, I was a cockeyed clown with a broken wing.

We couldn't drag my sensible father, Eugene Nolan Jr., to a parade, much less to a ball, except for the krewes to which his family belonged, Iris and Hermes.

His mother, my widowed Irish grandmother Nana, had turned back into the redheaded party girl she'd once been after her seven children were finally married off. She took fox-trot lessons at the Arthur Murray Dance Studio, and at age eighty-five met her second husband on a ballroom dance tour of Mexico. She ferried across the river to gamble at the keno dens in Algiers, smoked Salems, drank bourbon highballs, and always rode in the women's parade, Iris. One year, after her float pulled up to the Municipal Auditorium for the ball, Nana was too drunk to climb down, and had to be hoisted to the ground by the hook-and-ladder from a fire truck. Ada B. was what everyone called Ada Burk Nolan, and as a boy I imagined Nana's name spelled "Ada Bee," so much did she remind me of a queen bee. The Burks were an Irish clan that arrived in New Orleans in the 1840s and started out in the drayage business. Her father had been a Mason, and her brother William R. Burk was a church architect, one who at the turn of the century built her large Arts and Crafts house at 1438 Verna Court, just off of Esplanade Avenue approaching City Park. Although growing up I didn't know her family as well as I do now, they all agree: the Burk girls were born to dress up and go to town.

Nana had married a "Mr. Nolan," as she always referred to my grandfather. Eugene Nolan Sr., who arrived in New Orleans in 1900 from Nolan County in West Texas, was a founding agent at the Pan-American Life Insurance Company, a New Orleans–based firm that pioneered the insurance industry in Latin America. In the middle of the summer of 1939, he died of a heart attack at age sixty-five while pulling vines from a live oak in front of the house on Verna Court. Nana always swore she warned "Mr. Nolan not to climb up on that ladder in this heat." Evidently Mr. Nolan was of the mad-dogs-and-Englishmen variety of New Orleans transplants, among those who never adjust to the rigorous languor necessary to survive the infernal summers here.

All I know about Mr. Nolan is that, although he was a 33rd Degree Mason and a Presbyterian deacon, he did manage to do one interesting thing in life: according to Nana, he shot off his own foot in a hunting mishap involving, as she told it, "a colored boy and a snake." Shortly after the accident, an "*anuncio*" appeared in the Pan-American bulletin titled "*Nolan Pierde un Pie, Pero Conserva el Animo*" ("Nolan Loses a Foot, but Not His Spirits"). An older cousin told me that, as a little girl, she was always terrified by the sight of his wooden leg dressed in a black shoe and sock, dangling with straps and propped up against his bedroom chiffarobe. Although I never met him, I do feel closely related to anyone capable of shooting off his own foot. Most of his children, including my father, at one time worked at what became the family business, Pan-American Life. What this mysterious peg-legged insurance agent left me was both a middle and last name, along with a heart condition and a Bakelite paper clip container.

"Here, take it," my mother told me one day with pursed lips, handing me the lidded Bakelite dish. "This is the one solitary thing your daddy has from his own father. Those Nolans had no sentiments."

My mother curated her own family's possessions like a director at the Smithsonian, and by "sentiments" she meant the literal treasuring of practical objects passed down from one generation to the next. That is, tradition. Almost all of what I now use on a daily basis—furniture, cookware, a silver service that includes iced tea spoons, even my great-grandmother's tin watering can—belonged to various generations of her family, and as I handle them those people's long-gone lives touch mine. Tradition, or what my mother called "sentiment," is an inherently anti-consumerist and therefore un-American ideal, one that has dovetailed with my own frugal bohemian tendencies. My insurance agent grandfather's Bakelite container, true to tradition, is still filled with paper clips and is tucked inside my tobacconist great-grandfather's desk drawer, my only contact with the life of Eugene Nolan Sr., whoever he may have been. If he'd been part of her family, my mother probably would have had his wooden leg with the dangling straps made into a lamp, under which she'd have sat to tell the tale of the hunting misadventure involving "a colored boy and a snake."

Distinct as they were, both of my parents happened to be from the downtown area bordering Esplanade Avenue, although not from the same neighborhoods. My thirty-six-year-old father met my twenty-two-year-old mother at Third Presbyterian Church, located at Broad and Esplanade in between their two worlds, the church my mother and her brother Jimmy had started to attend during the lean years of the Depression. The photograph of my parents' first date, taken in 1945 at the swank Blue Room of the Roosevelt Hotel, shows the nattily dressed couple, together with my father's brother Raymond, another late-to-marry Irish bachelor who became the treasurer of Pan-American. His date, of course, is my mother's best friend, Wanda Siegel. Also seated at the table are a couple just returned from the war, still in military uniforms.

Even as my father lifts a cocktail glass in the Blue Room, I don't doubt that still seared into his memory are the piles of corpses his unit discovered at a concentration camp they liberated in Leipzig. He kept a shoebox filled with photographs that the GIs took of the camp, pictures mass-reproduced and distributed to the troops, who had to dispose of the rotting cadavers as soon as they took over the camp. Otherwise, they were afraid that nobody would ever believe what they'd discovered. As a boy, I would stare for hours at the contents of this shoebox of horrors, wondering if that was what the whole world looked like only two years before my birth. Like many veterans trying to reclaim normal lives, my father never talked about the war and could never fathom why I wanted to live in Europe, a place he left behind as a bombed-out ruin littered with corpses. Like the death of my mother's brother Jimmy, his war experience was part of a leaden cloud that hovered over our house. The towering figures of my parents could fall inexplicably gloomy, or lash out in anger over nothing, and I never understood why. It wasn't because of what was said but what wasn't: the unspoken.

Growing up, it seemed that my parents' families were from different galaxies. Nana was always telling a joke or mixing a highball. Mémère, brow furrowed, was forever fussing with something amiss, a scorched pot or a window that wouldn't close, as if she alone were responsible for the world turning. Like the iconic smiling and frowning masks of drama, they represented the comic and tragic to me, the dual sides of my own nature that have seldom addressed each other except in writing. The dark humor in my fiction has been a form of self-invention, my own way of finally getting both of these families together in the same room, the one in which I now live.

People become confused when I speak of "my socialist youth," so let me clarify. No, I wasn't raised in a Soviet village or a Havana tenement, but in New Orleans, a hotbed of right-wing politics. But during the fifties and early sixties when I was growing up, everything was "public," a word that now carries sinister connotations of radical socialism.

In those days, I rode the public bus to a public school, then stopped by the public library before we played ball in the public street. In the summers, I went to a public day camp at the Y.M.C.A. at Lee Circle, any illness or accident brought us to public Charity Hospital, and many weekends were spent at the public pool in City Park, where we picnicked, rode the flying horses, and my father played golf. During the Depression, the W.P.A. constructed both the hospital and the park facilities as part of Roosevelt's "socialist" public works program that rebuilt the infrastructure of the country. To us, the columned main branch of the public library at Lee Circle, the Delgado Art Museum in City Park, and the imposing Municipal Auditorium, where operas, concerts, and Carnival balls were staged, appeared as majestic temples of culture. My deeply conservative family took these public facilities for granted, and indeed expected them to be there, paid for by their taxes. Private schools, pools, concert venues, recreation, and transportation were in some other country, not the one where I grew up.

From age ten, I took buses and streetcars throughout the city by myself, often carrying little more than my fourteen cents round-trip fare. My mother told my sister and me that if we were ever lost or had a problem, to ask a policeman. That meant that the cops were highly visible, stationed on street corners or walking beats, maintaining the public order. The police weren't speeding past in squad cars, staring at computer screens, as they are today, but were operating on two flat feet, controlling the pedestrian streets. Despite the family's precarious finances, my childhood world seemed civilized, a word rooted in the Greek *civitas*, meaning public and collective. My insomniac grandfather, when he couldn't sleep, would often stroll at 3 a.m. through the Seventh Ward in his pajamas, bathrobe, and slippers toward Esplanade Avenue to "get some air," the same air now whizzing with drug dealers' bullets. Late on Saturday nights, drunken knife fights sometimes broke out in raucous corner barrooms in the neighborhood, but I never saw a gun, windows weren't barred, and it never occurred to me to be afraid. The public facilities that were part of my daily life cut across all class and ethnic lines, except, of course, for one.

This was before racial integration.

After integration, which didn't begin in full legal rigor until I was in high school, everything began to privatize, and the city turned over the ruins of the underfunded public sphere—the schools, parks, buses, hospitals, pools, and libraries we had always depended on—to what some white folks referred to as "you-know-who." Blacks were finally invited to be part of the general public, but only after everyone else had left for private schools, car pools, clinics, country clubs, and the suburbs, taking their tax base with them. And white people cut off their noses to spite their faces, radically reordering their lives, first and foremost to avoid any contact with blacks. By the late sixties, the bustling collective sphere I grew up in had crumbled, and the once lofty word "public" had become indistinguishable from the N-word. As far as I can tell, today the unwritten foundation of the Republican Party platform is quite obvious: *public was fine when it was for us, but don't give any of our money to you-know-who.*

W hat finally opened my eyes was a segregated sanctuary, of all things sacred, that most openly public of places. With head bowed, the uniformed black sexton sat behind the partition that separated him from the white congregation droning the doxology. His eyes squinted shut, he seemed to be praying so hard he was weeping. As a ten-year-old wiggle-worm roaming the church, I tiptoed past, dumbfounded at my first dim perception of injustice.

"Because Arthur is supposed to go to the colored church, that's why." My mother impatiently hushed my questions, oblivious to my sensible argument that the sexton both worked and lived, along with his eleven children, at ours. Arthur was my friend, I reasoned to myself, the only thing about church I liked beside the jelly donuts and when the choir sang.

This was during the late fifties, when what everyone called "trouble" was already brewing. The deacons had unanimously voted that should black worshipers appear at the vestibule door, an usher would stop them with directions to "their own church." They couldn't even pray with Arthur behind the partition.

Gnarled live oaks shaded the racially checkerboarded neighborhoods off Esplanade Avenue where I grew up. Third Presbyterian Church was located not more than a few streets, it then seemed, from where everybody in the entire world was born, rode the carousel, studied, lived, and was buried. I was as used to seeing black faces as white, yet the segregated bathrooms, schools, buses, and restaurants were as taken for granted as the humid air I breathed or the water I slurped from the fountains marked "white only." Discrimination is always invisible to those who practice it, but at a certain age I began to notice these partitions and to feel uneasiness in the pit of my stomach.

Something was wrong.

After church at my aunts' house on Bayou Road, Mildred the black housekeeper perched on a tall stool in front of the stove stirring the grillades. With her booming voice through the swinging door, she dominated

Great-great-grandfather Auguste Glaudot Sr.:
1830 Brussels–1908 New Orleans

Great-great-grandmother Marie-Josephe
Dieudonné: 1829 Alsace-Lorraine–1905
New Orleans

Great-great-uncle Sylver Landry, one
of Alice Landry's four siblings who
died of yellow fever, 1882–1884

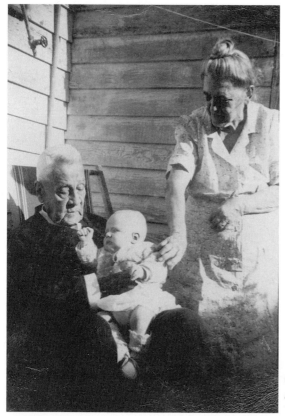

Great-grandparents Auguste Glaudot Jr. and
Alice Landry with newborn James Nolan,
1454 North Galvez St., 1947

Grandfather Lenow Partee (left) with brothers Alva, Cherry, and Raymond, Memphis, 1894

Great-grandfather Auguste Glaudot Jr. at his tobacco shop, 440 Chartres St., 1930s

Great-aunts' house, 2275 Bayou Road, 1930

Great-grandmother Alice Landry Glaudot, North Galvez St., 1947

Helen Alice and James Partee, Bayou Road, 1930

James Partee on paper route, Tremé, 1934

James Partee (right) with Leon Trice Jr. and Putt-Putt on French Quarter
balcony, Mardi Gras, 1936 (photo: Leon Trice Sr.)

Olga Glaudot Partee with newborn Helen Alice,
French Quarter, 1924

Helen Partee Nolan with newborn James, Bayou Road, 1947

Marguerite Glaudot, volunteer nurse,
Charity Hospital, World War II

Master Sergeant Eugene Nolan, France, World War II

First date at the Blue Room, 1945. Left to right: Raymond Nolan, Helen Partee, Eugene Nolan, and far right, Wanda Siegel

Great-aunt Marguerite Glaudot and James
Nolan, 2418 Columbus St., 1951

James Partee, the sad clown, Bayou Road, Mardi Gras, 1925

James Nolan, the happy clown,
6228 Lafaye St., Mardi Gras, 1952

the conversation at the dining room table like an invisible family member, telling each of us in turn what to eat and serving up side dishes of gossip and advice. "Miss Lucille right," her voice would thunder from the kitchen, instantly settling a difference of opinion between an aunt and my grandmother, "that man not good enough for that girl nohow." Standing, we would spend hours talking with Mildred, but were never supposed to sit face to face with her in conversation. She ate the food she prepared off "her own dishes," kept with the cleansers and scouring pads under the sink.

Again, I had begun to notice something was wrong, but didn't yet understand what.

Perhaps I had been fated to feel that way, since at the age of eighteen months I inadvertently desegregated the New Orleans Public Transit System for ten minutes. During one of our many moves between shotgun doubles in the neighborhood, my mother entrusted her baby to Marie, the black housekeeper, to bring on the Esplanade bus to the newly rented house. The driver immediately pulled the bus over, I am told, while a long, loud disagreement erupted among the passengers about where to put a black woman carrying a white baby, an exchange whose fine distinctions undoubtedly exhausted the unwritten bylaws of the institution of racism. I was finally placed judiciously in the bony arms of a white lady seated near the front. When I began to holler to high heaven, the driver wearily conceded that Marie could take me with her to the back of the bus, where I rode snugly in the "colored section" to my next home.

The buses and streetcars then were segregated by a maniacal system of moveable wooden signs pegged into the backs of the seats, indicating where the "white only" section ended and the "colored only" began. As a child taking the bus to school, one of the first lessons I learned was how to shift the signs toward the rear to free a window seat for myself. Later, when I understood exactly what was unjust about an apartheid that separated half the population from the other and denied dignity to the very people who had helped raise me, I would muster my courage to disobey the signs, causing the kind of "trouble" just beginning to make the newspapers.

By this time, my reaction was becoming so heated that the family was convinced that "outside agitators from New York planted a seed" in my brain, as if I hadn't grown up with a pair of slowly opening eyes in my head. During this period my parents, like many of their generation, fled to the suburbs, abandoning the wide avenues, high-ceilinged rooms, cemeteries, churches, public schools, and parks that had defined not only their lives but those of their parents and grandparents before them. There they learned how to edge lawns, commute for hours, and visit psychiatrists in an uprooted white-only bubble free from any encroaching "trouble."

And the old neighborhood my family left behind became mostly black, to this day identical in every tree root, shop sign, and porch rail, but of another complexion. Wherever I may live now, this still feels like home, and sometimes I find myself riding through it, usually the only white face on the Esplanade bus.

The Presbyterian church at the corner of Broad is still there, abandoned and for sale. The signboard that once noted the title of the Sunday sermon is blank. There is nothing left to say about "doing unto others." For decades the church remained inviolately white in a black neighborhood, reduced to only a handful of elderly parishioners who couldn't even afford a full-time pastor, much less a black sexton behind the partition.

When the bus stops at that corner, I peer out its tinted window in disbelief at the red brick building, a monument to the stubbornness and hate that tore my life apart at an early age. Something is still wrong, the pit of my stomach informs me: black and white Southerners are too much alike to live so divided. Seated around me on the bus are faces that could well belong to Arthur's children, to Mildred's or Marie's, or to their grandchildren. We have a childhood and a whole culture in common yet were never allowed to know each other.

As the bus wheezes past the church I divert my stare. My mind fills with the flight of fluttering paper sparrows, and I remind myself that I don't live here anymore.

5

A FANATIC HEART

Great hatred, little room,
Maimed us at the start.
I carry from my mother's womb
A fanatic heart.
—W. B. Yeats, "Remorse for Intemperate Speech"

Perhaps it was in the summer of my thirteenth year, as I lay sprawled under the whir of a window fan reading *The Communist Manifesto*, that my parents first suspected I wasn't going to turn out like other boys. The year was 1960, and the place New Orleans, where the muggy heat was already bringing to a boil the social turmoil of the upcoming decade.

As I concentrated on Marx's dangerous abstractions in a bedroom wallpapered with a motif of baseball bats crossed by fishing poles, I was aware, at the periphery of my squinty vision, of the civil rights marches in the South and the mounting Cold War confrontation in Berlin. In February the first sit-in had occurred at a Woolworth's lunch counter in North Carolina, and in October Khrushchev would take off his shoe and pound it on the United Nations podium, swearing he would bury us. Even in a weedy neighborhood of Caribbean-style shotgun houses in the torpid tropics, as far from Moscow or Berlin as anyone could imagine, I would take Khrushchev's threat personally.

I was a gangly, sunburned kid, face dabbed with Clearasil, lost in that interminable summer between childhood and adolescence. And I was ravenous, not for experience—sex had yet to cross my radar—but for words, ideas, and books that would line up events like my olive-green plastic soldiers, the Good Guys vs. the Bad. The chaos outside was a perfect match for the chaos churning within: I was rife for conversion to some cause. And just at that moment Mrs. Johnson, the next-door neighbor with the cigarette holder and a kitchen stacked with books, stepped in. She was young, childless, passionate about ideas, and belonged to some organization called the John Birch Society.

"When Joe and I first got married," she told me, "we read Thoreau's *Walden* together, then sold everything we had and moved to a cabin in the country to live off the land." She tapped a dangling ash from the cigarette holder and peered at me through black cat's-eye frames. "That didn't last long. And then we realized how the Communists were taking over our country," she said, picking up Whittaker Chambers's memoir, *Witness.* She loaned me that book and Ayn Rand's novels, with a conspiratorial urgency that bespoke times of crisis.

Mrs. Johnson's pillared house on the corner of Wamsley Avenue loomed like an antebellum mansion over our raised shotgun double next door. Hers was the big house where people entertained big ideas, facing a wide avenue that led to the world. Just behind it, our rental squatted on narrow South Gayoso Street, flanked by others exactly like it as far as the eye could see. The truth is I was infatuated with Mrs. Johnson, enthralled by what I took to be her cosmopolitan outlook and heroic depths.

Any news at all was news to me in 1960.

"Have you looked at a map of Europe lately?" I quizzed my father, brandishing a headline from the *States-Item* in his face. "The Communists are everywhere."

"What the hell are you talking about? I was in Europe fifteen years ago, and the Ruskies helped us beat the Nazis." That was as much as he ever said about the war.

"So are you a Communist?"

"Don't you ever call me that." He raised his hand to strike me. "Go feed the dog."

Except for my tipsy grandfather still living downtown, who sat up all night in a rocking chair reading Shakespeare in his bathrobe, nobody in my family read books. Any attempt I made to introduce intellectual debate wound up in horrible screaming matches. In our kitchen there were no books, only an unvarying weekly menu: red beans on Monday, brisket soup on Wednesday, fish on Friday, and roasted chicken on Sunday. I foresaw a lifetime of the same, even after I grew up, married, and moved next door, as children were expected to do then. My parents had seen the recent movie *Blackboard Jungle* and feared my teenage years might involve some shenanigans with girls, booze, and cars.

Nothing had prepared them for ideology.

Besides Mrs. Johnson in her bookish kitchen, the only people I could talk with about important ideas were several Jewish friends I had met at McMain Junior High School. I don't remember if they spotted me reading a right-wing book in the lunch line, but they told me they were "red-diaper-babies," their parents had been Communists, and I was wrong about everything.

"You're a petite bourgeois who will wind up on the ash-heap of history," Ricky informed me as I sipped through the straw of a cafeteria milk carton.

"At least I yearn to rise above the mediocrity of the masses," I yelled, trying to be heard above the lunchroom din with a line I cribbed from *The Fountainhead.*

We formed an odd circle, these kids with last names like Laventhal and Schulman, and myself, the sensitive blond fascist. We resisted sports almost as much as we loved ideas, and in gym class were always the last to be picked for any football game. We would face each other across the scrimmage line, debating collectivism and Hegelian logic, only vaguely aware of where the football was until it hit us in the face. I can't imagine what the other boys thought of us. Actually, they didn't exist for me. Nothing did but my cause.

"Have you ever known a Communist?" I grilled my mother, who was trying to relate to her suddenly militant little boy.

"I suppose so. I had a good friend in high school who was pretty mixed up. She became a Communist, then moved to New York."

My mother. A Communist friend in New York. I couldn't believe my ears.

"So what happened to her?"

"They say she's going to a psychiatrist now, trying to straighten herself out."

A psychiatrist. New York. My mother had another life I was trying hard to picture.

"Have I ever met a Communist, to the best of your knowledge?"

She shot me a funny look. "Remember those twins you used to play with in second grade? What was their name? White?"

"Yeah, you said they got polio and had to move away."

"That's what they told everybody. The truth is the F.B.I. had their mother under surveillance. Then they came and took her away. Said she was some kind of cell leader. Remember how she used to make y'all those sandwiches after school?"

"You mean Miss Nancy was the kingpin in a Communist spy cell? Just like in Whittaker Chambers? And I used to eat her tuna fish sandwiches." The revelation gave me goose bumps. I, too, had been duped by subversives.

At the time I recalled a happy childhood of Indian forts and church picnics and Boy Scout camp. Only years later, when I read the history of the 1950s, did I remember to what extent our daily lives had been marked by the polio epidemic, the McCarthy witch hunts, and the threat of nuclear war. AIDS and the Patriot Act and color-coded terrorist alerts are a déjà vu to anyone who made it through the fifties. Even more elaborate than duct tape–sealed safe rooms, families then were advised to dig underground bomb shelters in their backyards for when the Communists dropped the big one on Canal Street, sure to happen any minute. A shrill siren went off every day at noon, testing the alert system for a nuclear attack. As it does now, the government kept us docile, ill-informed, and terrified.

Children weren't being raised by television sets, not quite yet. Our parents shielded us, censoring the world. This was why the duck-and-cover air-raid drills at school, when we were instructed to place our hands over our heads while crouching under our desks, seemed like such a goofy game. Nobody ever explained to us what an atom bomb actually was. A fall from innocence was still possible. And I hit hard.

Communists are everywhere, they assured us. But often as I looked, I could find only dust bunnies and stray Lego blocks under my own bed.

The next year, when I was in ninth grade, Mrs. Johnson invited her fervent young disciple to meetings of an anti-Communist group that gathered in her living room the first Tuesday evening of every month. A dwarfish man who I seem to remember sported a black eye patch (although perhaps I have him confused with a character in a Sunday comic strip titled "Brenda Starr") had prepared a mimeo booklet with a baby-blue cover that explained Marxism, exposing the pack of lies it really was.

I dared say nothing, scanning the words in my fake-tortoise-shell reading glasses while I studied the splotchy, wrinkled faces of wildly gesticulating adults. Most of them reminded me of my Mr. and Mrs. Potato-Head creations. I had never been in a roomful of adults before who weren't relatives fussing with food and telling corny jokes. Mrs. Johnson, regally perched in a brocade armchair puffing her cigarette holder, controlled the meetings with quiet intensity. She looked as glamorous as a movie star portraying a leader of the French Resistance, and the dwarfish man was her mechanical monkey, which she turned on and off at will.

Quite on my own, I decided that dialectical materialism was really a neat idea, and that Hegel was right about the historical movements of thesis and antithesis. Loathing Communism, I became fascinated by its theory and terminology. Outside of Sunday-school Christianity, which I was leaving behind with my Oz books and pet gerbils, this was the first explanation of the world I had ever encountered.

Of course, it was Satanic and menacing, enslaving millions. I was thrilled. Like the evangelizing Milton, perhaps I was on the devil's side all along.

Mrs. Johnson arranged for a guest speaker to address a general assembly at my junior high school on the Communist blueprint for world domination. Dr. Schwartz was an Australian with a mustache prickly as a toilet brush. He was the director of the Christian Anti-Communist Crusade, and his lecture was titled "Will You Be Free to Celebrate Christmas in 1980?"

That seemed like an entirely reasonable question during those most unreasonable times.

I was mesmerized, and my red-diaper-baby friends scandalized. Our civics teacher, Mr. Huet, widely known as a pinko comsymp, viewed the speech as a violation of the separation of church and state. Much to his credit, he ignored our bland text and taught the class from paperback copies of Max Lerner's *America as a Civilization*, a liberal analysis that

at the moment reeked of commie propaganda. Our classes degenerated
into fiery debates between the teacher and me, and word soon spread
that Mr. Huet was practicing "indoctrination." It was my favorite class, a
vocabulary and critical-thinking boot camp, and in an adversarial role
my mind sprang to life.

"Stand up for what you believe," Mrs. Johnson encouraged me. I was
her foot-soldier in an apocalyptic battle with evil, and was beginning to
create disturbances. All I lacked was a bullhorn and an insignia.

The nadir of my prepubescent fascism occurred during a ninth-grade
science project on race. Even though I grew up white during Southern
apartheid, I wasn't raised to be a racist. We'd lived in downtown neighborhoods off of Esplanade Avenue that alternated between one block
of black families, one block of white, and one where nobody could tell
what the families really were. My mother's family may well have belonged
to that ambiguous third category, although like many New Orleans natives from a French background, I've never been sure. Paging through
a nineteenth-century album of my Creole family photographs, African-
American friends recently have pointed out that my Landry ancestors
were mixed. None of these subtle color-code complications ever entered
my mind at the time. As far as I was concerned, my relatives had only
been placed on earth to aggravate and embarrass me.

Along with J. Edgar Hoover, Mrs. Johnson was convinced that the civil
rights movement was chockablock with Communist dupes and spies.
She slipped me a copy of *Race and Reason*, a white supremacist tract
that became the basis of my so-called science project. I forget the book's
exact arguments for white supremacy, but let's just say they hit their target
audience in the unformed mind of a fourteen-year-old boy drunk on
right-wing ideology. By way of a visual, I cut out photos of ballplayers
from the sports pages of the *States-Item* and pasted them with flour and
water onto a piece of poster board, with arrows linking the Caucasoid,
Afroid, and Mongoloid types to their continents of origin. Actually, the
sports pages of the evening newspaper were green, so for all the emphasis
my report placed on skin color, all of the "Races of the World" pictured
on my poster turned out a uniform mint green.

After several presentations about photosynthesis and cross-pollination,
my science report turned into a shouting contest between me and my

red-diaper-baby friends. We had managed to move our scrimmage-line debates into science class. Our teacher, a member of the White Citizens Council, sat back, arms folded, and gave me a grade of E-100. Later that year, as the mint newsprint faces of the races of the world cracked and buckled on the poster rolled up in my closet, James Meredith was assaulted by a mob of angry whites when he registered for classes at the University of Mississippi. The governor of Mississippi, no more of a scientist than I was, explained that "God made the Negro different to punish him."

Most boys my age would have jumped at the opportunity, but I was horrified.

The moment had arrived to decide where I would go to high school. My parents were astounded that a lackluster student had turned "smart" on them, and weren't quite sure what to do with me, frothing at the mouth about dialectical materialism. My mother had asked what that mess was in the closet with all the lumpy ballplayers caked on it, and when I explained my scientific research, had tossed it in the trash without comment.

Mrs. Johnson had an idea.

"The boy just needs discipline," she said. With a sly smile, she asked me to meet with her husband one afternoon to discuss my future. Mr. Johnson had been lifting weights in their basement, and greeted me red-faced and sweaty in a white terry-cloth bathrobe.

"Let me tell you about a wonderful school where I went as a boy your age. Made a man of me." It was an exclusive military academy in Indiana and he was sure I could secure a scholarship as his "legacy" student. Maybe he could help out with any expenses my parents couldn't afford. He presented me with his senior-class yearbook from Culver Military Academy. "I'll make a few phone calls tomorrow to the right people." Then he shook my hand.

It was all settled. I was being sent to reform school, a classy gulag for individualist dissidents somewhere as cold and remote as Siberia.

The school looked like hell on earth: page after page of sour-faced cadets in uniforms marching around quadrangles under gun-metal skies, doing chin-ups and hitting punching bags. Cigarette holders and eye patches, yes; grunting in the mud and saluting pimply superiors, no way. It suddenly occurred to me that I didn't want to be Mr. Johnson but Mrs. Johnson. At the moment I didn't know what to do with that revelation.

First I had to escape *Blackboard Jungle,* the fate that awaited me at a regular high school.

So I took the test for the honors high school. Modeled after the Bronx High School of Science, Benjamin Franklin was a public school created in the wake of the Soviet launch of Sputnik, dedicated "to teaching Johnny what Ivan knows." I wasn't particularly keen on the trigonometry and physics that Ivan knew, but there I joined my red-diaper-baby friends doing the six hours of homework a night that would catapult our country to the forefront in the space race. Evidently Ivan was so overworked he didn't have time to fight Communism, and neither did I.

And there life changed.

By that time we had moved to another house in Broadmoor on Louisiana Avenue Parkway, then a predominantly Jewish neighborhood. After a black vagabond raped and murdered a grandmother in her garage down the block, most families fled. Strains of the theme from *Exodus,* a popular movie at the time, accompanied the moving vans down the street. My parents bought a brick ranch house far away from Mrs. Johnson, in the suburb of River Ridge. After a single summer in the burbs, I hightailed it to my grandparents' basement, where I fashioned my own rat-infested *garçonnière* in what used to be my grandfather's office. I grew my hair until it curled over my collar, fell in love with a Buddhist named Harriette Grissom, dressed like Woody Guthrie, and began to smoke Gitanes. I started to write poetry under the tutelage of Mr. Charles Suhor, a poet-teacher who was also a jazz drummer, to hang out at integrated coffee houses in the French Quarter, and to attend meetings of the civil rights movement. Since I didn't have a record player, Harriette played Bob Dylan's entire first album to me over the phone. I also had "the freight-train blues, down to the bottom of my rambling shoes."

"So," said my grandfather one afternoon, looking up from Shakespeare in his rocking chair, "I hear you're a member of the Communist Party now." He gave me a wink. I thought that was the funniest thing anyone had ever said to me.

I was probably already stoned.

On November 22, 1963, I was sitting in French class when a student delivered a note to our melancholic teacher Mrs. Schueler, who immediately burst out crying. "Class, I have such terrible news," she informed us between choked sobs. "The hootenanny has been cancelled." After the bell rang, we learned the afternoon hootenanny had been called off because the President of the United States had been shot dead in Dallas.

Not only had Kennedy been assassinated, but by a Communist from New Orleans. His name was Lee Harvey Oswald.

Maybe Mrs. Johnson had been right, and I had fallen down on the job. I called her.

"Kennedy was soft on Communism," she explained. She was feeling no pain.

"Then why would a Communist kill him?"

"Jesus is the only way." Mrs. Johnson had become a born-again Christian, and there was no way to interrupt the evangelical tape loop with questions about who stood where on a grassy knoll.

Later it turned out that Lee Harvey Oswald either had been a Communist posing as an anti-Communist in New Orleans, or an anti-Communist spy infiltrating the left. My heart sank. My past had come back to haunt me. His face looked unsettlingly familiar, pasty and fanatic, like mine. Fanatics don't care which side they're on, as long as they're fighting.

My great-aunt Marguerite was a schoolteacher and great friend of Jim Garrison, the district attorney. She had taught all of Garrison's children in third grade at Bienville grammar school. Reete, as I called her, lived with my grandparents, or rather my grandparents and I lived with her, since her salary was our sole source of income. During Garrison's investigation into the New Orleans background of the plot to assassinate Kennedy, she taught with an armed security guard in the rear of the classroom. The district attorney was convinced someone was trying to kidnap his children. And every evening at home I received Reete's up-to-the-minute bulletins about the Garrison investigation over gumbo or red beans and rice. At the time, it never occurred to me that this whole murky, provincial broth might be served up one day in a great film or novel. Only years later, when I saw Oliver Stone's *JFK*, which lionized Jim Garrison, or read John Kennedy Toole's *A Confederacy of Dunces*, with its madcap cops rooting out "the communiss," did I gain any tragic or comic perspective on the political hysteria that formed the backdrop of my high school years.

After all, I was a teenager by then, starring in my own secretive melodrama. And as a repentant John Bircher, with each report about the Garrison investigation, my heart sank even further.

Somehow I was to blame.

According to the district attorney, the assassination wasn't a Communist plot but an anti-Communist conspiracy involving anti-Castro Cubans, the mafia, the C.I.A., and several prominent right-wing kooks in New Orleans. He uncovered a dank, wormy loam of local connections, all of which I tried to digest at dinner. Scanning the newspaper photos of characters like Clay Shaw, a sadomasochistic gay businessman from the French Quarter, and David Ferrie, a pedophile pilot with swatches of cotton glued to his bald head who also had lived on Louisiana Avenue Parkway, I kept searching for the dwarfish man with the black eye patch. Every sinister detail of those anti-Communist meetings came back to me in full force: the shadowy faces in the smoke-filled room, the bundles of pamphlets passed hand to hand, the occasional foreign accent, the blind fervor. And when I'd gone home at nine—bedtime on a school night—what were those characters plotting? I never dared mention my suspicions to anyone, especially Reete, who conferred with Garrison on a daily basis.

Had I been part of a group that conspired to assassinate the president even before I started to shave?

In the midst of this, I was visited at home by an investigator from the Orleans Parish School Board. He was trying to get the goods on Mr. Huet, my ninth-grade civics teacher. Was he a Communist? Everyone said I thought so.

"Absolutely not," I reasoned. "I don't think he's intelligent enough to be a Communist." Such was my exaggerated respect for the brains behind dialectical materialism. And I was relieved the investigator didn't interrogate my grandfather about whether I had become a Communist.

Mr. Huet was fired anyway. For teaching Max Lerner. And the president was dead.

My own bomb had exploded in my face.

I was seventeen years old.

What causes this lostness, this fierceness, in the teenage fanatic? Looking to Freud, we might suspect sexual repression, since the male libido supposedly peaks at eighteen, when opportunities to express it are scarce. Or according to Jung, it might be an atavistic regression to the role of tribal warrior, whose rite of passage is to protect his ancestral turf by slaying any threatening dragons. Marx would say that in capitalism the adolescent is an economic parasite alien to the means of production, destructive because he is a freeloader.

All we know is that the fanatic is usually male, very young, and that these days he threatens us from all sides: from Islamic madrassas and training camps, from hilltop colonies in the West Bank, from white survivalist ranches and dens of skinheads, and from the violent fringes of every conceivable ethnic and linguistic nationalism and every stripe of religious fundamentalism. He is willing to die for his cause, he has the world in an uproar, and his ranks are swelling. He is a ski-masked ISIS militant, a Nazi Youth, a Young Pioneer, a Red Guard, a Basque separatist, a Balkan ethnic cleanser, a Hamas suicide bomber, an Israeli occupier, Timothy McVeigh, Mohammed Atta, Lee Boyd Malvo, the Uzi-totting African soldier with peach fuzz above his upper lip. He is Cain and he is Abel, and we already know how this story ends.

What do they want, these young fanatic hearts?

Or rather, what was I looking for? I was trying to line up my fragile, emerging self behind an idea that would lead to an adult identity different from the one I was being offered. Almost any idea will do—or both sides of the same idea, as was my case—just so long as it bestows a sense of belonging to something greater, a connection denied by society or family, history or circumstances. And far above the ranks of young disciples are the manipulative adults, cynical or sincere in their manic purposes, directing their recruits with great puffs of ideological smoke from their cigarette holders.

So, you may want to know, what happened then? Mrs. Johnson continued as a holy roller, and I never spoke with her again. David Treen, one of her anti-Communist cronies, eventually became governor of the state of Louisiana. I have become a teacher, a tribute perhaps to those early teachers who helped me grow beyond my own fanaticism. I was an antiwar activist in college, spent years supporting various Latin American revolutions, and taught for a time in China just after the Cultural Revolution. My collectivist ideals did not accompany me on the return flight from Beijing.

Did I ever actually become a Communist?

Am I now, or have I ever been, a terrorist?

I don't care to answer those questions right now. I'm sitting in my grandfather's oak rocking chair under a whirring ceiling fan, just about to finish a rereading of *King Lear*:

> The weight of this sad time we must obey;
> Speak what we feel, not what we ought to say.
> The oldest hath born most: we that are young
> Shall never see so much, nor live so long.
> [*Exeunt*]

6

THE DIAMOND QUESTION MARK

My grandfather lost everything in the crash of 1929 and never again trusted banks. My grandmother was always inadvertently washing ten- and twenty-dollar bills that he had squirreled away in suit pockets and rolled-up socks. With wooden clothespins, she would clip the soggy bills to her wash line between the step-ins and sheets. By the time I was growing up, in the newly prosperous fifties, the subject of my grandfather and his lost money had become something of a family joke. Yet I suspect that during the penurious years when my mother's family moved from one shabby rental to another in downtown New Orleans, the joke wasn't a particularly funny one.

No, they weren't poor people. One look around at the antique furniture, the crystal and silver, the opera programs fanned out on the coffee table, and the embossed editions of classic nineteenth-century literature, and it was obvious that they were once used to a more luxurious life. They happened to be rich people who just didn't have any more money. The golden age in which they had prospered was over, and had been for such a long time that their grandchildren studied about it at school. Disillusioned, they survived the rollercoaster ride of their era with some degree of grace. With wry grimaces, they distrusted the instant riches that flourished around them in their later years, afraid that once again they would live to see the financial system come crashing down around them.

Luckily they didn't. They missed the crash of 2008 by almost four decades.

My grandfather, Lenow Alexander Partee, had been a spoiled teenager in Memphis during the gloriously spendthrift 1890s, the era that Mark

Twain satirically labeled the Gilded Age, or rather, the *first* Gilded Age. The youngest of five brothers and sisters, my grandfather was doted on by a loving family and waited on by a staff of servants. Cotton trading may have been the family business, or perhaps it was dry goods, I'm not sure, but the Partees lived in a mansion in the Pinch District, had an office in a building they owned on Front Street, and sent their children to the finest schools.

"When I was seventeen," my grandfather told me, chomping on a cigar like W. C. Fields, "my father said I could do anything in the whole wide world I wanted to. He would send me to Yale, say, or buy me a bicycle. I took the bicycle, and after I rode around the block for a couple of years, headed West."

His mother Jessie's family, the Lenows, were probably assimilated Jewish immigrants who originally bore the name Lenowitz. In 1852 Jessie Lenow's father founded Elmwood Cemetery in Memphis, one of the first park-like burial grounds established during the rural Southern cemetery movement. When my grandfather's only sister Etta died unexpectedly on her wedding day in 1911, the family commissioned an Italian artist to sculpt a life-sized statue of her out of Carrara marble. The statue was shipped from Milan to Memphis and still graces Elmwood Cemetery, although now is blackened by time and decay.

Jessie Lenow was graduated in 1876 from the Tennessee State Female College, and I've always been amused by her graduating essay, written in the curlicued calligraphy of the day, titled "The Influence of Beauty." Flowery estheticism was the muse of the first Gilded Age, much as postmodern theory has been the muse of the second. "Thus beauty sits in regal state," my great-grandmother penned, "and rules with royal hand the million loyal human hearts; and, if knowledge then be king, and the mind of man the throne on which he sits, we must, at least, proclaim fair beauty queen, and woman's face her chosen seat." Although my snickering boyhood reading of this lofty passage conjured images of a bosomy beauty queen sitting on a woman's face, clearly a florid classicism marked an age with the aristocratic pretension that its prosperity would never end.

I'm not certain when my grandfather's fortunes first began to decline. His three successful brothers in Memphis—Cherry, Alva, and Raymond— considered their younger brother "shiftless." For a few years he wandered the country on his inheritance, and could gab at length about Frisco and Buffalo and St. Louis, the bustling world of redcaps and porters and bellhops. Shortly after World War I, Lenow Partee drifted to New Orleans, where he married into an affluent Creole family of tobacco merchants. Although not a French Catholic, he was charming and had elegant penmanship, that watermark of a true gentleman. But his inheritance was dwindling, so he eventually found a job as an auditor, a profession that valued his fine hand and smart appearance, even while he continued to rely heavily on family stocks and bonds. It was still the Roaring Twenties, and the country was rolling in dough.

For a gentleman of his breeding, certainly everything would work out.

And it did, until October 29, 1929. Overnight his portfolio turned into worthless paper.

Panicky bank runs followed the weeklong "bank holiday" in New Orleans. As banks began to fail across the country, the Lenow Partees realized they had nothing. *Rien de rien.*

My grandmother Olga Glaudot bundled up her two young children and moved back into her family's home on Ursulines Avenue while my grandfather, tail between his legs, took a room in a boarding house. This was to be a temporary arrangement, of course, only until the experts in Washington straightened out the unfortunate financial mess. President Hoover himself announced on the wireless that "prosperity was just around the corner." A few years later, the Auguste Glaudots lost the tobacco business in the French Quarter, along with their stately house on Ursulines. As the Depression deepened, the three generations lived crammed into a single shotgun rental in the run-down Seventh Ward with their vases, crystal, mahogany furniture, and fin de siècle library. My grandfather, "too good for any job," as his Creole in-laws complained, eventually landed work with President Roosevelt's W.P.A., and somehow the family scraped by.

My mother told me that while she was growing up during the Depression, "many were the nights when my brother, sister, and I got by on just rice with a pat of butter." Every gnawed bone was tossed into the eternal *pot-au-feu* simmering on the stove. For a while she was shipped off to live with her spinster aunts on Bayou Road who had relatives in the country, from which came a reliable supply of food. Although the shelves at home were stacked with books to read, they all had been published before 1910. The only other entertainment was the funny papers.

And this was the genteel poverty into which I was born. My grandfather advised that unless I studied Latin, I wouldn't amount to much in life. He would point out the flamboyant curves of the signature on the flyleaves of his books and cluck as I practiced my own clumsy penmanship. As a teenager, when anyone encouraged me to choose a profession in which I could make tons of money—insurance, investment banking, real estate— my grandfather sighed. He could picture how that would end, with men in top hats leaping out of office windows. At that point he might repeat one of the various refrains he called his "thoughts of the day," no doubt cribbed from souvenir ashtrays in the French Quarter: "I'd rather be a dirty bum riding a slow freight train way behind than a multimillionaire in a golden casket on a fast express in the baggage coach ahead."

Then he and I would laugh and laugh.

One thing that my grandfather did believe in was jewelry. Diamonds and gold, to be exact. That was wealth you could hold in your hands, and didn't lose value. You could add to it, an ounce of 24-carat gold or a diamond at a time. He felt that when you were sporting a diamond stick pin on your tie, you really had something.

The wads of bills deposited in his clothes that my grandmother regularly ran through the rinse cycle were actually down payments or monthly installments on the various purchases he was negotiating at the jewelry stores on Canal Street. Every day he would rise at noon—a gentleman never did business in the morning—and carefully dress himself to ride the streetcar to Canal Street to mail a letter, buy a cigar, have a cup of coffee, shoot the breeze with hotel doormen, and haggle with jewelers.

Even though he was in his late eighties by this time, he didn't dress like the turn-of-the-century dandy you might expect. It was the swinging sixties and he dressed Mod, in clothes I would have killed for. I was in high school then, living with my grandparents, and often I'd sneak into his bedroom to splash on English Leather cologne before a date, or to borrow a Madras shirt. The striped double-breasted sport coats with the wide lapels were off limits.

"You've got to keep up with the times," he told me, admiring his spit-shined Bass Weejuns. "Is this too loud?" He pointed to a red paisley tie over a shocking-pink body shirt.

"Groovy," I said.

My grandfather, natty man about town, claimed to be the spitting image of that dapper haberdasher Harry S. Truman. On May 8, 1969, he typed a fan letter to the former president, extending effusive greetings on his eighty-fifth birthday and commenting on their "resemblage":

A nice person stopped me in the street a few years back and said, 'Cap, if you were just a bit taller and some heavier, I'd swear you were Harry S. Truman.' I went him one better and said, 'Major, you've just paid me a high compliment, for I've always considered Mr. Truman one of my favorite persons.' The next time you are up and around Walnut and 12th, you might 'salute' the old drugstore on the Northwest corner for me, my favorite haven of rest 61 years ago.

The letter is signed, "Just an old-time Democrat from the Very Deep South." Truman never responded, but I've saved the carbon copy for the shred of biography it provides: at one time my grandfather hung out at a corner drugstore in Independence, Missouri, no doubt dazzling the girls with his wit and wardrobe during the economic panic that hit the country in 1907.

Although I coveted my grandfather's clothes, I was less enthusiastic about his jewelry. Gold cuff links weren't my bag.

When he would return from those daily expeditions to Canal Street jewelers, huffing and puffing, he'd often be mumbling under his breath, "Jesse James stuff. Might as well hold me up with a gun in broad daylight." Then he'd slip out of his vest pocket the piece of jewelry in dispute to ask what I thought.

I first saw the diamond pendant when it was a rectangular chunk of 14-carat gold with a single diamond at the center. My grandfather would lounge on the unmade bed in his room, listening to a radio perpetually stuck in the static between two stations, chewing on a cigar and holding jewelry up to the light. My grandparents had separate bedrooms because my grandfather used the metal wastepaper basket as a spittoon. And sometimes missed.

"Diz-gusting," my grandmother would say, curling her lip. Long-suffering Mémère was no Mae West to her husband's W. C. Fields. Picture one of those devout widows dressed in black on their knees in the shadows of Notre Dame.

In my grandfather's room, every scrap of paper—matchbook covers, calling cards, the backs of envelopes—was covered with columns of minute calculations as he juggled his various accounts with the Jesse James jewelers. He was obsessed with the diamond pendant for more than a year. He couldn't decide whether it should be a pendant, a tie tack, or one of a pair of cuff links. At the time I was starting to buy my threads at Army Surplus, so didn't offer an opinion. Nobody I knew was wearing diamond tie tacks to hootenannies or protest marches.

Beaming, he called me into his room late one night to show me something. We'd often share a midnight beer with cheese and crackers. After all, he was well into his second childhood as I was emerging from my first.

The pendant was finally finished.

"What is it?" I scratched the peach fuzz on my chin.

"That's what the folks at Pailet & Panetta wanted to know. Every time I had a few extra dollars left over from my Social Security checks, I'd ask Pailet to mount another diamond on it." He was always so nonchalant about money. He'd scrimped and saved years for this piece of jewelry. "Finally he said, 'Mr. Partee, what are we making here?' And I said, 'Mr. Pailet, I don't know. So make it a question mark.'"

And there it was, a diamond question mark, a paisley-shaped curl of stones bordered in silver and set in gold. On the back it was signed "Pailet."

"What does it mean?" I asked.

"Got me."

"Cool." I was reading Jean-Paul Sartre, and it struck me as so . . . existentialist.

"I see all these folks running around wearing their religious medals—St. Jude, St. Joseph, Virgin of Whatnot. This expresses what I believe. Saint I-Don't-Know." And then he chortled.

Earlier that year my grandfather had shocked the Sunday dinner table with his agnostic dream. "I had a dream last night," he announced over demitasses of black coffee.

"Pass the sugar." My grandmother rolled her eyes.

"I was in a tiny cement cell, and the floor, ceiling, and four walls were slowly closing in on me a few inches at a time. I knew that when they met, I'd be gone, and nothing would be left—no time, no life, no death, no God—nothing."

"Diz-gusting." My grandmother crossed herself.

Everyone jumped up at once to clear the dishes, leaving my grandfather and me at the table. Eyes watering, he was shaking his snowy white head, stirring the spoon inside an empty cup.

Years later I found out what the diamond question mark was really about.

It was my inheritance.

At the end of the second Gilded Age, I'm sitting here studying the stash of jewelry that my grandfather left me. Here's the Swiss Universal gold watch that I once brought to be adjusted at Matteucci's, the San Francisco watch shop located in North Beach. It hadn't worked in years.

"I know this watch," the elderly Mr. Matteucci told me. "Look, here's my mark with the date inside. I last cleaned it in 1962."

"Was PawPaw in San Francisco in 1962?" I asked my mother on the phone. I didn't remember that trip of his, but the jeweler's mark proved it.

"Of course not," she said. "He won that watch in a poker game in the French Quarter."

"Then the San Francisco sucker he won it from lived in my neighborhood here. He and I go to the same Italian jeweler."

There is a diamond tie clip shaped like an arrow, also signed by Mr. Pailet, along with a monogrammed gold belt buckle—LAP—and matching cufflinks. A gold bill clip with a large P. And here are the various rings that my grandfather wore all at once: a chunky emerald, an ornate amethyst, and the only one I've ever worn, a smoky aquamarine. Right after his death in 1971—at the time I was a long-haired journalist writing for the radical magazine *Ramparts* in San Francisco and wasn't invited to the funeral—my mother mailed me his favorite ring, a square amethyst mounted in gold. Like the Romans, I'd drop it in my wine glass so that I wouldn't get drunk. But a street urchin from Berkeley soon ripped it off, and so for years I didn't see the rest of my grandfather's jewelry in Mother's custody.

These days I couldn't wear any of this bling to walk the mean streets of New Orleans, the same streets my bejeweled grandfather strolled forty years ago. I'd be devoured alive by fourteen-year-old thugs like Sebastian in *Suddenly Last Summer*. If the public display of jewelry is a sign of civilization, then we Americans live in savage times.

Except for Puff Daddy's bling, I doubt that my grandfather would have approved of the Gilded Age that has just slammed to a close. He would have found the gas-guzzling S.U.V.s, suburban McMansions, $40,000 Birkin handbags, vacation condos and beach houses, private jets, nouvelle cuisine, $500 bottles of wine, and kindergarten résumés aimed at the Ivy Leagues all vulgar and stressful. The Rockefellers, Guggenheims, Vanderbilts, and Carnegies of his youth at least exercised their noblesse oblige to endow museums, universities, and libraries before they bowed out. What have the present robber barons left us except a trillion-dollar deficit, mountains of plastic junk from China, and an obscenely wasteful and foolish way of life?

The only aspect of the current recession that surprises me is that anyone is surprised. I've been tapping my foot for years, waiting for the present Gilded Age to fold. And I knew it would, like clockwork, as surely as the booms ended that caused the economic panics of 1837, 1873, 1907, 1929, 1987, and 2001. During the past thirty years I've witnessed the savings-and-loan debacle, which cut short the greedy yuppie era, the delirious dot-com boom, when San Francisco was invaded by hordes of twenty-five-year-old millionaires with nothing real to sell, and then the housing bubble. When I vacated 1405 Kearny Street, the rent-controlled apartment on Telegraph Hill that I'd had for twenty years, and the rent soared from $375 to $2,800 a month—the new slumlords didn't even fix the doorbell—I thought of tulip bulbs. Like the tulip bubble in seventeenth-century Holland, a crash was inevitable on such an absurdly overvalued commodity.

And then came Katrina, which finally convinced me that nobody was in charge.

The moment I decided to abandon the flooded city on the third day after the hurricane hit New Orleans, the first thing I stuffed into my satchel was my grandfather's jewelry box. Mr. Pailet's jewelry shop had long since disappeared from Canal Street, along with almost every other reputable business, and as I sloshed down the once venerable street through knee-deep water dodging bullets from the looting free-for-all, I knew the time had come to flee. Seated on the floor of a stolen school bus driven by a Cajun pirate, I rode through the impenetrable darkness with the diamond question mark dangling from a gold chain under a ratty T-shirt, plastered by sweat over my heart. Breathless but glad to be alive, I felt like my grandfather's "dirty bum riding a slow freight train." As the bus rattled over the Crescent City Connection bridge and out of the city, I thought of the four generations of bones afloat in our family tomb and wondered if I would ever be allowed to return home. I finally understood why overseas Chinese, Jews, Gypsies, and other displaced people value gold so much.

When the time comes, you can run with it.

But the inheritance from my grandfather is more than jewelry. If culture is experience refined through the passing of generations, then I received the equivalent of an inexhaustible trust fund. He bequeathed me the last living vestige of a democratic country skeptical of wealth, streetwise, smart-mouthed, and defiant, one in which any loser can set out to reinvent himself like Huck Finn in that "territory ahead of the rest." Over the years, I've come to view the various booms and busts of our times through the prism of my grandfather's diamond question mark. The towers may crumble, the stock market crash, and the levees break.

Don't trust any of it. Jesse James stuff.

When I told my mother's sister Doris that I had escaped from New Orleans wearing the diamond question mark, she reverted to the family joke about her shiftless father and his lost money. "Oh you know him," she said, laughing. "It's probably not worth very much."

7

THE OPEN ROAD

For a brief summer I was a teenage runaway, and I have just one regret. Only once can you run away from home to San Francisco. After the first time you either live there or you don't, each of which presents its own problems.

Yet in 1966, when I left New Orleans heading west, I began an adventure that would lead me not just to another city but to a road, and at the end of it, to myself.

My Depression-era parents, allergic to risk, were horrified at my plans to give up my "good job" as a grinder's assistant on Tchoupitoulas Street to "go gallivanting around the country" during the summer of my freshman year in college. "You're seriously compromising your university career," read the note my father taped to the mantel of the French Quarter apartment where, with a dozen friends, I was practicing hard to be a beatnik.

My grandfather had a different perspective. He had spent his youth riding the trains coast to coast at the turn of the century, depositing his inheritance in the hands of Western saloon-keepers and New York red-caps. "Why, Frisco's the best burg west of Canal Street," he encouraged me, chomping at the cigar he chewed on more than smoked, as gentlemen of his era did. PawPaw traced the decline of Western civilization from the day the bronze cuspidors were removed from the lobby of the Roosevelt Hotel.

So it was he, dressed in a seersucker suit and Panama hat, who escorted me to the railway station, greeting everyone inside as "chief" and "governor" as if he'd known them his whole life. After making certain the conductor would take good care of his grandson, he slipped me some "portraits of George Washington and Abraham Lincoln," as he called the few bills he always managed to give me from his Social Security checks. "Don't take any wooden nickels," he admonished, waving goodbye.

I was on the way to meet up with my high school friend Harriette Grissom, and in no way did I consider myself some penniless flower child, a figure soon to be invented by the media. I was a serious would-be writer pursuing his destiny with almost $60 in his pocket and the friend-of-a-friend's address.

The perpendicular streets of San Francisco loomed as a religious revelation. The night of my arrival I was so intoxicated by climbing the hills, by the bracing wafts of fog and the exotic smells of Chinatown, not to mention a jug of cheap burgundy, that somehow I believed the cable cars made no regular stops on Nob Hill but that the passengers pirouetted off like Fred Astaire as the cars passed in front of their pastel Victorians. I spent my first morning in San Francisco at a hospital emergency room, and the rest of the summer with a broken elbow tucked into a dirty sling.

But no matter, because with Harriette and two other summer runaways there was room on the living-room floor of an older writer named Ben Jennings, who worked as a telephone repairman, and the cable-car conductor down the hall who listened to Bach all night welcomed our shaggy company for his impromptu spaghetti dinners. John Foret, the Satanist poet, made brief appearances, if only to rave about the saintly thief Jean Genet and steal Ben's typewriter so he could buy speed. When I nervously read one of my high school poems to these older artists—it was titled, I'm afraid, "I Was a Brooding Young Man in My Night"—and they snapped their fingers in approval, I knew that I was on the right track.

My only luggage, my father's World War II duffel bag, held only books of poetry and denim work shirts, nothing to prepare me for what Mark Twain called "the coldest winter I ever spent," a summer in San Francisco. Someone gave me a khaki army blanket that, with a flourish of my one good hand, I would toss over my shoulders like a Carnival duke's cape to flutter in the sudden descents down Nob Hill.

Ben Jennings's girlfriend soon tired of stepping over sleeping kids on the way to her kitchen, and we runaways took the hint. The four of us pooled the last of our money to purchase what the label described as a "junior umbrella tent," with which we took off hitchhiking to Big Sur to look for Henry Miller on the beach. The green tent pitched, Harriette and I entrusted Howard Groger with our last $3.58 to buy a week's supply of potatoes to roast over a fire we carefully built in the sand.

The fire died out and we went to sleep hungry that night. Howard turned up the next afternoon with a jumbo-sized bag of Tootsie Roll Pops and a story that, to this day, I don't believe.

And so like hungry bears, we began slinking around the edges of family picnic areas, pointing with widened eyes at extra hamburgers. A park ranger took pity and gave us work clearing trails in the forests, where we sweated all day to earn our nightly deliveries of provisions to the tent. It wasn't until we returned to San Francisco several weeks later that we realized the undergrowth we'd been yanking at was poison oak.

My face puffed up into a big bright raspberry and I took to wearing a mitten on my free hand so I wouldn't scratch it. This condition finally dried out during the endless hours that Harriette and I spent waiting in the Mohave Desert for friendly truck drivers on the long hitch back to New Orleans.

A complete disaster? To the contrary. Now that I'm teaching I sadly realize that my college-age students will never slip past Aunt Sally to find themselves on the river like Huck Finn. This essential ritual of the American experience may be closed down for good. These days, of course, it's too dangerous to run away from home. So these adolescents remain safely nestled in the Styrofoam packaging of the suburbs, piercing and tattooing themselves in their own fierce rites of initiation. Outside is not an alluringly romantic picture. The streets are dominated by a steely distrust, by the tragedy of the homeless, by abused runaways selling themselves to survive, by the threat of homicidal mutilators. Students must now buckle down in a competitive panic to insulate themselves from the great unknown with credit cards.

Yet the real American dream has never been security but freedom, Walt Whitman's "open road" that points to a common ground between all people. Traveling this road inspires belief in yourself and those around you, in the vast goodness of the land itself, where any loser can set out to reinvent himself as a winner. My grandfather's generation knew this

America, and mine may be the last to have glimpsed the full expanse of this myth.

There I stood, this skinny Southern kid looking out over the Pacific Ocean as if I were Balboa himself, my arm in a sling, shivering under an army blanket, my skin corrugated with poison oak, and with less than a dollar in my pocket. I was cold and hungry, shaking with the scary uncertainty of my new self. Surely I've been more comfortable since, but I've never been so happy in my life.

II. AWAY AT SEA

'What am I?' asks the seaweed for the first time.
Another wave, another wave, another wave answers:
the rhythm is born and destroyed and rolls on:
only the sorrowful movement is true.

—Pablo Neruda, "End of the Party"

- 8 -

STAIRWAY TO PARADISE

Was anyone ever so young?
—Joan Didion, "Goodbye to All That"

The night Mick Jagger picked me up in San Francisco, I was spending my last two dollars on a Heineken at a terrace table of the Savoy Tivoli in North Beach. It was another chilly fall evening of 1970 in a city where, for someone who had just turned twenty-three, anything and everything seemed possible. From the back, one of the two Brits at the next table looked familiar, and then he swiveled around, eyebrow arched with a question, finger pointing at the lighter on my table. The lips, the cheekbones, the silk scarf knotted around his neck—it was *him*—and when our eyes met, I could tell he was looking for more than a light.

I nodded, and then Mick lit his cigarette, taking me in at a single glance: blond hair past my shoulders, velvet pants, kohl-lined eyes, and a ring on every finger of the hippie sitting alone nursing a beer.

"Mind if I join you?" he asked with a wink.

Stunned, I again nodded, pushing out the chair next to mine.

"It gets a bit boring chatting with one's chauffeur." The man he'd been seated with was wearing a driver's uniform and cap.

"Please allow me to introduce myself," I said.

Those fleshy lips twitched at my joke. I couldn't take my eyes off them. And for the first time I smiled back. Then he took out a silver coke spoon, twiddling it between his fingers.

Our preliminary conversation was something about New York, a tour, how hard it was for him to go out publicly. Soon we were sitting behind the tinted windows of his limo parked around the corner on Union Street, holding up the silver coke spoon to each other's nostrils. I was surprised to feel his hand on my knee, and then farther up my thigh, which I took as permission to lunge toward those lips with a gelatinous kiss that seemed to go on forever. I'd never had sex with another man before but under these circumstances, didn't hesitate. To my embarrassment, the cheap zipper on my hand-stitched velvet pants stuck, and Mick had to tug at it, but the zipper on his tight goatskin trousers eased down like a first bite of ice cream.

We finished fooling around just as the chauffeur was settling into the driver's seat in front of the screened partition. When the engine was turned on, the speakers in back blasted: "Pleased to meet you / hope you guess my name / and what's troubling you / is the nature of my game." Then the short, muscular English eccentric pecked me on the cheek, opened the limo's back door, and said, "It's been a gas, Jimmy. Ta ta."

Clenching my jaw and sniffing sticky fingers, my boot soles barely touched the sidewalk as I practically skipped along Grant Avenue toward the neon lights of Chinatown.

This, of course, never happened.

Not to me, in any case, although I wouldn't have doubted it for a moment if somebody else had told the same story.

Maybe it was being out of school for the first fall since I was four, or the way the fog tumbled over the Golden Gate Bridge late every afternoon, draping the city in a stage scrim of make believe, or that feeling, as Janis Joplin was singing at the time, of "nothing left to lose." Maybe it was just being young, but I was convinced something this thrilling could take place at any hour of the day or night, given the collective fantasy we inhabited during the early seventies in San Francisco. By "we" I mean the droves of young people from across the country who had taken over the city during the past few years, all of us in various scraggly stages of reinventing ourselves, complete with new names for our divine reincarnations. We were poised for the magic heading our way, heralded by every moan of a foghorn resounding across the Bay: each of us was destined to become a rock star, the inevitable revolution was almost here, the

Vietnam War would soon be over, and our culture of zonked-out peace and love would triumph around the globe. Any day now the Black Panthers would take over City Hall, the troops would come home to plant organic vegetable gardens, and food, rent, theater, and clothes would be free—if only we could figure out how.

We were educated, talented, liberated from the old Judeo-Christian shackles, and seething with visionary optimism. Like Mickey Rooney announcing to the other kids in one of his thirties musicals, "Hey, I have a barn we can turn into a theater—let's do a show," we had an even better idea: *let's make a new world together*. The old one we left behind had gone to hell. In Aldous Huxley's phrase, we had "cleansed the doors of perception" with psychedelics, and now saw life as grown-up children did, the unfettered children we were never allowed to be.

Like previous generations of pioneers, we had flocked from across the country to its Western edge to push the limits of the possible way past the parameters of our parents' dismal lives. We weren't in Kansas anymore. At the cusp of those libidinous sixteen years between the introduction of the birth control pill and the first AIDS cases, we thought we could reinvent sexuality and stage a prison break for pinch-lipped Puritans. Armed with little but bulk brown rice, food stamps, and second-hand clothes, we also could take back the economy. And if the Promethean fire of freedom were indeed the devil, we felt an enormous sympathy for him.

What could possibly go wrong?

My introduction to the ongoing orgy, or at least to the gay part of it, happened differently than in a limo with Mick Jagger tugging at my zipper. Yet it blew off the top of my head. One evening a performer with the Cockettes, a gender-bending theater collective I was hanging out with, showed up at my door on Arguello Street. Sprite-like Gary Cherry had a mane of crinkly chestnut hair past his shoulder blades, and we'd only had one previous conversation. Odd as it seemed at the time, his name wasn't made up, and it turned out we were both related to the Cherry family in Tennessee. Southern traditions die hard, and so it would take a cousin, so to speak, to get my gay cherry.

Twinkle-toed as Puck, Gary held out his hand. "I have a hit of mescaline. Want to do it with me?"

I invited him in, and we split the turquoise tab.

Gay life, as I saw it until then, had never attracted me. A few years earlier, in the French Quarter demimonde of older bohemians that formed my introduction to adult life, many of the men I knew were bisexual, fathering children with wives and girlfriends but cruising for tricks in the gay bars, sometimes for money, other times for kicks. During college and grad school, I'd had several serious girlfriends. Although I felt some homosexual inclinations, I'd never acted on them because I was self-identified as a beat or a hippie, not—how can I delicately put this?—as a fruit. Those were the clean-cut boys in the band who smoked Kools, wore mohair sweaters, hung out in piano bars sipping cocktails and singing Barbra Streisand songs, and worked as florists, decorators, or hairdressers. I liked these people, counted several among my friends, but it wasn't me.

Once, as a high-school senior, I'd been taken to a Quarter gay bar by a few of these friends, students from the Tulane Architecture School who seemed to know more about me than I did. All four walls of the tiny bar were mirrored, which made it seem crowded, and everyone looked as square and craggy as my uncles. I had no idea what to do or say.

A man in a fuzzy sweater tapped me on the shoulder. "Hey," he said, "what you doing?"

Anxious to leave, I wasn't doing anything. "I'm looking in the mirror," I said, as if there were anywhere else to stare.

"Oh," he said, turning away abruptly, "you're one of *those*."

I'd never met a gay hippie and didn't recognize my ambiguous sexuality in the mirror of the times. That is, until I arrived in San Francisco in September of 1970 to crash with some college friends.

On my first morning, fresh off the plane from New York, where I'd finished a Master's in English, I awoke in a two-storied Victorian on Washington Street to a beehive of activity. In the cavernous living room where I'd slept in a corner, guys dressed in work boots and kimonos with glitter in their beards were painting cardboard scenery and singing in falsetto chorus:

> I'll build a Stairway to Paradise
> With a new step every day.
> I'm going to get there at any price,
> Stand aside, I'm on my way!

The air was musky with the scent of pot and patchouli, cut by the sharp smell of poster paint and glue. Somebody with a joint between his ruby lips was running around with glittered nipples and a staple gun, affixing yards of sequined ribbon to the borders of cardboard cutouts. Dressed in denim overalls, a blond woman who looked like Heidi clanked in with a bucket and shovel she'd just used to compost the organic vegetable garden in the backyard.

Upstairs, my college friend David MacMillan turned on the Rolling Stones.

These were the Cockettes, explained another college friend, David Wise, their in-house photographer. The group had been started on New Year's Eve by someone called Hibiscus. By July, *Rolling Stone* already had published the first of several articles about them. Hibiscus, a.k.a. George Harris, was from a New York theater family, and in the wake of the 1967 Summer of Love had traveled with his lover Allen Ginsberg to San Francisco, stopping along the way in October at the protest march in Washington, D.C., against the war. "Flower Power," the iconic photo of the blond young man in a white turtleneck inserting a carnation stem into the raised muzzle of a National Guardsman's gun—that was George—on his way to becoming Hibiscus, the long-haired guy with the glittered beard and staple gun whom I was studying as I rolled up my sleeping bag.

The troupe was getting ready for a fifties-themed show called "Hell's Harlots" that would open at midnight on Friday at the Palace, a former North Beach Italian opera house and movie theater now used during the early evenings to screen kung fu flicks and stage Chinese operas. This was to be the seventh of the Cockettes' loony, homemade shows at the Palace, following that year's big hits of "Paste on Paste," "Gone with the Showboat to Oklahoma," "Madame Butterfly," "Fairy Tale Extravaganza," "Tropical Heat Wave," and "Hollywood Babylon." As I stood gaping, the new "hot number" wandering onto the scene, Hibiscus came over and planted a lipstick kiss on my cheek, inviting me to the new show—for free.

That Friday, as the elderly Cantonese audience came tottering out at 11:30 p.m., the sidewalk in front of the Palace was already swelling with a dazzling mass of costumed freaks, the likes of which I'd only seen during Mardi Gras in the French Quarter. Both men and women had bracelets up to their elbows, rings on every finger, and madcap bonnets on their frizzy heads. They were shimmering in vintage designs of satin and velvet, turning the corner of Columbus and Powell into a thrift-store runway. Everyone had a unique, elaborately put-together look, or as put-together as you can get while dressing up on LSD. "Love your drag," people in the ticket line squealed to each other. And this was just the audience. The performers were inside, setting up the scenery. The admission was two dollars, although some people paid with joints or by laying out lines of coke at the cashier's window.

When the two college-pal Davids and I entered through a stage-door entrance in the alley, the theater already reeked of reefer. Backstage was mayhem, a rainbow whirl of glitter, sequins, toppling cardboard scenery, and half-dressed men and women strapping on high heels. Nobody could remember their lines or knew their cues, although a normally dressed, goateed redhead stood by with a clipboard trying to organize the performers' entrances and exits. Hibiscus struggled with an enormous papier-mâché flying saucer while a regal looking black man named Sylvester zipped himself into a satin sheath. While David MacMillan threw on a skimpy biker skirt and David Wise snapped away with his Pentax, I took a seat on the front row, studying the faded chinoiserie that decorated the walls and ceiling.

Was I ready for "complete sexual anarchy," as John Waters would later describe his time with the Cockettes?

The previous year I'd gone to Stony Brook on a Woodrow Wilson fellowship to study with the death-of-God theologian Thomas Altizer, after taking seminars with his colleague William Hamilton at New College in Florida. Recently their photos had appeared together on the cover of *Time*, under the caption "Is God Dead?" My Master's thesis had been on the *nouveau roman* and the death of traditional narrative. As an undergrad, I had fallen under the spell of the Freudian Norman O. Brown's books, which proposed that the repressive ego dissolve into "polymorphous perversity," along with media guru Marshall McLuhan's books, which prophesized the end of linear, print-oriented thinking. Marxist writers such as Herbert Marcuse convinced me that capitalism was over. When I decided to end my graduate studies with a Master's and forgo the Ph.D. path, it appeared that, as a culture, we had thought ourselves to the very end of thinking.

That show was over.

God, traditional narrative, the repressive ego, linearity, and capitalism may have become obsolete, dead as the four student war resisters shot by National Guardsmen at Kent State that spring, but I was just getting started. So sitting stoned out of my skull on the front row of the Palace Theater waiting for a Cockette show to begin at midnight, was I in the right place?

I thought so.

Then the people waiting outside poured in like a flurry of winged angels, and I was soon to discover that the audience was half of the show. We were all on stage as, one by one or in chorus line, the performers tripped onto the proscenium, did their impersonations of slutty greasers, sang and danced—often not so well—while the audience jumped to their feet with catcalls. Hibiscus's papier-mâché flying saucer came crashing through the scenery, ending the *West Side Story* gang fight. Sylvester did a silky Billie Holiday number that knocked me out, and then, backed by a rock 'n' roll band, someone named Rumi barreled onto the boards dressed as Tina Turner, belting out "Proud Mary" while two boys done up as the Ikettes harmonized behind him. No, these weren't lip-syncing drag queens striking poses in a mirrored gay bar, but for better or worse, real performers marked by an elfish lack of guile.

They weren't trying to sell us on anything, either sexual roles or their own musical talent. Men played women, and women men, most performers falling somewhere in between. They were the androgynous body celebrated by Whitman and Blake resurrected in all of its sensual glory, far from the ashen sense of an ending that hovered over my graduate seminars during the post–"Waste Land" days of Western civilization.

They were the joy that happened after Godot finally arrived.

And so they stole my heart.

Well, that was fun, I thought, as Gary Cherry slipped out my bedroom at dawn, leaving me naked between the sheets of my mattress on the floor. He did me, I hesitantly did him, we got high, got off, and a good time was had by all. Why had I been so wary about caressing another man's body all these years? A weight lifted off of my shoulders. Now if people thought I was gay, well, guess what? I was, sort of. At the time I had a girlfriend in the Haight whom I sometimes visited, although those late-night booty calls suddenly seemed less urgent.

Evidently, there was another sexy world out there.

And it soon moved in with me.

One night Rumi, the Tina Turner impersonator, came a-courting in the same way Gary Cherry had. Gary never dropped by again, and I suspect that triple-Scorpio Rumi, as determined a creature as I'd ever known, had sent Gary as a scout to test-drive me. When Rumi finally got my pants down around my boots, he told me that since the moment we met, he'd set his cap for me. In October I'd seen him do a riotous Mick Jagger impersonation at "Les Ghouls," the Halloween show, pouting carmine lips and shaking maracas in gold harem pants while singing "Sympathy for the Devil," which inspired the raucous audience to leap up dancing on their seats.

Even though this wasn't the back seat of Jagger's limo, I was ready.

The next morning Rumi woke to tell me about his dream. He was in a room with Tina Turner and Mick Jagger and they were "doing," or impersonating, each other. When he moved in with me, this grad-school poet learned how to behave as a proper stage-door Johnny.

At that time I was also living with photographer David Wise in an elegant two-story Victorian on Arguello that we scruffy types were able to rent only because one of our roommates, Janet, had persuaded her ex-husband Jerry Jeff Walker, a musician I knew from the French Quarter, to sign the lease for us. Another of our roommates was the drummer for the Hoodoo Rhythm Devils, and the fourth a fading Yankee belle named Sheila, who kept a pet ferret, tolerated only amber light, and was a least ten years older than we were. Wispy Sheila counted among her ex-flames Leonard Cohen, the satirist Paul Krassner, and Gary Brooker, the piano player for Procol Harum. That Halloween, when Brooker came to stay with us while the band played the Fillmore West, he wound up in Janet's bed, not Sheila's, and the two never spoke again. As always, I carved a pumpkin, and when my jack-o'-lantern wound up perched atop Booker's grand piano during the gig, I was ecstatic, such was my reverence for lyricist Keith Reid's "A Whiter Shade of Pale."

"Rumi," Sheila would say, "would you please tell Janet that I say not to hang her wet socks over the shower curtain in the bathroom?" The two women's silences grew loud enough to fill the chilly Victorian.

Sheila once walked in on Rumi and me having sex in front of the blazing fireplace in the living room. "We need to establish a firm rule in this household," she primly announced as we sat cross-legged on tatami mats over our Hunga Dunga food co-op dinner. "No fucking in the warm room."

But because of my jack-o'-lantern on Procol Harum's piano, I forgave Sheila her fitful Blanche DuBois scenes. Compared to the chaos, clutter, and catfights at the Cockette commune then on Haight Street, our ménage was as sedate as a Jane Austen novel.

My room soon filled with Rumi's drag—mothy feathers, tasseled dresses, silver stars, mascara pencils, and pineapple tits—although I remained an austere ragamuffin not drawn to the Palace stage. One way I did participate was to write a cover article on the troupe for *Organ*, a San Francisco monthly, my first piece of published journalism. It featured David Wise's photographs, and he and I had a grand time brainstorming among the proof sheets in his basement darkroom. The piece was called "Picture Postcard Home: The Cock on the Right Is Mine," a title inspired by the 1936 photograph of my mother's murdered sixteen-year-old brother in Carnival drag, in which Jimmy is posed on the right. Appropriately, the article is a faux letter to my mother attempting to describe the Cockettes, written in the hyperbolic rush of images inspired by Tom Wolfe's and Hunter S. Thompson's New Journalism, my nonfiction muse at the time:

Now, Mother, you told me a number of things about your life during the Depression: nobody had any money, no one had a job, you had two dresses in your closet and everyone, being in the same leaky boat, had fun. Things are not too different here, and sometimes I've wondered if it might be your same dresses because, honey, they're old but were quite a bargain at the Third Hand Store. You said you and your friends made things—none of this TV business—stood in welfare lines, put on your own shows when you didn't have a quarter for the movies, dreamed of revolution but schemed at getting rich. If anything, the thirties are happening again in the seventies: the talk is big, the soup is thin, and we have a blast.... The Cockettes are queens in their mothers' fur coats and their fathers' buckle-up army boots. Fools, beautiful fools, in love.

I still wasn't communicating with my parents after they'd committed me three years earlier, so I never sent this make-believe letter, published in a West Coast magazine that I hoped would never reach New Orleans. But the letter device was more than rhetorical, as close as I was ever to stray toward coming out to them about my fluid bisexuality. After all, I reasoned, I didn't want to know about theirs, so why should I burden them with details about my sex life? Besides, as far as my family was concerned, I was now "away at sea," like my great-Uncle Numa, the Merchant Marine engineer. Whatever he did during his long voyages to India, China, or Egypt didn't concern them. Only what happened in New Orleans counted.

A week after the piece appeared, I got a call from *Ramparts*, the national leftist magazine.

"Is 'Jimmy Nolan' a pseudonym?" asked Peter Collier, the editor. That was how I'd signed the piece.

"Yes," I said in a high-pitched lisp. "My real name is Truman Capote." Capote, a Cockette fan, had been to many of the shows.

Collier laughed. "Whoever you are, we'd like you to write for us. Please drop by our office in Berkeley to discuss doing a feature piece for us on another topic. We need your kind of jazzy cultural commentary."

Late that December, I finally made my first and last stage appearance with the Cockettes at a show called "Winter Wonderland New Year's Eve Anniversary Extravaganza," held at a swank mafia nightclub in North Beach, Bimbo's 365 Club. Rumi insisted that I do it, since at some point the star performers' "hot numbers" or current boyfriends were expected to parade on stage as boy-toy trophies. But, to say the least, the Cockettes and the mafia weren't a good fit, so while I was prancing about the stage in a red Sergeant Pepper–style military jacket, Mr. Bimbo was running around the bar wrapping naked Cockettes in tablecloths, shouting "I've never seen so many fucking *finocchios* in my life." Rumi was supposed to close the show with his Tina Turner number, which he'd tirelessly been rehearsing for this big break on the club scene. But just as he was about to go on stage with his band, Mr. Bimbo cut off the lights.

"Union rules," he announced, triumphant. "This show got to shut down at two in the morning."

Rumi was heartbroken, weeping all the way home in the taxi while I held his Tina Turner wig in my lap. He disappeared the next day, and still crestfallen came back a week later to collect his drag. What's love got to do with it? I wondered, already up to my neck in secondhand emotions and thirdhand dresses.

That February, Hibiscus left the troupe he'd founded, aghast at the hippie-capitalist direction the group was taking. An internecine war broke out between those who supported free theater and those who, unhappy with the twenty dollars per show they earned each month, wanted a more lucrative success to match their spreading fame. Hardly anyone had a real job, and most lived either on funds from home or on a pittance of state welfare called Aid to the Totally Disabled, for which they auditioned by acting out for a social worker their most bizarrely psychotic fantasies. A welfare acceptance letter was considered an Academy Award.

Hibiscus, a purist at heart who gathered day-old bread and wilting flowers from restaurant garbage cans, had fallen under the early influence of the Kaliflower commune, where Allen Ginsburg had installed him before returning to New York. The commune, whose window curtains were blood-stained sheets free from the city morgue, was run by the dictatorial ideologue Irving Rosenthal, author of the novel *Sheeper* and a former editor of the *Chicago Review*. Although I avoided Rosenthal, at least two decades older than I was, years later, when I came to know Allen Ginsberg better, I could well imagine how the two could have been friends (or perhaps aging makes fussbudgets of us all). Kaliflower banned tobacco and alcohol, conducted surprise midnight meat raids on other communes' fridges, cutting them out of the Hunga Dunga food co-op if they discovered so much as a hot dog secreted among the mung beans, and insisted art should be free. Hibiscus soon founded another gender-bending theater troupe called the Angels of Light, more like the Living Theater than Busby Berkeley, whose sporadic free shows were even more spectacularly chaotic than the Cockettes'.

Ambivalent, I continued to hang out with both camps, but the bloom was off the rose. As a veteran of political movements, I'd been wondering how long it would take for tribal factions to square off in some atavistic clash and people to start screaming at each other. I'd also been waiting for Puritan America, which we thought we'd left behind, to pinch its judgmental lips and butt in. As it turned out, Cain and Abel, along with the dour figures in "American Gothic," had been waiting in the wings the whole time, clubs and pitchforks raised, even while the rest of us thought we were tap-dancing our way to paradise.

I turned back to writing. Louis Simpson, my poet mentor at Stony Brook, managed to place one of my poems in the 1971 edition of Ted Solotaroff's *New American Review*, where it followed the first English translation of my idol Gabriel García Márquez's story "A Very Old Man with Enormous Wings." Heartened by this and a visit to the *Ramparts* office, I surveyed the California scene for a suitable subject for a Gonzo-style feature. What I came up with were the burgeoning fundamentalist Christian communes of so-called "Jesus freaks." I'd grown up in the straight-laced Bible Belt, where I memorized scripture at Sunday school, and was fascinated by the oxymoronic concept of hippie evangelicals. Even though now a self-proclaimed pagan, I certainly looked the part and could speak the Southern-inflected talk of "born again" and "praise the Lord." So I launched my first experience in immersion journalism, staying for days at a time in various Jesus-freak communes, smiling, nodding, and making everyone there think I was one of them. Although practicing an insidious form of brainwashing, the kindly older evangelists who ran these rescue missions for drug-zombie dropouts weren't bad people, although I couldn't wait to escape their suffocating prayer circles and group hugs.

In my room at home, the portable typewriter was set up on a closet door thrown between two sawhorses. Although a weak speller, I was so poor that I couldn't afford a dictionary. So while I wrote, I made lists of words with dubious spellings, which I took down to the corner drugstore, where standing at the revolving metal book rack I looked up the words on my lists in the paperback dictionary for sale. It wasn't easy to find the solitude to write in a household booming with four roommates, plus boyfriends and girlfriends, but like David Wise holed up in his darkroom designing rock album covers, they considered my prolonged withdrawals just another eccentricity.

I'd had one previous stint in commercial writing, during which I fell in love with publishing. In Stony Brook, I'd rented a damp basement apartment in the gothic seaside mansion of Joe Simon, the creator of Captain America and other Marvel Comic superheroes. When the middle-aged Joe and I discovered we both stayed up all night working, we'd meet over the light table in his studio to consult about his latest project, a magazine called *Something Else*, a groovy version of *Mad* magazine for bellbottomed teenyboppers. Eventually he hired me to write some of the copy and dialogue while he did the art, and amid clouds of his cigar smoke, we sipped coffee, tossed around ideas, and cracked each other up until dawn. Joe saw me as a down-home Southerner, so he asked me to put together a section for black kids, one I titled "The Plain Brown Rapper." Meanwhile, I was writing poems to slip under Louis Simpson's office door, and working on seminar papers about the impending death of everything. Nietzsche by day, teenage *Mad* by night: I barely had time to rattle the maracas in our student band, Brain Damage.

When my first *Ramparts* article came out as a cover story called "Jesus Now: Hogwash and Holy Water," I felt a bitter aftertaste of betrayal even as I cashed the modest check. As they say, a journalist is always betraying somebody, and I wasn't sure that I was cut out for immersion journalism, worming my way into people's lives then serving up portraits of them skewered by my own perspective. Although I hadn't liked them in the least, I felt guilty about my wry depiction of the fundamentalist hippies, who mailed me boxes of homemade cookies with notes tucked inside saying Jesus loved me, anyway.

After the Cockettes released a movie called *Tricia's Wedding*, in which an Eartha Kitt impersonator spikes the nuptial punchbowl with acid at the Nixon White House, those remaining in the troupe were aflutter with plans for their upcoming premiere in Manhattan. I was growing weary of the nonstop hype of San Francisco's counterculture, in which somebody always seemed to be hatching yet another slick new scheme. I wasn't cut out for the adrenaline-fueled whirligig of a pop journalist's life. I spent a few days in laid-back Sonoma County visiting John Foret, the Satanist poet from New Orleans, who was running a funky craft shop in Sebastopol called the Rising Sun, filled with homemade candles, incense, and embroidered clothes. In flight from the city, I wound up buying the business from John for three hundred dollars and moved my scant possessions into the Rising Sun's storage room. I turned out to be a disaster of a businessman, giving away the consignment items or trading them for the gallons of fresh goat milk I lived on.

When Hibiscus came to visit me, he was critical of my pathetic attempt at hippie capitalism, and convinced me to sell the business for exactly what I paid for it. Then he and I discovered a decrepit two-story house in a shadowy cathedral of ancient sequoias in Rio Nido, a hamlet on the Russian River. So I moved from the sleepy Rising Sun into a ruin named

Sunset. The monthly rent was a hundred dollars, which included both stories together with a small apartment over an empty garage. Dressed in a flowing kimono, Hibiscus immediately wandered barefoot into the forest only to return with a sack of dried leaves, which he glue-sticked with glitter and thumb-tacked onto Sunset's shabby walls as décor. A week later, half of the Angels of Light were hanging out in every clammy nook and cranny of the old redwood house, practicing Kathakali dance steps in saris in the front yard and making pots of vegetables and brown rice in a kitchen crawling with banana slugs.

Like Hansel escaping into the woods from the witch's oven, I was enchanted by my mushroom kingdom. Far away from the media buzz of the city—no phone, TV, or newspapers—a new phase was beginning for me, one that would inspire the title of a poetry collection I was working on: *Why I Live in the Forest*.

Hibiscus had been right. Amid much fanfare in the press, that winter the Cockettes did make it to the Anderson Theater on Second Avenue, where they presented a show called "Tinsel Tarts in a Hot Coma" and fell flat on their greasepaint faces. Half of the distinguished New York audience had walked out by mid-performance. Sylvester, by far the most accomplished of the group, resigned in a rant on stage. The *Post* published a review titled "The Cockettes—The Show Was a Drag," and Gore Vidal summed up the spectacle, quoting a line from *Gypsy*: "No talent is not enough."

New York didn't get San Francisco, and the feeling was mutual.

Leaving Sunset in the care of various Angels of Light, I began to travel abroad during the winters, when the sequoia forest was so dark that the streetlights were on twenty-four hours a day. On the Russian River I'd connected with writers living in other communes linked to ours, including my lifelong friend Andrei Codrescu, along with the poets Harold Norse, Hunce Voelcker, and Paul Mariah. The Jesus-freak article was anthologized in a collection on religion published by Macmillan, and the Canadian Broadcasting System invited me to Montreal to discuss it on a televised roundtable with a preacher and a priest, along with a rabbi, one who later, on leaving the TV studio, arm draped across my shoulder, congratulated me on my "common sense."

In spite of these heady successes, my final assignment for *Ramparts* was a flop. It was supposed to be an interview with Jane Fonda while she and Donald Sutherland were performing their F.T.A. (Fuck the Army) antiwar shows on military bases. After the photographer and I snuck onto the base in a camouflaged jeep, I was so intimidated by stony-faced Hanoi Hannah that instead of requesting an interview with her I submitted a zany Tom Wolfe–ish portrait of the Hollywood-star-as-revolutionary, which the magazine killed. The photographer accused me of acting unprofessionally, which I did. Like the Cockettes in New York, I'd fallen flat on my face in the big time, and for the moment was finished with journalism.

But the flute-and-bongo-playing processions with sarong-clad Angels down to the nude beach on the Russian River made up for it. At the time I had a hippie girlfriend who wore long India-print skirts, lived with her setter named Kiowa, and hitchhiked with fifty-pound bags of dog food and a gold vial of speed. This didn't stop me from putting the make on visiting "hot numbers," the good-looking young men from the city who crossed our rustic threshold. Our mix of woodsy communalism and free love was a potent one, or as Andrei Codrescu once told me, remembering our days together on the Russian River, "Every time I smell burned brown rice I get a hard-on." There, instead of the shy seduced one I became the horny satyr, and learned to be careful of the sexual roles I assumed: sooner or later the script would require that I play the opposite one.

This was an abrupt role reversal that, in some way, paralleled what happened to purist Hibiscus in 1973, when he returned to New York to found a branch of the Angels of Light, which soon became "Hibiscus and the Screaming Violets," a glittery rock show he performed with his three sisters. After this, at some point he turned back into George Harris, cut his hair, shaved his beard, acted in commercials and soap operas, and, *GQ*-handsome in his Armani suits, became a high-end escort for wealthy sugar daddies. In 1982 he was my first friend to die of the rare "gay cancer," but by that time, we were becoming accustomed to loss. Many of the former Cockettes had already ODed on drugs, including the deflowering Gary Cherry and, years later, my college friend David MacMillan. AIDS swept away most of the rest, such as Sylvester, who by then had turned into a disco-diva sensation with his hit "You Make Me Feel (Mighty Real)."

The Stairway to Paradise had collapsed into a slippery slide to hell. By the time we realized that we ourselves—not Mick Jagger's limo—were the magic we'd been waiting for, it was already gone.

The last time I saw Hibiscus, during a bleak New York winter, he was still Hibiscus, bearded and long-haired. Sunset in Rio Nido had been condemned and torn down, and I was returning from South America by way of New York to move in with Cockette photographer David Wise. Of all the naïve notions, we planned to get "back to the earth" by renting a farm in sub-zero Vermont. In a ratty loft in the East Village, Hibiscus was putting on the last of his Angel of Light extravaganzas, one in which he and the cast were costumed as sequined mermaids writhing their fishtails along the bottom of a glittery cardboard sea. Although his parents sat on the first row, bursting with pride, the show was sparsely attended, and by the time it was over, most of New York's Beautiful People were already at Max's Kansas City, cavorting with Warhol superstars such as Holly Woodlawn and Candy Darling.

David Wise and I, the last ones left in the emptied theater, were helping Hibiscus lug his bulky cardboard waves down the narrow steps of the drafty factory. Still dressed in my Colombian wool poncho, I had a pint of brandy in my back pocket to brace myself against the stinging cold, and was already drunk. "Goddamn this shitty hellhole," I raged, barely hanging on to my end of the cardboard scenery, "and fuck New York and the snotty assholes living here."

Hibiscus swirled his sequined mermaid fishtail around on the grimy stairway to face me with a sweet lipstick smile. "What are you so mad about?"

After all, it had been his show.

But this was what had become of our California dreaming. It was January of 1975, and I really didn't understand yet what I was so angry about. The Vietnam War was raging toward its shameful climax, that past summer the criminal president had resigned, the snarling punk era was just beginning, and disappeared Chilean poets were being tortured in dungeons. As adrift in life as J. Alfred Prufrock, I could still "hear the mermaids singing, each to each," although they no longer sang to me.

9

THE GARDEN OF EDEN

I was flying over the earth, looking for a place to be born." Snug in her pink flannel pajamas, three-year-old Jessie Blue startled her parents with this pre-uterine memory. "I looked down at these two nice people in a cottage by the sea, and they seemed like a good mommy and daddy. So I swooped down and got born here."

Years later, Jessie Blue's parents, lifelong friends of mine, told me this story on their redwood deck in Santa Cruz, California. She was such an astonishing child that I believed she really did sail through the sky, arms akimbo, searching for a port of entry into this life. So I wasn't surprised when Jessie Blue became a trapeze artist. But I was shocked to the core when she was killed at age twenty-seven in San Francisco during an aerial rehearsal with Cirque du Soleil.

Her harness broke.

My harness also broke at age twenty-seven in San Francisco, when I came plummeting to earth. It was 1976, the year of the American Bicentennial, not that I was interested in celebrating what I considered the inglorious history of the United States, particularly in regard to Latin America. U.S. OUT OF NORTH AMERICA was one of the signs I carried during an anti-imperialist march down Market Street, protesting the American involvement in toppling the progressive Allende government in Chile three years earlier. In the fall of 1973, I'd been living in Colombia, on my way to the "Chile of the poets," when I heard the news of the violent military coup on September 11 and the death of Pablo Neruda a few weeks later. At the time I was translating Neruda's *Stones of the Sky*, and saw the tragedy in Chile as a rallying point, the Spanish Civil War of my generation.

During the year of the Bicentennial, I'd just returned to the States from extended stays in Central America, where I'd befriended Chileans tortured by soldiers trained at the C.I.A.-run School of the Americas in Panama. I was livid at my country's complicity with the dictator Augusto Pinochet's regime. I had held the hands with missing fingers, sliced off in the stadium in Santiago after the coup. I had sung Victor Jara's and Violeta Parra's folk songs with the survivors, and translated poetry by the "disappeared." Then I returned home to the red, white, and blue bunting of a yearlong orgy of national patriotism.

The anger must have made me particularly horny, because something else was brewing that year. My unborn children were circling the globe, searching for me. It was as if they wanted to reinforce the laws of gravity, to anchor my Ariel spirit bouncing around the world on a pogo stick of poetry and politics. These embryonic souls must have taken pity on me, because unlike my friends in Santa Cruz, in no way was I mooning by a window overlooking the sea, lighting joss sticks and dreaming of a bundle of joy.

I was a sack of angular bones with a long blond ponytail, a circuit of misconnected wires waiting to short out, overeducated and underemployed. Among my few possessions I counted copies of *Why I Live in the Forest*, a volume of my poetry published two years earlier by Wesleyan University Press, a suitcase of clothes, a few boxes of books and papers, my Creole great-great-grandmother's Persian carriage shawl from the French Quarter, and the skull of a Brahman bull that I'd found in a dewy field of psilocybin mushrooms among the Mayan ruins at Palenque, Mexico.

This was when the unborn spirits of my children decided to come calling. Between March and September of that year, three unplanned pregnancies occurred with two different women. Never before had I gotten a woman pregnant, or have I ever since. Previous girlfriends had been on the pill, other lovers had been men, so I wasn't prepared for this type of consequence. I had meditated at length on the twin funnels that connect us to the beyond—birth and death—but never confronted the procreative miracle that puts the other two ends of the spectrum in perspective.

After all, I was still busy giving birth to myself.

I want us to have this baby," I told my girlfriend Maureen that morning, wrapping her in a hug. I hadn't slept a wink the night before. Since getting her news of the pregnancy, I'd been spooked by the eerie shadow of my own mortality. *I'm going to die,* I kept thinking between fitful turns in bed, *I'm going to die one day.*

"But," I announced, "only if we raise the baby in Cuba. I don't want our child to grow up in a capitalist, imperialistic country."

Did this fool even know what he was saying? What I must have meant was that I myself didn't want to grow up—here or anywhere.

"I see," she said, nodding as if now she understood what she had to do. And it wasn't moving to Havana.

As if we were in some corny television drama, she and I called ourselves "the young professors" as we sped about St. Petersburg, Florida, in a cloud of hilarity and pot smoke. It was the spring semester of 1976 at Eckerd College, and we both were new to university teaching. Maureen was a redheaded dancer from Brooklyn, had graduated from the Performing Arts High School and Juilliard, and was back from conducting dance research in Ghana. That fall I'd returned from Panama, where I served as an interpreter for the Solidarity with the Panamanian People Committee, invited to tour the country by the Marxist dictator Omar Torrijos, who was trying to assert national sovereignty over the Canal Zone. Who wanted an American colony dividing their country in half?

Maureen thought she was African and I thought I was Latin American, and it felt unreal to both of us to be teaching at a private white college in the South. She wore African headscarves and I sported huaraches and hand-embroidered *camisas,* and on that planetary Floridian campus of sand spurs and squat brick buildings, Africa and Latin America magnetically drifted toward each other until they occupied some imaginary third-world continent in the middle of a mattress thrown onto a terrazzo tile floor.

Even educated fleas do it: we fell in love.

I had attended Eckerd during the sixties when it was called Florida Presbyterian, so my infamous reputation there preceded me. When I was offered the appointment as Poet-in-Residence for one semester, I was warned that the college couldn't afford any drug or sex scandals. So, of course, I arrived on campus after a night in the slammer in Bay St. Louis, Mississippi, where with Frans, my Dutch lover from San Francisco, we'd been busted for carrying an ounce of marijuana while hitchhiking from New Orleans along the Gulf Coast. Frans was going to be deported and I had to appear in a Mississippi courtroom.

Welcome to the profession, Professor Nolan.

As it turned out, Frans was never deported and soon returned to San Francisco. As immersed as I was in the culture of that city, it never occurred to me an ounce of pot, a foreign male lover, a ponytail, and my fringed red Peruvian bag would raise eyebrows in the Deep South. We'd been released from jail after I mentioned an uncle who owned a summer house in Bay St. Louis. I pleaded *nolo contendere*, and Judith, a former girlfriend in Los Angeles, wired the court three hundred dollars from her trust fund.

I never had to go to trial, but the unborn spirits must have taken note. Judith would be the next on their list.

Such was our confusion about the abortion that I drove Maureen back from the procedure in her car, the only time I'd driven since I flunked the California driving test. We both felt sheepish and guilty, particularly Maureen, the Irish Catholic. We returned to my paneled tree house on a quiet back lane and spent days rocking back and forth in the Mexican hammock on the screened porch, saying little. What I learned is that despite the blustering postures of men—*sure, let's strap the infant on our backs and join the guerrillas in the jungle*—women decide these matters. And whatever their choice, it is they who bear the consequences. I've never understood how men could presume to make laws about what women decide to do with their bodies. It would be as if women made male adultery a felony. But we'd never let them, would we?

So the dancer went back to dancing, lithe body intact, and the poet went back to rabble-rousing. We concluded that semester with Maureen's outdoor student dance concert featuring an African drum circle, and my own Third World Solidarity Conference. At the last minute, the pro-Castro speaker from Miami couldn't make it. His legs were blown off in a car-bomb explosion engineered by anti-Castro forces. That same week I was riveted by the news that a U.S.-backed military coup in Argentina had just overthrown Isabel Perón and was initiating what the generals called a "dirty war" against union leaders, students, journalists, and Marxist guerrillas, a campaign that would last for seven years and during which up to thirty thousand people would be "disappeared," tortured, and then dropped drugged from helicopters to drown in the Plata River. I had no idea of the sheer brutality with which I was dealing. Right-wing Latin Americans were out for blood, and I was irate that in military dictatorships such as those in Chile and Argentina, progressives could be plucked off the street and "disappeared" into dungeons.

People like me and my friends.

And then that summer my worst nightmare was to come true. I was.

In June, Maureen and I were off to Guatemala, the next place we hung our hammock.

L ittle did we know that in 1976 the Guatemalan civil war was coming to a full boil. This protracted battle, which began in 1960, would engulf the country in the early eighties and by 1996 leave 200,000 indigenous people dead. Leftist priests from Spain inspired by Vatican II's liberation theology would square off against conservative evangelical missionaries from the States. Paramilitary death squads supported by the government and financed by the U.S. would raid the mountain villages of Kiché Maya peasants and confiscate their farmland for exploitation by mining companies. Already labor unions were being smashed and agricultural cooperatives disbanded. The country was beginning a terrifying descent into genocide, and the clarion voice of Rigoberta Menchú was a long way off.

And there we were, golden-haired gringos trying to get "back to the earth" with travelers' checks.

Maureen and I could sense the incipient violence the minute we crossed the Mexican border and landed in Guatemala City, a grim gray metropolis of choked traffic and stricken faces patrolled by teenaged soldiers toting submachine guns. After a hassle at the border crossing, during which the wallet containing my entry permit was stolen, we took off for Panajachel, one of the small towns that ringed Lake Atitlán. This was among the few pockets of foreign tourism that survived the devastating earthquake that had shaken the country that February, leveling the city of Antigua. When you come to heal yourself among the Maya, the most grounded people on earth, only to encounter relief workers freely handing out Valiums to them on the street, you know something is wrong.

Even in those days Panajachel was a Yankee-friendly *gringolandia*. On the picturesque Calle Santander, backpackers munched granola and burgers in cafés blasting Neil Young while outside Kaqchikel Indian women went about their ancient tasks, baskets of vegetables balanced on their heads. We rented a blue two-room house with a wide veranda by the placid lake, canopied at night by stars. This idyll was set behind the high iron fence of an effusive rose garden meticulously tended by an Indian gardener. We felt like Adam and Eve in the Garden of Eden. The house had intermittent electricity, outdoor running water, and a kerosene stove, a place that must have seemed like a château to the Indians who lived in the reed houses surrounding us. Maureen braided her long auburn hair with colorful yarn into native plaits and used a batik cloth as a skirt, even learning to carry a basket on her head. We entertained the fantasy that we were "one with the people."

"Going native?" an American backpacker asked us as we traipsed along the lake in our indigenous garb, basket on head. That burst our bubble, but didn't dispel for long the delusion that we were one with the people.

We were one with the people until the Indian women whom we invited to enter the gate to fill their vessels with our tap water started walking off with our plastic dishes and drying laundry. Then we put a padlock on the gate to keep the people out. We were one with the people until the gardener accused me of trying to steal his native language. He and I had been exchanging lessons in English and Kaqchikel until he became suspicious that I would sell his language in the United States. From those lessons I remember only one word—*whiskilé*—the name of a squash we call *mirlitons* in New Orleans, for which there is no English term. The gardener taught me to add mirlitons to my Creole red beans, and I felt right at home eating the diet of the people.

We thought we were one with the people until Maureen told me she was pregnant again.

"What about the copper IUD you had put in after the abortion?" I asked, stunned.

"It didn't work." She looked down. "I've missed my period."

"But that's impossible." I crossed my arms.

She shot me a look that said *as if you would know.*

Frankly, I didn't believe her. Women can be so emotional, I thought, always making mountains out of molehills. I decided that she was reliving the trauma of the abortion, that the guilt was literally making her sick and provoking symptoms. My ebullient Ginger Rogers, the playful, tap-dancing redhead, became pale and morose. Her freckles disappeared. She bought a black wool *rebozo* at the market in Chichicastenango and wore it draped over her head like a nun. I figured that her Catholic-school education was catching up with her.

"What am I doing with this dead baby's blanket?" she said one day, throwing the black shawl down on our veranda.

I picked up the shawl and hung it on the clothesline. As the rainy season approached, the dead baby's blanket turned into the leaden sky above us. I stomped off to take long solitary walks around the lake. Maureen made friends with another New Yorker, writer Vicki Lindner, whom I'd met three years earlier when Judith and I were in Peru. Together they discovered there were no reliable pregnancy tests in Guatemala, so Maureen flew back to St. Petersburg.

Ten days later her letter arrived. She was indeed pregnant for the second time in four months. And it was clear what she'd decided to do about it. There would be time, she wrote, after her dance career to have children. But not now. Would I please come back to St. Petersburg to help her deal with this?

The dead baby's blanket was gone from the clothesline but now I moped around the suddenly desolate lakeside idyll. How could I not have trusted Maureen to know what was happening inside her own body? I felt like a real son-of-a-bitch. Pregnant Kiché women with empty buckets on their heads stared at me accusingly through the locked gate as they trudged on bare feet down to the lake to fetch water. Banks of low dark clouds rolled in from the shore and it rained every day, swelling the yellow and pink roses in the Garden of Eden to an obscene size until their petals dropped off, one by one.

In this moody haze of drizzle, I drifted back to where I'd started. The revolution.

I soon met a Chilean named Paulina who lived in Guatemala City but was vacationing in Panajachel for the summer. She'd survived the September coup three years earlier in Santiago and was committed to the resistance against the military dictatorship, as concerned as I was about the fate of the disappeared languishing in jail. She pointed out that, as in Chile, the C.I.A. also had staged a military coup in Guatemala in 1954, toppling the democratically elected government of Jacobo Árbenz

Guzmán. From a prosperous family, Paulina had been able to escape Chile, and now was married to a Guatemalan businessman of evident means. She was connected to a group of exiled Chileans who had also made it out of the country, and her house in the city served as a launching pad for their attempts to seek political asylum in Europe. Several were already in Sweden and Denmark, and others spent their days making the rounds of European embassies trying to secure residency visas to start new lives.

One weekend Paulina and I climbed the extinct volcano San Pedro on the other side of Lake Atitlán, overlooking a town called—of all things—Santiago. That day Paulina was also one with the people, and wore her maid's flowered house dress with a length of clothesline fastened around the waist as a belt. We began the exhausting climb at dawn with an Indian guide, and by noon we made it to the top, panting. Below us the lake was an unblinking blue eye, pure as the ancestral soul of the Americas. That was where she invited me to a party, a very special one.

"I'll be getting together with other *exilados* next Thursday in Guate to send one of us off to Paris," she said. "French political asylum is tricky to get, so this will be a real celebration. Marco was traumatized by his time in prison, and really needs to get out of Latin America. In Santiago he was one of the leaders of the student Communist party, and he won't last long in this country. Soldiers are already tailing him."

The next Wednesday I took a bus into Guate, as the capital was known, and spent the night in a cheap hostel. On Thursday I hitched a ride on the back of a motorcycle to the Colonia Club de Golf, a luxurious suburb where the party was to take place. I was carrying a copy of Neruda's memoir *Confieso que he vivido* as a sign that I could be trusted. When I entered the mansion where the Chileans were gathering, with its expansive manicured grounds, I was surprised that it was empty of any furnishings. They were meeting in a friend's vacant estate so that if the soldiers showed up, the party wouldn't jeopardize anyone's home or family.

The soldiers didn't show up at the party, but I was certain we were being watched and that they followed me back into town on the bus that evening. During the festivities, the rubber band I used to fasten my ponytail had snapped and my long hair was falling past my shoulder blades. I looked like one of the Allman Brothers, a sitting duck for the uniformed agents of public order.

"*Documentos,*" demanded a beady-eyed soldier the moment I stepped off the bus.

As always, I had my worn passport with me. After paging through it, the soldier asked me for my entry permit into the country. I explained that it had been stolen at the border along with my wallet, and unfortunately no stamp in my passport indicated my legitimate entry into the country three months earlier.

The soldier shook his head. "Looks like you're in the country illegally and need to go to jail until Immigration determines your status. Who were those other foreigners you were with in that house at the Club de Golf?"

"What Club de Golf?" I didn't intend to say a word about the Chileans. "I'm renting a house in Panajachel and am living here legally."

A small crowd gathered on the sidewalk to watch the soldiers arresting the blond hippie. An older woman approached to ask if I needed help. I scribbled Paulina's phone number on a scrap of paper.

"Please call this friend and tell her I'm being put in jail. And, by the way, do you happen to have a rubber band to tie back my hair?"

Out of her purse she produced an elastic ponytail holder festooned with a plastic daisy. She glanced at the local phone number and promised to call that evening. Then the soldier frog-marched me down the street to the district jail. Unless the señora called Paulina, nobody in the world would know where I was.

So this was what it felt like to be "disappeared."

After surrendering my new wallet, belt, watch, and house keys at the front desk, I was led through a series of cement courtyards to a narrow iron gate, beyond which was a large yard filled with about a hundred men. Slouching against the walls, most of them looked like hardened criminals, glaring at me with hooded eyes as I walked past. Gathered in one group were a few dark-skinned Kiché Mayans, and in a corner stood another fair-complexioned American, who approached me immediately.

The words tripped out of our mouths. Short-haired Jeff from Michigan also had been picked up in Guate, in his case for not carrying a passport on the street, although I suspected a bit of marijuana may have been involved. Jeff didn't speak Spanish and was oblivious to the political situation in the country. He had been in the yard for two days now, and showed me the ropes. A single reeking toilet for the hundred men. A straw-thatched concrete enclosure littered with dirty pieces of packing cardboard for sleeping. And beyond a far gate, another yard filled with real desperadoes doing hard time. The only telephone was in the adjacent courtyard, on the other side of the locked gate I'd just entered. After several requests, Jeff hadn't been allowed to leave the compound to use it.

Nobody knew where he was.

Together Jeff and I seemed to attract attention, and soon a trustee told me the leader of the already sentenced prisoners in the back courtyard wanted to meet us. I figured that this honcho might be of value to us, so we were ushered into an airless cinderblock room lit by guttering candles and smelling of sweat. Cigarettes glowed in the dark, and among the Goyaesque shadows I could soon make out the silhouettes of grizzled men atop straw mats on the packed earth floor, eating roasted chicken with their fingers. Jeff and I were both shaking, but I managed to answer their inane questions about American girls and baseball. The honcho told me that his cronies in the other yard would keep an eye on us, and advised we stick together for our own safety. He didn't offer us any of his chicken.

Looking back, I wonder if we were another course of chicken. The older men gaped at us with twitching eyes, greasy lips, and something approaching lust.

Once back in the main yard, the other prisoners were milling toward the dark sleeping shed, where they got into fistfights over the pieces of cardboard. Jeff and I hunkered down in a corner and finally found a tatter of cardboard to share. He pointed out that the men weren't armed and we had nothing to steal. The other prisoners were probably as afraid of the two gringos as we were of them, but I didn't close an eye the entire night. Obsessive thoughts flooded my mind: of Maureen in Florida, of the disappeared in Chilean and Argentine jails, of the real possibilities of being tortured, raped, or killed.

At dawn a cart piled with stick brooms was pulled into the yard, and we prisoners set about sweeping the cement for another long, messy day under the broiling sun. Following chores, another cart distributed beans and tortillas, which I could barely choke down. Shortly after, a guard entered the yard and called my name. He told me that I was being transferred to the adjoining yard, the one with the phone. I asked if Jeff could come along with me and was told no. My American friend freaked out.

"Look, man," he said, sweating profusely, "we swore we'd stick together. It's the only way we'll survive this, like that guy said last night."

"But after two days, they still haven't let you call the American Embassy. We'll just rot together back here. At least I'll have a chance in the other yard to get us both out."

His eyes pleaded with me not to leave. It was one of the hardest decisions I'd ever had to make, and I did it in a split second. I signaled to the guard and stepped out of the yard, the iron gate clanging shut behind me.

And to my amazement, when I asked the guard if I could use the phone, he said yes. Then he offered me a cup of coffee, as if I were a visiting dignitary. I was the only prisoner in the yard, which contained not only a heavy black phone but a private toilet.

The man who answered my call at the American Embassy took down my name as well as Jeff's, and our whereabouts. "Don't worry. Sometime this morning an attaché will be out there to see y'all. Can't miss him. He's a colored fellow."

I couldn't believe my ears.

In a few hours, the "colored fellow" appeared in a tie and starched white shirt. He told me not to worry. "After a week here, they'll probably send you both to the work farm, and I pass by there every month to bring *Playboys* to the Americans."

"Are you joking?" I sputtered. "They can just pluck American citizens off the street on trumped up immigration charges and keep us on a work farm for months?"

"Sometimes years," he said, shaking his head. "We pay these cops' salaries with our foreign aid, but can't tell them what to do."

I explained that the immigration office must have a copy of my stolen entry permit, as well as Jeff's, now tucked inside the passport in his hotel room. Could the attaché at least bring us copies of those documents from Immigration?

"Sorry," he said. "That's not how they do things down here. But I'll see you at the work farm if they send you there."

I got the name of the ambassador from him: Francis Melroy, a Nixon appointee from whom I didn't expect too much sympathy. But I planned to call him directly.

The African-American attaché then entered the main yard to speak with Jeff, who had been wildly gesturing to me with a thumbs-up through the gate. Little did either of us suspect that the only help we'd get from our government when thrown into a foreign jail would be a subscription to *Playboy*.

As soon as the attaché left, a wooden door creaked open from a small stucco room adjoining the courtyard and a hand beckoned to me. I stuck my head inside to find a corpulent middle-aged man with a florid, pockmarked face sitting on a mattress. The wall of the cell was plastered floor-to-ceiling with pastel pictures of Jesus: on the cross, in the Garden of Gethsemane, rising from the tomb. The pockmarked man motioned for me to sit down on the floor.

"I saw you yesterday," he said, eyes devouring me, "and from the back thought you were a woman." He reached over to flick my ponytail, still held in place by the elastic with the plastic daisy.

I scooted away from him.

Then he told me his story. He was a colonel in the army who one drunken afternoon had plowed his car into a school bus, killing seven children. Soon after, he found Jesus and became an evangelical Christian, like the country's next military dictator, Efraín Ríos Montt. The colonel had been sentenced to ten years, which as a military officer he was serving in a private cell with an unlocked door to this courtyard. He hadn't been with a woman in several years, and was feeling sort of lonely. So he'd had me transferred to this patio. He patted the mattress next to him, inviting me to sit there.

I jumped to my feet. "I'll be out of here by this evening." It was already mid-afternoon on Friday, and Immigration closed at six p.m. until Monday. Somehow I would get there. A hundred mournful eyes of Jesus stared down at me from the smudged walls.

"No you won't," he said with a wink. "*Te vas a pasar este fin de semana conmigo.*"

Those were among the most chilling words I'd ever heard: you're going to spend this weekend with me. I scurried out of the cell to his leering smile and called over the guard. I needed to call my ambassador.

The Ambassador Extraordinary and Plenipotentiary Francis E. Melroy Jr. was, of course, in a meeting, but I left him this message: *at six p.m. this afternoon, American citizen James Nolan will kill himself by jumping off the courtyard wall at the local jail unless he is taken to the immigration office where his status can be ascertained.*

The embassy clerk took down my message in shocked silence. "Didn't y'all meet up with that colored fellow?" he asked.

"Please deliver that to Ambassador Melroy." Then I sat on the ground to figure out how I could scale the wall in order to throw myself off it, picturing rivulets of my blood tricking across the cracked cement.

At 5:15 a guard entered the courtyard carrying my passport and informed me that he was taking me to Immigration. He handcuffed me and, since my wallet was still at the front desk, paid our way on the rush-hour bus. I kept asking him the time: 5:30 . . . 5:45 . . . 5:55. To my relief, we arrived at the office only to find that it would be open late, since they were processing a stack of urgent visas for Honduran migrant workers.

After a lengthy wait, an immigration clerk took me into a separate office to tell me that they hadn't located a copy of my entry permit into the country. The last notation in my passport was an exit stamp from Panama in October of the previous year. So Immigration assumed that I was a foreign subversive who had illegally crossed the border and had been living in Guatemala for almost a year, connected in some way to Chilean revolutionaries and the Communist insurgency. But as a courtesy to the ambassador of my country, which was generously helping Guatemala to rid itself of such vermin, I was to be deported within seventy-two hours. He stamped a deportation order in my passport and handed it over to the escort policeman.

After this ordeal, I was overjoyed to be deported. On the bus ride back to the jail to collect my belongings, I made a mental to-do list: buy a return ticket to the States, check out of the hostel, empty the house in Panajachel, and get the hell out of this totalitarian country.

When we arrived back at the jail, the desk clerk asked the policeman escorting me for my release paper from Immigration. The policeman shrugged and said he hadn't been issued any release paper.

"There's no release paper," I chimed in. "Look in my passport. I'm being deported," I bragged, as if it were an honor.

"Bring him back into the yard until the release paper arrives," the clerk muttered, jerking his thumb toward the back of the jail.

Caught in an embarrassing mistake in his paperwork, my cop escort turned violent. He grabbed me by the handcuffs and dragged me screaming down the corridor toward lock-up. It was 7:30 on a Friday evening, and I knew that Immigration was finished with me. No "release paper"—whatever that might be—was on its way.

"There's no fucking release paper," I shouted as I was thrown back into the private yard, where my handcuffs were removed. I was beside myself with panic.

The pockmarked face of the convict colonel popped around his cell door and gave me a smarmy smile. *Te vas a pasar este fin de semana conmigo.* His words that afternoon echoed almost audibly. The Embassy had closed, and soon so would Immigration. And I would be alone with this rapist for the weekend.

Just at that moment—with a timing to this day I can hardly believe—a guard appeared with a covered basket for me that a señora had brought to the jailhouse door. Inside was a small apple pie, of all things, along with a brief note in English from Paulina: "What can I do to help you?" I borrowed a pencil from the guard and scrawled in English on the other side of the paper: "Go to Immigration <u>now</u> and bring the jail desk clerk my release paper!"

"Please take this thank-you note to that kind señora from church," I told the guard. Hungry as I was, I couldn't bring myself to eat the apple pie, so when the guard returned, I handed it to him. Then I hid in the toilet from the colonel convict.

Within an hour, I was escorted back to the front desk, where I was handed my belongings along with my passport. When I stumbled outside, there stood Paulina, dressed to the nines, waiting for me in front of the jail. I dove for her, wrapping her in a bear hug. "Why an apple pie?" I screamed between kisses to her cheeks.

"Isn't that what Americans eat?"

"Quick, let's get out of here," I said, grabbing her hand and scampering around the corner.

We took off down the crowded street, finally hiding in the back booth of a Chinese restaurant. She had gone to Immigration, she said, and after much coaxing, persuaded them to write out a release paper, although they insisted that with the deportation stamp in my passport, one wasn't necessary. She reported that a pleased-looking American man was waiting in the office when she arrived, who I assumed must have been Jeff.

"And how did you get them to send over the paper?" I asked, wide-eyed.

"Easy," Paulina said. "I came on to the immigration officer like a crazed whore and offered to sleep with him. We have a date for right now," she said, glancing at her watch. "How do you think we got people out of jail in Chile?" This was obviously a date she didn't plan to keep, so we ordered another round of beers.

"Your rapist should meet mine," I said. "Poor guy's really lonely."

Within forty-eight hours I was on a flight, not back to Maureen in Florida but home to my great-aunt Marguerite's house in New Orleans. As the plane roared through the cumulus clouds over the Gulf of Mexico, I stared out of the window, trying to visualize the insistently searching souls of my unborn children. Sorry, I told them, I'm a deported jailbird who just escaped certain death in a foreign cooler by the hair of his chin. Four years later, at a consulate Fulbright reception in Barcelona, I told this story to an American cultural attaché who had served at previous posts in Central America.

"You're the only American I've ever heard of who got out of a Guatemalan jail alive," he said, slapping me on the back. By then it almost seemed funny.

The third time did it.

Tail between my legs, I was slouching back to San Francisco, even though I had no apartment or job there. On my way to vanish once again into the city's permissive fog, I stopped off in Los Angeles to see my former girlfriend Judith, now settled in a comfortable house in Topanga Canyon, where she ran a New Age bookshop.

Judith grew up in Beverly Hills, her father was the shower-door king, and she was heiress to her grandfather's Lucky Strike fortune from South America. She had paid my court fees in Mississippi, and claimed that she was worried about me. I could talk with her, even if I had to ignore the often wacky woo-woo of her New Age beliefs. A dark, passionate Russian Jew, she was into the violet ray, St. Germaine, the Pleiades, vegetarianism, cleansing fasts, and some spiritual leader named Elizabeth Clare Prophet, who took her followers for every cent they had. I referred to this charlatan as Elizabeth Clear Profit, and at least Judith possessed the earthy perspective to laugh at my joke.

Once together in Topanga Canyon, we mostly talked about the year we'd spent traveling in South America with a tribe of international hippies drawn by the dramatic appearance in the southern sky of the Comet Kohoutek in 1973. Together with another lover of mine, a gay man named Lance, Judith and I had rented a banana farm in Timbío, a small village outside of Popayán, Colombia. Our Indian neighbors amused themselves wondering which one of the two blond men the brunette dish belonged to, but the truth was that I slept in the middle of our grass-mat bed on the floor, and sometimes rolled to the right and sometimes to the left. This didn't confuse me in the least, although it did everyone else. Before leaving for South America, I had written a cover story for *Ramparts* magazine about an androgynous phenomenon of the new sexual liberation that I called "pansexuality." In some circles, the word I coined stuck, although the feminist poet Adrienne Rich attacked me in the next issue of the magazine as a sexist male pig.

Judith broke her cleansing fast to join me for dinner at a Mexican restaurant, where we slurped down two rounds of margaritas. After telling her about the pregnancies with my new girlfriend in Florida and Guatemala, I was just getting to the scariest part of my jail escape saga when, ecstatic to still be alive, I leaned over to kiss her on the mouth.

"We'd like another round," I told the waiter, pointing at our empty glasses.

"Are you trying for a third?" she asked.

"You bet."

We spent a single night together in Topanga Canyon before I boarded the plane to San Francisco. There I rented a room at a shabby Basque residence hotel in North Beach called the Hotel Du Midi, a room with a bay window recently vacated by a Basque shepherd whose horse had died in Spain. The grandmotherly Basque proprietor kept the linoleum floors and sheer curtains spotless, and it almost felt like staying with my great-aunt Marguerite in New Orleans. I lived on take-out food from Chinatown and, flat on my stomach, heated water for instant coffee with an electric coil whose short cord only plugged in under the bed.

I didn't hit rock bottom until a late-night conversation at a phone booth in the Café Trieste. Judith told me she was pregnant and it was mine.

"When I asked you that night in the Mexican restaurant if you were trying for your third," she said, "I meant pregnancy."

"Thought you meant my third margarita. What now?"

"I'm going to have the baby. I received this mind-blowing vision from the Pleiades in a flash of violet light. Are you ready?"

"Not really."

"This child is going to be the messiah of the New Age."

I was prepared for almost anything but unstable Judith as the Virgin Mary. I comforted myself that at least she had the means to raise the messiah of the New Age on her own, far from my meager manger in the Basque hotel.

"At the moment I can't contribute anything materially," I said, eyes brimming, "but I'll help as much as I can to raise the child."

The news was a sucker punch to the gut, and I could barely make it back to the chenille spread on my bed. I spent a few weeks aimlessly wandering the back alleys of Chinatown in the fog, shaking my head in disbelief. I wondered how I was going to tell Maureen, with whom I was exchanging weekly love letters. She was planning to quit her college teaching job at the end of the semester and come live with me in San Francisco. She didn't want just to teach dance but to work as a performer, and she knew there were plenty of gigs among the small theaters in town. Yet now another woman was going to give birth to our baby, the one we didn't have.

Eventually luck turned my way. I rented a studio apartment in a ramshackle brick building on an alley in the Barbary Coast and sent for my possessions from Florida. I bought a foam mattress to throw on the floor and placed my portable typewriter on a squat wooden bench I found in the courtyard. The brick walls outside were covered with fuchsia bougainvillea whose petals carpeted the worn stones of the nineteenth-century building. My neighbors were eccentric artists and filmmakers. Sliding open my glass door that gave onto the quaint courtyard, I felt as if I were back in the French Quarter.

Two months later Judith called. She was in San Francisco, she explained breathlessly, on a pilgrimage to Mount Shasta. No, she couldn't see me right then. She was with a new boyfriend named Bobby, a Vietnam vet. That afternoon he'd forced her to order a hamburger, and eating meat for the first time in years made her sick.

"Pregnant women need extra protein," I said. "How's the baby?"

Silence.

"You know," I said, "our child?"

"I've been meaning to tell you . . . I decided not to have it."

"You aborted the messiah of the New Age?"

"Look, I knew I couldn't count on you for any support—"

"But I said that I'd—"

"You're way up here and I'm in L.A. with. . . ." She broke down sobbing.

In that moment, as a twenty-seven-year-old would-be revolutionary at the end of his rope, I finally finished growing up. Consequences were no longer what happened to other people but to me. I'd been clinging by my fingernails to cherubic innocence, floating on a cloud of myopic idealism, and I hit the ground with an abrupt *splat*. This was how the world really was, hemmed in by the all-too-human limitations of what we call original sin. The central myth of the New World always has been one of a self-renewing innocence, of the purity of Indians, rainforests, wild animals, children, rainbows, and the faith that we can return our corrupted continents to their prelapsarian origins. This was the guiding principle shared, each in our own ways, by both the headbanded American hippies of my generation and the Latin American Marxists of the same generation, who adopted Indian warrior noms de guerre. As if we could bolt shut the gates to the Garden of Eden from the inside, start a commune, grow our hair, live like Indians, wear rope sandals, and eat only fallen fruit. As if each of us weren't carrying around within ourselves that stolen apple, worm and all. As if everyone, at one point or another, didn't take a fatal bite.

After that phone call, I decided that, no, I couldn't pretend to live in that imaginary world any longer. I was out of New World air freshener. I cut my long hair and, like the exiled Adam, bowed my head in shame as I shambled out of the Garden, sentenced for life to an ancient world weighed down by generations of violence, grief, and sorrow. The year my children came looking for me, I wasn't at home. So like Jessie Blue, they may have swooped down from on high but were born elsewhere, to other parents. Unbeknown to me, I've probably met them here and there, and they seemed happy enough to be who they were.

That fall Maureen drove from Florida to live with me. We had no idea at the time, but soon our travels would take us to new lives in Barcelona and then Beijing. A few days before she arrived in San Francisco, Manu, a stray cat I'd adopted from the bougainvillea-covered courtyard, had kittens.

Three, to be exact.

I nailed a board over the lower shelf of my closet bookcase to create a crib where Manu could nurse her newborns. But every morning the feisty kittens woke us up. They would scamper over the board and, on shaky paws, skid mewing across the wooden floor toward us, then scramble onto our foam mattress.

"Here come the kittens!" we'd say, as the first squeals approached.

And we'd sit in bed and hold up each spotted kitten to the light, their just opened eyes gazing out on a brand new day.

10

WHAT WAS BEHIND THE GREEN DOOR

When I saw my first porn movie, I wasn't carried away by waves of lust. After the opening sequence, I was more in a state of shock. My Argentine friend Raúl told me that he once entered a porn theater on Times Square only to find his sister, an aspiring actress, writhing on the screen. So imagine my surprise when Marilyn Chambers, star of the feature I was watching, was pulled from a car and thrown through my front door.

I rubbed my eyes. It couldn't be true.

Although *Behind the Green Door* was first released in 1972, it took me a long time to get around to porn flicks, much less to go see one at an X-rated movie house like the Mitchell Brothers. This was during the late seventies, and in bohemian San Francisco everyone was already comfortably settled into whatever vices we'd acquired during the previous decade. Even in the post-hippie era, sex was open, spontaneous, and available everywhere. To tell you the truth, we were humping like bunnies, and a porn movie was like trying to tempt someone at an Italian wedding feast with a TV dinner. That day I must have been extra hungry, or maybe my countercultural resolve was weakening. We were still busy making ourselves up in San Francisco, and maintained a steely distrust of mainstream culture. In this fading era of food co-ops and communal living, of free love, free boxes, and free theater, I never got around to investigating anything even vaguely commercial until it appeared inevitable. Believe it or not, I didn't get high-speed Internet service until last month, and only bought a digital TV a week after my mother's rabbit-ear model became obsolete.

I'm still slow that way.

I was living in an apartment at 37 Osgood Place, a little-known alley of nineteenth-century brick buildings dating from the pirate days of the Barbary Coast. Just off Pacific Avenue, the building was situated on what was once the wharf of San Francisco Bay, and originally had been an Australian whorehouse run by a murderous gang of pimps called the Sydney Ducks. The renovated crib-like apartments were arranged around a crumbling brick courtyard that could have been in the French Quarter. I paid $130 a month rent and didn't mind the shoe-box sized studio, especially since my sliding glass door opened onto a brick wall of cascading fuchsia bougainvillea in the courtyard, which we entered from the street through a creaky wooden door with peeling green paint. On lazy afternoons, the other tenants and I would gather in our underpants on the rooftop to sunbathe, smear each other's backs with coconut oil, and share joints and brownies. The women went topless, of course, and what I called the Underpants Brigade usually wound up howling with hilarity as the sun set pink behind the wall of bougainvillea and the theater lights on Broadway and Columbus began to twinkle.

Allen Ginsberg had lived in the building, the photographer Steven Arnold rented the basement apartment, and eventually the German film director Wim Wenders would move in. The place percolated with creativity, as did the whole neighborhood during that era, when North Beach was filled with small theaters like the Committee, the Montgomery Playhouse, Club Fugazi, and the flamenco show at the Old Spaghetti Factory. Francis Ford Coppola had just bought the Little Fox up the street, where Randle McMurphy railed against the system in an eternal run of the play *One Flew over the Cuckoo's Nest*, and turned the theater into his film studio, American Zoetrope. My upstairs neighbor Cheryl, an actress, had the first answering machine I'd ever seen. She bought it so that she didn't have to wait by the phone all day for audition callbacks. It took me another fifteen years to get my own, but as I said, I'm slow that way.

The Mitchell Brothers cinema was located at the corner of Polk and O'Farrell in the borderline Tenderloin, and was one of the first movie houses dedicated to X-rated movies, mostly those made by the two Mitchell brothers. Filmed in the wake of *Deep Throat*, their feature *Behind the Green Door* was the original porn blockbuster. Years later, after the movie house became a sleazy strip club and live peep show, it was raided by the police, and to get even, the wily Mitchells posted a notice on the theater marquee, "For Show Times, Call . . . ," followed by Mayor Diane Feinstein's home phone number. Eventually, Jim Mitchell would shoot his drug-addict brother Artie to death, and the business would be sold, but in its first incarnation the Mitchell Brothers was still a must-see stop in swinging San Francisco. In those days the building was covered with lush nature murals and inside was done up like a Storyville bordello, with red velveteen walls and brass chandeliers. It was nothing like the dreary porn barns and sex shops that would soon mushroom in the Tenderloin, of the kind frequented by lonely, grey-faced old men in raincoats.

At the time, I was a robust young man with shoulder-length hair, dressed in drawstring pants and a Guatemalan shirt, a tourist in my own town out for an adventure. At first, I was disappointed that the Mitchells didn't sell popcorn: that was how well I understood the porn business. The darkened theater was filled with middle-aged Japanese men and women seated in groups, and feeling squirrelly about this new experience, I slipped into an aisle seat in the back. Let's see what it's like to watch people ball on screen, I thought. I was game.

As the film began, a car swerved through the night into a narrow brick alley that looked all too familiar. Then two thugs yanked Marilyn Chambers from the back seat and threw her through a green wooden door—my door—the one to 37 Osgood Place. Was Behind the Green Door going to take place in my apartment? I lunged forward in the seat, waiting to recognize the courtyard, my Pullman kitchen, or the other members of the Underpants Brigade. Had I rented an apartment on a porn set?

"Green door," as a pop song of the fifties went, "what's that secret you're keeping?"

The rest of the movie actually occurred in an enormous circus-like sound studio, where Marilyn Chambers was screwed before a live audience by long-haired men swinging on trapezes. As in The Story of O, she was enslaved by these hunks, but didn't seem to mind. I quickly understood that people didn't watch porn movies for the character development. The sex was mechanical and repetitive, and struck me as a fairly ridiculous endeavor unless you were participating, which I wasn't. Yet slouching lower in my seat, I was hopelessly aroused, wondering how I was going to walk out of the theater in that condition.

After the first male orgasm, one third of the Japanese in the audience stood up and marched out of the theater. I assumed that, offended, they were going to demand their money back. After the second orgasm, another group of the Japanese audience jumped to their feet and also paraded out. After the third, almost everyone else filed out, leaving just me and a few other American men sitting by ourselves in the theater, adjusting our clothes.

I felt obligated to watch the whole film, just to see how the, *ahem,* plot turned out. I was expecting Marilyn Chambers to prance naked through my courtyard, puffing on a post-coital cigarette, but not a trace of 37 Osgood Place appeared again. After the credits rolled, I quizzed the ticket taker, a gruff older man with a sallow complexion.

"How come all of those people left in groups after the orgasms?"

"The Mitchells bus in Japanese tourists," he told me, "and they sign up for the one-cum-shot tour, the two-cum-shot tour, or the three-cum-shot tour. They sit together, according to how many money shots they paid for, and then get back on the tour bus waiting outside. That's how we make our nut in the dirty movie business. We'd go broke waiting for hippies like you to drift in."

I was flabbergasted.

Walking home down Polk Street, I began to view the city in a garish light, one colored by tourism, money, and sex. Many years later in New Orleans and Barcelona, I'd witness those cities' cultures also slicked up into hot commodities, but at the moment didn't understand exactly what was happening here. The freewheeling spirit of San Francisco was being packaged and sold, and people were lining up to pay for the freedom we'd fought to establish in our funky parallel cosmos. As delicious as the freedom you struggled for could be, I suspected that the freedom you bought rotted the soul. As far as I was concerned, the idea of a sex shop was as incomprehensible as an air shop: what in the world was there to sell? Underpants? Coconut oil? Sunsets? I suddenly noticed the sturdy bars on our androgynous playpen of earthly delights, and the horny faces staring in from the uptight world on the other side looked sinister indeed.

I passed a shop on Polk Street called Hard On Leather, which at first glance I took for a trendy shoe store. But the window display consisted of male mannequins in buttless black leather chaps, along with whips, handcuffs, harnesses, spiked dog collars, and painful-looking clips, clamps, and plugs. I shivered. To my mind, this creepy tableau invoked death, like the altar at a Black Mass. I walked on, hugging myself as the wind whipped a chill fog down Polk Street. Along the way I wandered past the glittering gay clubs blaring the new pumped-up dance music called disco, where the fresh-faced, short-haired young men who were streaming into San Francisco from small-town America perched all in a row on bleachers like factory chickens, feeling free for the first time in their lives, if only for the duration of an amyl nitrite rush or a twirl of the mirrored ball overhead. The bathhouses and sex clubs would eventually get them, and most of these young men wouldn't live long. Within the next two years the first cases of a "gay cancer" would be discovered in the city, the disease now known as AIDS.

Before the model and actress Marilyn Chambers made *Behind the Green Door*, she appeared as a ruddy-cheeked milk maiden beaming at a baby on boxes of Ivory soap. But when the film was released, Proctor & Gamble promptly fired her. As naïve as we were back then, she assumed that her role in the porn film would naturally cross over into legitimate acting parts. As she later confessed in an interview, "Boy, was I wrong."

I didn't know it at the time—Harvey Milk would be assassinated within a few months—but a lot of us were starting to get things wrong. The secret behind the green door turned out to be a Pandora's box of greed, lust, and self-destructive behavior. Soon expensive lines of coke would replace nickel-bags of weed, sexual encounters would become predatory and specialized, and San Francisco would change, or revert to its original character in a way that would have delighted those nineteenth-century sex traffickers, the Sydney Ducks. The second Gold Rush was under way, one that would peddle to the rest of the country a dubious product called "lifestyle," as the first had exploited natural mineral wealth. One morning in the not-too-distant future, we Summer of Love veterans would wake up to realize there was no way back, and that we had little choice other than to finish growing up in the money-grubbing world in which we'd been raised. I still think about this day whenever I torment myself with the question: how did the liberating joy of free love and psychedelic drugs evolve into the grim scenario of AIDS, crack, and crystal meth?

I had just turned the dreaded age of thirty, after which my generation assumed that idealistic flower children would shrivel up into the homun-culi of cynical adults. Yet that evening as I bounced over Nob Hill through the fog, walking home from my first porn flick, I was still bobbing along like a cake of Ivory soap. I was probably writing some goofy poem in my head as I floated toward 37 Osgood Place and then disappeared behind the green door.

11

SCENE OF THE CRIME
A Love Story

The only time anyone has ever held a gun to my head, I was leading a double life in Madrid.

It was September of 1979 and, just arrived in Spain, I was attending the orientation for Fulbright fellows. Soon I would be on my way to Barcelona to teach American literature at the Universidad Central for a year, and little did I suspect, for many more years, beginning a long expatriate relationship with Spain. I was lodged at a cheap *pensión* on Calle Cervantes, where every morning I dressed up in a plum corduroy sports coat and double-pleated khaki trousers, with wide-collared Sta-prest shirts whose polyester-blend fabric made me itch and sweat in the late-summer sauna of Madrid. I barely recognized this spiffy thirty-year-old man in the mirror.

I was trying to look as respectable as I could. The previous year I had spent in southern India, smoking bheedis, drinking hashish-laced lassis, and wearing the loudly batiked sarongs called *lhongis*. So my dapper seminar-wear was just another change of native costume. I figured that the State Department officials with whom I sat in conferences probably worked for the C.I.A. Even though these were the relaxed Carter years, a Cold War tension hung in the air. These steel-jawed officers were trying to get what they called "more bang for the buck" out of the Fulbright program, tired of pouring money "down the rat hole of literature." So by day, I was dressed to play my role as an earnest young professor with a name tag, wrestling with the Cold Warriors.

Night was another world entirely.

Franco had been dead for only three years, and the entombed Spanish capital was beginning to explode with the fierce creativity and sensuality repressed during the past four decades. Discordant rock music blared out of club doorways, prostitutes lined the streets, and the sweet scent of Moroccan hashish floated everywhere. I had stepped into the formative moments of the crazed *movida madrileña*, an underground demimonde later immortalized in the films of Pedro Almodóvar. The bars never closed, and life began at midnight. My only friends in Madrid at the time were a Spanish writer named Eduardo Lago and his pregnant wife, Amparo. I had met them in Benares, India, the previous year, just after I received the telegram informing me of the teaching fellowship to Barcelona.

Seated at the next table of the hostel breakfast room, Eduardo and Amparo had been engaged in a violent argument, only half of which I could make out. They were cursing each other as only Spaniards can, shitting on the communion wafer (*me cago en la hostia*) and calling on the whore who gave birth to you (*la puta que te parió*).

"Er, *perdóneme*. Are you by any chance," I asked in my best Latin American Spanish, "from Spain?"

They shot each other incredulous looks.

"I'll be moving there in September to teach at the university in Barcelona. I'm a poet from San Francisco, and this is my girlfriend, Maureen," I said, introducing them to the redheaded jazz dancer at my side. Maureen and I had lived together three years earlier in Guatemala, and her Spanish was also good.

The four of us became fast friends along the ghats of the Ganges, talking of our travels as we wandered among the smoking funeral pyres. Eduardo was another scruffy poet, well-read, ironic, and fair-skinned, an English teacher by day. Born in North Africa, he was the son of one of Franco's generals. Amparo was as fiery and dark as a gypsy, the daughter of Communist union organizers. I could picture her on the barricades as La Pasionaria. That they were married to each other was my first indication that life had changed in polarized Spain since the dictator died. Their only child, Susana, conceived during their stay in Benares, was born weeks after I hit Spain.

So Eduardo and Amparo became my guides to the Goyaesque marvels of Madrid's underground nightlife. Without changing clothes, after my seminars I would join them at a bar called La Campana, or the bell, a hangout for writers and painters in the working-class neighborhood of Lavapies. Every time somebody tipped the bartender, he rang a bell over the bar to hoots and applause from the rowdy denizens of the place. Poems were read as hashish cigarettes were passed, and I became fond of *fino*, a dry sherry. Nights would end near dawn with the second-to-last drink—"one last drink" strikes superstitious Spaniards as unlucky—at an eerily lit stoners' bar called the Only You. Reciting García Lorca and humming Roy Orbison, we would circle the dark, labyrinthine streets, rejoicing in the sheer freedom to do so. I had lived through the late 1960s in San Francisco (which extended long into the seventies), and now I was double-dipping, exulting in another moment of sixties-like euphoria.

Like everything else worth doing, once was not enough when it came to youthful rebellion in the streets.

Late one evening I stumbled toward my shabby *pensión* on Calle Cervantes in the neighborhood of the Muses, as it was called. I was discovering that the entire *Siglo de Oro* of Spanish literature had taken place on its cobbled streets. In the arched doorway of Hostal Cervantes, two shadowy figures lurked in the halo of a dim streetlamp.

"Got a light?" one asked in what I recognized as a Colombian accent.

As I dug into my pocket, the man with the unlit cigarette dangling from his lip pulled out a pistol and pressed it to my head. Even though I was raised in New Orleans, murder capital of the United States, I had never actually seen anyone hold a gun before, much less to my head. So when the two Colombians dragged me through an open gate into a pitch-black alley, I was fascinated as much as shocked.

They demanded my wallet, and I complied. They glanced in disgust at the few pesetas inside. Then they pulled the plum corduroy sports coat off my back, and made me take off my new loafers. They took the gold watch my father had given me, and then noticed the lapis lazuli ring from India, the one that barely fit over my knuckle.

"Take off that blue ring, or we'll cut off your finger," one commanded, pulling out a switchblade. I stuck the finger into my mouth, slickened it with spit, and slid off the ring.

They still looked disgusted. Was this all the rich blond foreigner had?

"Where's your dough?" they demanded.

"In traveler's checks in my room." My entire fortune consisted of several hundred bucks in twenty-dollar American Express checks. And I'm not sure why I blurted this out, but I did: "If you wait here, I'll go get them for you."

They looked at me as if either I were the complete fool that I was, or I were making fun of their mugging techniques. They shoved me into a corner under a staircase, and warned me not to move.

"The next time," one spat out, "we'll kill you." He waved the gun in my face. Then they were gone.

Coatless and shoeless, I crouched in the corner for several minutes and then stood up trembling. I peeked out of the doorway onto the empty street, illuminated by the first rays of dawn, and then crept on stocking feet to the door of the *pensión,* climbed the massive staircase to the second floor, and fell into one of the cast-iron twin beds in my room. For several hours I watched the grizzly morning light creep through the sheer curtains framing a window that gave onto the air shaft of a central patio. The snub-nosed gun flashed in front of my eyes, and over and over I heard the threat: "*La próxima vez le mataremos.*" Would they be lurking under the streetlamp the next night to kill me?

Then I rose to tell the *pensión* owner what had happened.

"Things like this didn't happen under Franco," he shouted. "Just last week my niece was kidnapped from in front of El Corte Inglés." He pounded the counter for emphasis. "El Corte Inglés!" he repeated, outraged that this could occur in front of the fancy department store towering over the crowded Plaza del Sol in the heart of the city.

The *pensión*-owner insisted that I file a police report. With some reluctance, I dictated my *denuncia* to a gruff cop who typed it up, stopping every few minutes to swear and wrestle with the wrinkled carbon paper that was obviously much more important than my robbery. I immediately understood that this kind of labyrinthine bureaucracy came from Spain, both in Latin America as well as in my torpid native city. After my arrest and deportation in Guatemala, I already knew the ropes: stacks of papers sealed, stamped, signed, and in triplicate. With a flourish, I signed all three copies, and left.

My first identity in my adopted country was as a crime statistic.

In jeans, T-shirt, and a worn-out pair of Adidas, I crept into the morning meeting at the Fulbright Commission, and took a seat in the back. Finally I raised my watchless arm.

"Last night I was mugged by two gunmen," I began. Following the audible gasp, I told my tale. The moral: be cautious in Madrid. Dress down. Don't stop on the street to speak to anyone. And above all else, avoid the Muses at night.

During the remaining days of the orientation, I dressed like the yard man. I continued to hang out with my new Spanish friends, but asked to be accompanied everywhere. I practiced a fuck-you sneer, and always looked like I knew where I was going, even though I never did. For good measure, I would kick trash cans as I passed them, and flick lit cigarette butts into the gutter. Soon Spanish people started to ask me for directions. I fit right in.

But Madrid terrified me. Scuttling alone at night down a shadowy street, I'd suddenly reverse my steps, sensing that danger lurked just around the next corner. I would go here, but not there. I would take this route, but not that one. In the streets, I was sure that I was being followed. In the cafés, I was certain I was being watched.

Several days later, when I stepped off the train in Barcelona, I breathed a sigh of relief. As I made my way past the newsstands and flower kiosks on Las Ramblas, taking in the fizzy Mediterranean air, I felt safe. I was home.

Whenever Madrid came up in conversation in Barcelona, I voiced my distrust. "Dark and chaotic," I raved. "Filled with cutthroats," I ranted. I didn't realize that I was playing right into the historic rivalry between the two cities. The Catalans and I got along quite well indeed.

"This is Professor Nolan from the United States," the Catalans would say by way of an introduction. "He hates Madrid."

My drinks were on the house.

I spent two extraordinary years in Barcelona, and traveled throughout Spain lecturing and reading my poetry. But I always came up with any excuse to avoid Madrid, only an overnight train ride away. When my fellowship was renewed for a second year, I was obliged to attend the Fulbright orientation the following September in Madrid. Eduardo and Amparo had moved to Málaga, and I knew few people, so I stayed to myself and returned to Barcelona as soon as possible. The Muses were still holding a gun to my head.

Maureen, the redheaded jazz dancer, came to live with me in a huge tiled apartment just off Las Ramblas with seven balconies overlooking the street. An operatic canary trilled and warbled in its cage on a balcony facing a row of palm trees. My girlfriend danced in a weekly variety show on Spanish television called *Exterior Día* as well as in the musicals that then thrived on the theater strip of El Paralelo, Barcelona's Broadway. I taught my classes at the university, started a fledgling American Studies program, wrote and translated, and then at night played stage-door Johnny to Maureen's tap-dance diva. Walking home late from the bars, we took a curtain call belting out show tunes to street sweepers at work with whisk brooms.

As these storybook times tend to go, everything was wonderful until it wasn't. I fell in love with somebody else. Sebastián was a Mallorcan writer who lived in a medieval village of *campesinos* at the center of the island. I began to spend weeks at a time with him on his family farm, discussing Flaubert while we baled hay. Back in Barcelona, the canary escaped, or perhaps Maureen let it go. We fought constantly, as Eduardo and Amparo had been doing when we met them in Benares. Finally Maureen flew the coop, too, amid slamming doors and harsh words screamed from the balcony. This wasn't the first time we'd gone our separate ways, and wouldn't be the last.

In 1981 I returned to live in San Francisco, traveling back to Spain whenever I could. I became a frequent flier on the Air France route between San Francisco and Barcelona. But I always sidestepped Madrid. Until six years later, when I couldn't avoid my fate there any longer.

This time it wasn't the Fulbright Commission.

It was my mother.

She called from New Orleans to ask that I meet her in Madrid. A provincial Southern lady, my mother was no jet-setter, so this both startled and delighted me. She would be traveling with her close friend Marta, a Nicaraguan related on one side of her family to the Sandinistas and on the other side to Violeta Chamorro and the opposition. Marta's family stories were riveting. My mother and Marta wanted me to show them Spain. It was to be a whirlwind tour, all my expenses paid, beginning in Madrid.

"But Madrid is just awful," I told my mother. "Remember that's where I was mugged. It's hectic and congested with traffic. Barcelona is more elegant and leisurely, like New Orleans." She had left home few times during her life.

"We want to see the Prado, and besides," Mother said, "Madrid is where our el cheapo flight lands. And after that ordeal, we're not getting on any old train until we have a good rest in a *nice* hotel. And don't try to drag us into any of your holes in the wall."

Marta was energetic and adventurous, while my mother was already becoming a fragile old lady. This was my mother's first visit to Europe, and I knew it would be her last. I suspected she was doing this to get to know her long-lost expatriate son, "away at sea" all these past years. She wanted a peek into my world. I was at her command.

My mother, the efficient medical secretary, gave me a date, the address of their hotel, and a time. I made my own arrangements, and my flight to Madrid was, in fact, an ordeal. I didn't sleep a wink on board, and was up the whole night before with roiling anxieties about Madrid, about my mother, and about my mother in Madrid. The improbable combination was Daliesque. I was a melting watch, a bundle of nerves, sure everything would go wrong.

I arrived in a daze at midnight, caught a shuttle bus from the airport to the Plaza Colón, and then hopped into a taxi. When I opened my mouth to the driver, I had no idea where I was going.

"I need to find a cheap *pensión*," I told him, "somewhere near the center of town."

I never made reservations, always relying on—as my mother put it— holes in the wall.

I sat back, delirious as we swung past the fountain at Cibelus, staring out of the cab window at my nemesis, the city as dark and forbidding as I remembered it. We veered left and then right in no discernible direction. The driver was taking this foreigner for a ride.

"Stop here," I said, tired of the scam. "Look, there's a *pensión*." I could make out a dim *hostal* sign hanging from a balcony across the street. I got out, trudged up the stairs, and as luck had it, there was a room.

As I handed over my passport to register, the balding clerk behind the counter squinted at the picture and then back at me.

"Don't I know you?"

"I don't think so. Listen, I haven't slept in two nights. I'm about to collapse. I'll sleep like a dead man."

The next morning I woke up groggy in a cast-iron twin bed. The sun was already high in the sky, light streaming through the gauzy curtains from the air shaft outside. I suddenly experienced a strong déjà vu, no doubt a symptom of my jetlag, as if I had woken up in this bed before. I showered, poking around the room until the jagged pieces of a familiar puzzle gradually fell into place.

When I walked out to the counter, I didn't even need to glance at the *pensión*'s name on the business cards in the plastic holder. I knew where I was. Out of the thousands of hotels, *pensiones*, and inns in the city of Madrid, I had checked into the very same room of the same *pensión* in front of which I had been mugged seven years earlier. I found myself in the Hostal Cervantes on Calle Cervantes, at the scene of the crime.

I couldn't stay away.

"It *is* me," I told the balding owner when he made his appearance, "the American who was mugged outside."

He slapped a hand to his forehead. "So that's where I know you from." We chatted until lunchtime like old friends.

And then I stepped out onto Calle Cervantes, standing at the exact spot where I'd been mugged. Light filled the street, cumulus clouds swirling above in the lapis lazuli blue of an El Greco sky. Giggling schoolchildren were skipping home, leather school bags strapped to their backs. I'm not certain which subconscious impulse lured me back to that nightmare spot, but in an instant my dread dissolved into one of the most peaceful states I've ever felt. As I floated toward the Plaza de Santa Ana, birds were twittering.

I'd never heard birds before in Madrid. I felt like a character in a Looney Tune, wandering around with swirls of bluebirds and hearts orbiting my head.

All afternoon, I continued to look around me in wonder, as if a sprinkling of fairy dust had turned me into another person in a new place. Yet here I was, and this was still Madrid. What had changed was the rusty window screen of fear through which I'd viewed the city. It was gone.

I had a day to kill before Mother and Marta arrived, so I called María Luisa Maillard, a writer friend I'd met through Sebastián years ago in Barcelona. She'd since moved home to Madrid.

"I never thought I'd hear from you in Madrid. Guess who else is in town?" she squealed. "Sebastián! He called me an hour ago. He's on his way from Berlin home to Mallorca."

"Give me his number." I was dancing at the phone booth.

"He's in some *pensión* off Calle Fuencarral and didn't leave one. He's flying to Palma tonight. Give me your number. He said he'd call back."

"I'm at the Hostal Cervantes on Calle Cervantes but I don't know the number. I must see Sebastián. He thinks I abandoned him. Look, if he calls back, tell him . . . tell him to . . . I don't know what to say. Tell him I love him."

Five minutes later, I was walking into a travel agency on the Paseo del Prado.

And Sebastián was walking out.

Neither of us could speak for several minutes. It had been five years. During that time, he had returned all of the letters I'd sent him from San Francisco, even the ones from Beijing, where I'd been living again with Maureen. No one has ever accused me of traveling in a straight line.

"But what are you doing in Madrid?" he finally asked. "I thought you hated it here."

"I did. But my mother is meeting me here tomorrow."

"Your *mother*? From New Orleans?" It was as if he'd had a date to meet his mourning-clad peasant mother carrying her egg basket at a coffee shop in West Hollywood. He couldn't quite grasp that my Southern-belle mother was coming to the punky streets of Almodóvar's Madrid.

Neither could I.

He postponed his flight to Palma and checked into my fated room in the Hostal Cervantes with his worn yellow valise. When he took off the clunky black shoes, I gagged. He'd been walking for sleepless days and nights in Berlin and Madrid, his socks had disintegrated, and his feet were ulcerated and reeking. I bathed his wounded feet in duty-free vetiver cologne, and then we yanked the mattresses from the cast-iron twin beds into the middle of the floor and lay down together, staring for a long time into each other's eyes.

When we had finished making love, we were both in tears. Of joy, release, disbelief, the tears you cry when an ancestral curse has been lifted, when the occupying army has retreated in defeat, when the sun pokes its snout out after a hurricane, when the vampire lies with a wooden stake through his heart. I had returned to the cocoon of a recurring nightmare, unraveled it, and now butterflies were streaming around the room.

And then it was morning, time to greet my mother and Marta at their hotel. Sebastián suggested we return the mattresses to their beds, aware, as Mediterraneans are, that the price of personal freedom is often keeping up the most minimal appearances.

Already late, I sailed through the swank glass doors of a hotel in the towering modern part of Madrid. My mother and Marta had arrived at midnight, so they should already be up. When I stepped into the hotel room, there they were, in various stages of undress, putting on makeup.

And the mattresses from their twin beds were joined in the middle of the floor.

"These beds are too soft, so we couldn't get to sleep," my mother complained, massaging the small of her back. "So finally we just put the mattresses on the floor."

My face still raw from Sebastián's stubble, I stood there trying to take this in. My mother and Marta held hands as they walked down the street, but that's what Latin American ladies do to show close friendship. But hadn't my mother once told me that her favorite book in high school was the lesbian classic *The Well of Loneliness*? And what about her best friend Wanda Siegel and her female partner, a Navy officer named Tiny?

This was no time for a heart-to-heart talk about the mysterious goat paths of love. For the second time that morning I dragged mattresses from the floor onto twin beds, and then we plotted our itinerary. The rooftops of a glorious city called to us through the picture window.

I couldn't wait to be back on the streets of Madrid.

Three years later, in September of 1989, I moved to Madrid on another Fulbright fellowship. I rented an attic apartment with a terrace in Lavapies, not far from La Campana where Eduardo and I had read our poetry a decade earlier. The city struck me as vital and open, raw and edgy, bursting at the seams with creative energy. By that time, the neighborhood of the Muses—where a gun had been held to my head—was no longer sinister but becoming gentrified. My mugging there had served as an initiation rite. How could I live in Madrid unless I were willing to die there? Just as Pegasus, god of poetic inspiration, flew out of the severed snaky head of the Medusa, my life sprouted wings at the site of my once darkest dread.

Now I couldn't imagine *not* living in Madrid.

The national Filmoteca was steps away from my apartment on Calle Olmo. La Sanabresa, one of the best and cheapest restaurants in the city, was a block away. And the bustling open market of Antón Martín was at the corner. Every evening that I went out was a wacky world unto itself. Roving groups of friends pushed their way into the endless variety of crowded tapas bars, staging an impromptu party as if they were in their living rooms, passing sloshing drinks and tiny plates of shrimp and meatballs over everyone else's heads. Eventually the groups would merge, new alliances would be formed, and then off to the next place. I would usually end the night with people I'd met at taverns along the way, strangers who didn't know the friends I'd begun the evening with. These strangers then became the friends with whom I christened the next night, and so on. Nobody cared where I was from, or that I spoke Spanish with a foreign accent. Everyone was a *Madrileño*, immediately and jovially, a private club with only one exclusionary clause: you had to be there.

When I discovered that the next year a teaching job would take me back to Barcelona, I moped for a month. I lived in Barcelona during the next six years, eventually becoming a legal Spanish resident. But every chance I had, I hopped onto the Talgo, the overnight train to Madrid, humming what I called my "Salgo en el Talgo Tango." In Barcelona I became known as Professor Nolan from the United States who loves Madrid. My relations with the Catalans, and especially with the rise of their linguistic nationalism, turned testy. Barcelona was a refined bourgeois city composed of closed circles of loyal friends, but I preferred the earthy, working-class democracy of street life in Madrid.

I'd discovered what James Baldwin calls "the murder at the very heart of love." I thought of those words every time I walked past the Hostal Cervantes, which churned up visions of the snub-nosed pistol and the two mattresses thrown together in the middle of the floor. For me, what Madrid now possessed was what the Spanish call *morbo*, that morbid mingling of love and death, longing and fear, beauty and decay. This is the *duende* that García Lorca identifies as the fount of inspiration, the elegant passion at the heart of the bloody bullfight.

Not long before I gave up my apartment on Calle Olmo, I was walking with Miguel, a young Lebanese-Dominican dentist who had also just immigrated to Madrid. He was as taken with the city as I was, and at the moment, we were both pretty taken with each other. It was only one in the morning, still early by Madrid's standards, and we were strolling past the fountain at Cibelus backlit against the midnight-blue sky. Rivers of people were coursing past, taxis honking, high heels clopping, boys bellowing soccer chants, the city exploding around us in a lusty delirium.

"Madrid!" Miguel shouted, staring at me bug-eyed.

"Madrid!" I shouted back, sweeping my arms to take in the gleaming façades and pulsing crowds and raucous traffic.

"Maaadriiid!" we roared in unison. And then leapt into each other's arms.

- 12 -

FIRST MORNING

For many of us, the morning-after of the 1960s didn't occur until at least a decade later.

The first morning of the rest of my life took place on September 6, 1981. By then what we called the "revolution" or the "counterculture" was undeniably over, along with whatever ideals may have lingered on through the seventies. Ronald Reagan was president, and even in San Francisco everybody had cut their hair short, cleaned up their acts, and gotten regular jobs. The decorator color was office-machine gray, ties were thin, heels sensible, clothes trim and snappy. Women had put their bras back on, men were growing mustaches and sculpting muscles, and everything in sight was cold, metallic, and designed to death.

My generation had finally turned thirty, only to discover sex-roles and money, exactly as we feared would happen to anyone reaching that dreaded age. The disorderly line of joint-toking young people draped in paisley in front of the Times, a cheap repertory cinema on Stockton Street, had given way to the impatient queue at Kinko's, where everyone was waiting to copy their résumés. After a year in India, and two years in Barcelona, I'd just moved back to the United States. I felt like the last kid on the block still in the make-believe Indian fort after it turns dark.

I wasn't ready yet to go home and be normal.

But the truth is, I was broke, and all I knew how to do was write poetry. My second book, *What Moves Is Not the Wind*, had just come out with Wesleyan University Press, I'd been awarded some fancy fellowships, and had taught university classes for a few years in honorific, low-paying positions such as writer-in-residence and Fulbright lecturer. But so far I'd managed to boycott my own career. I'd never done anything hard, unrewarding, and boring, that is, never had a real job. So I typed up my vita on a Smith-Corona and mailed it out to colleges in San Francisco. I was thirty-three and, like Jesus, ready to be mocked and crucified.

H ave you ever taught freshman comp?"
    The wake-up call came while I was daydreaming in my under-wear, staring out of the kitchen window of my rent-controlled apartment on Telegraph Hill at the wall of fog tumbling over the Golden Gate Bridge. I'd been wondering whatever happened to everyone on our commune at the Russian River, to Hibiscus, Rumi, and Andrei Codrescu, to all of those poets and painters, drag queens and composters, sequined groupies and muddy children. The days of peace and love, free boxes and demonstrations, seemed never to have happened. I hadn't figured out yet that every ten years in California the past is erased like an old videotape.

"No," I answered. "Mostly literature and creative writing."

"But I notice here on your vita," said the businesslike baritone of the chair, "that you have worked with international students. So you must have experience teaching English as a Second Language as well as the rudiments of exposition."

"Not really." I wasn't exactly trying to sell myself.

"Look, the deal is we need someone to cover a nine a.m. section of freshman comp starting tomorrow morning. Meet me in my office at 8:30. This will be a part-time, one-semester contract without benefits." I had no idea what that meant, but would find out soon enough. The Reagan revolution had begun, during which higher education was reorganized to resemble migrant agriculture, depending on a shifting pool of seasonally unemployed, part-time instructors paid by the class. In other words, if the university had tomatoes to pick, they'd call you the day before. So with a grand total of $178 in my bank account, I jumped on the truck, although not with the gratitude expected of me.

That evening I borrowed an iron from my neighbor, a former actor working in a bank, and pressed a shirt and what I hilariously referred to as "slacks." I considered borrowing a tie, but decided on limits to my humiliation. I finally got to sleep at dawn, twisting in the sheets all night in dread of the alarm clock.

Then I rose like a sleepwalker among foghorns to face my first day on the job as a young urban professional.

As if yuppies and Reagan weren't enough, in those days doctors in California had diagnosed the first cases of a rare "gay cancer." I had never heard of Kaposi sarcoma or T-cells, never attended a memorial service, and couldn't have begun to imagine that half of my friends in San Francisco would die of AIDS by the end of the decade. A few people around me had ODed on drugs, but they weren't close friends, I didn't do hard drugs, and I was still bursting with the sheer invulnerability of youth. Although I was already too old to die young, that remained a romantic possibility—until I received the news about Karen.

Karen had been so pale and so French, with her kohl-lined eyes, black lipstick, and velvet cloaks, her long hennaed hair held in place at the nape of her swanlike neck by a single ivory chopstick. She spoke English with a French accent, French with an English accent, and Spanish with a Turkish accent. Her mother was from Paris, her father an American diplomat who, I suspected, worked for the C.I.A., and she'd grown up all over the world. We first caught sight of each other during the early seventies in San Francisco at "Earthquake Cabaret," an event put on by the Angels of Light, Hibiscus's gender-bending theater collective that followed in the wake of the Cockettes. I'd been dancing around ecstatically on stage behind Allen Ginsberg dressed in drag as his Aunt Rose, pumping the harmonium and chanting William Blake poems. My mane was long and wild, and except for a few pounds of glitter, I was naked. After our little show, Karen approached the stage to ask me if I were real.

She said she wasn't either. And from that moment on, like the unicorn and the maiden with the mirror, we didn't lose sight of each other for the next few years.

We lived together with her cousin in Paris, and then on a houseboat in Amsterdam. She painted, I wrote. We both considered ourselves androgynous, and were often involved with other lovers of the same sex. Hers were invariably fashion models who played with the fringes of le hippi américain as if I were a new doll from California. Karen and I recited Baudelaire and García Lorca to each other from a bed that was a mound of tasseled silk shawls, and on New Year's Eve painted our faces blue as Gauls to take the metro. She was at home everywhere and nowhere, the first cosmopolitan I'd ever been close to. We swore that we didn't believe in frontiers or countries or passports, only in the borderless realm of art and beauty. She was my "sad-eyed lady of the lowlands," and we clung to each other like orphans, like Cocteau's *enfants terribles*, passionate and unfaithful, hallucinating together a world that never existed.

A few years later in San Francisco, Karen married a Colombian cocaine dealer with whom she had two children, both named after Bob Dylan songs. And what I found out from her cousin in Sausalito, within a week of returning home from Barcelona, was that while I'd been out of the country for three years, the whole family had been slaughtered in a drug deal gone bad. For several months I lived with that news like a wedge of ice in my spine as I circled the streets, catching glimpses of us together on every street corner.

Karen was my first dead lover, there to welcome me home to San Francisco in 1981, even before the others began to fall, one by one.

A nd so nursing a sour stomach at 7:45 in the morning of September 6, I made my way through the downy fog blanketing Telegraph Hill to board the 30-Stockton bus. The chill air tasted like toothpaste and fried eggs, and in my pressed slacks and button-down shirt, I felt late for my first day on the job as a part-time professor of freshman comp. I had stuffed a few pens and blank sheets of paper in my Nepalese backpack—make the students write something, I reasoned.

Sts. Peter and Paul Cathedral struck me as an enormous gray elephant looming over Washington Square, the first sign I was either still dreaming or delirious from lack of sleep. The bus wheezed to a stop, I dropped my coins in the slot and took a seat, wondering what the students should write. At that indecent hour of the morning, I decided . . . their dreams.

The neck of the woman seated in front of me caught my attention, so elongated and somehow familiar. She was clutching a silver lamé bag, and then I spotted it—the chopstick that held her hennaed hair in place at the nape of her pale neck. My eyes fixed on the powdery rose of her cheek as she turned ever so slightly to glance out of the window.

I couldn't see the face, but was sure it was her.

I should tap her on the shoulder, I decided, and scoop Karen up into my arms. Then I wouldn't have to face a class of surly freshmen and we could run away to Marrakesh to live with the tribe of blue Berbers. "*Luxe, calme, et volupté.*" Lines of poetry began to crowd my thoughts, Baudelaire, then García Lorca: "*Trescientas rosas morenas / lleva tu pechera blanca.*" All I had to do was touch the woman seated in front of me on the shoulder, time would stop, then we would be young and free again.

But I couldn't.

As the bus passed through Chinatown, filling with droopy-eyed Chinese off to another day at the laundry or sweatshop, I became increasingly agitated, crossing and uncrossing my legs, pawing through my backpack. What if Karen's cousin in Sausalito, whom I'd never actually met, had lied to me, and she wasn't dead, but only wanted to separate from her past? "Tell anyone who calls I'm dead." That sounded like something she might have said at a moment of high drama. How else could she have rid herself of a life with a Colombian cocaine dealer?

And what, I considered, if I was a complete lunatic chasing a ghost, late for his first day on the job in the real world? Now I'd never get benefits.

The woman seated in front of me on the 30-Stockton bus stood and, without turning around, got off at Union Square. And even though I had to transfer at Market Street, I slung the fringy backpack over my shoulder and followed her. She picked up her pace, reaching back to fasten the chopstick in her hair, the silver bag swinging at her elbow. And I was lunging behind, my throat tensed to call out: *Stop. It's me.*

Then the woman turned around.

Tears were streaming down her face. After all, she was being pursued by some crazy man at eight in the morning. Or maybe because she was late for her salesclerk job at Macy's or Gump's, or because she also had no benefits and Ronald Reagan was president and she could sense that soon all her friends were going to die. And tears were streaming down my face, too, because it wasn't Karen. The woman was shorter, stouter, worn-out looking. But for a full minute two perfect strangers stood staring at each other with wet cheeks and watery eyes on the corner of Stockton and Geary, before we each turned around and walked away.

I caught my bus on Market Street and was a smashing success as a tomato-picker at various universities, which I did for two years before accepting a teaching position in China, convinced that the system had to work better under communism. And, considering that and other delusions, it will perhaps take the rest of this life and part of the next to understand what happened to me and to my generation during that decade. But by the time I turned to walk away from the stranger on Union Square who, for a fleeting moment, reminded me of the dreams we once allowed ourselves to dream, there was nothing I could do about it. As in a child's nightmare, the monsters were lined up in the closet, waiting to appear.

The eighties were already under way.

13

I'LL BE WATCHING YOU

Every bond you break
Every step you take
I'll be watching you
—Sting (1983)

This is almost like real life, I thought for the first time since August. A bottle of rice wine in hand, I was climbing a cement stairwell stacked high with a bumper crop of socialist cabbage. Under a galvanized sky, I'd just bicycled through a labyrinth of alleys where most of Beijing's population lived at the time. I felt almost invisible for a change, and doubted that many cyclists had noticed the pair of determined blue eyes staring out from behind my white surgical mask and mummy layers of bulky winter clothes. To them, I was merely another buttoned-up bundle jostling through the rush-hour throngs of clanging bicycles and blaring street-corner loudspeakers.

"Don't spit, don't litter," barked the staticky recordings, "and if you meet foreigners, don't tell them any secrets."

I was on my way to a dinner party at a Chinese friend's home, although "party" might be an exaggeration. This was the China of 1983, as closed and restrictive as North Korea is today. The terrors of the Cultural Revolution had just ended, and the country was at the beginning of the Four Modernizations, one of which was supposedly an "Opening to the West." That was what I—a so-called "foreign expert"—was doing in Beijing, opening the minds of post-grad and undergrad English

majors to American and British literature. Yet no doubt in reaction to
the influence of "foreign devils" like me, a new slogan was in the air, the
"Campaign Against Cultural Pollution," which excoriated such contami-
nating elements as humanism, science fiction, and *Time* magazine, along
with women's long hair and earrings. Whenever I cycled past Tiananmen
Square, I always checked the portrait of Chairman Mao mounted over
the entrance to the Forbidden City to see where his mole was. Rumor
had it that as the political winds shifted, the mole on his face migrated
from left to right and then back again.

Chairman Mao's mole was as good as any other political weathercock
in the topsy-turvy People's Republic.

At the moment, "correct action" was to avoid contact with foreigners,
and so Ziang, my hostess for the evening, was a secret friend, not one of
my official handlers. She was a colleague at the Beijing Normal University
where I taught. On the morning she showed me my office, she casually
mentioned that four years earlier several colleagues had jumped to their
deaths out of the window over my desk after being branded "capitalist
roaders." A graying widow with a teenage son, Ziang had a daring sense of
humor, one that matched her bravery in inviting a foreigner to her house.
Tonight we were to dine with a calligrapher and an opera singer, both
older artists who seldom met with foreigners. The invitation, which lit up
my life, had been arranged through a series of clandestine notes, which
I then burned. I was beginning to think that—just maybe—ordinary life
was indeed possible for foreigners in China.

Abruptly, a door swung open on the apartment building's second landing and I found myself staring into the narrowing eyes of the building's
committee woman as she memorized my features, arms folded across
her chest. She was the one to whom neighbors reported on each other
about the most intimate details of family life, a monitoring shark in the
so-called "goldfish bowl" of the Chinese home. A visit from a foreigner
was potentially explosive information, surely to be reported to the offender's work-unit. Continuing around the mounds of cabbage, I came
back to reality, to the danger I was putting my friend in, the future risk
to her family, and the impossibility of living here.

Within the cramped confines of Ziang's two concrete rooms, we talked
animatedly of this and more. The stir-fry was simple but excellent, and
I fell under the spell of the chain-smoking calligrapher Ta Yin, who told

me that his nom de plume meant "hermit in the city." He emptied cup after cup of rice wine and, with his wispy white goatee and bushy eyebrows, looked like I'd always pictured the Tang dynasty poet Li Bai. I was so impressed with Ta Yin's calligraphy hanging on Ziang's walls that I commissioned him to translate the titles of my two books of poetry into classical Chinese characters and write them on scrolls. He warned me that even though I'd pay him some modest amount for his art, he'd be forced to note in the margins that these scrolls were gifts. Foreigners were only allowed to buy art in government-run shops, and any sales between individuals were illegal. I felt at home, as if I were with some older boho artist in North Beach or the French Quarter, where over the years I'd known many such crusty hermits-in-the-city. This late-night conversation about calligraphy and poetry could never have been simulated by any government exchange agency.

And yet our meeting, along with everything else that felt real to me, was forbidden.

Later that evening, as I pedaled my tipsy way home in and out of the shadows of gnarled ancient trees along the deserted streets, I wondered what would become of these friends within three years—or next month— because of this visit. Who knew where Chairman Mao's mole would be by then? At the moment, I never could have imagined what would occur at Tiananmen Square five years later, but I worried about this threat all the way home to the apartment in which my girlfriend Maureen and I were living. It was located in a bleak residential compound that the Soviets had built in the fifties for their advisors. We called it the Pound, although the official name of this guarded, walled Alcatraz for foreigners was the Friendship Hotel.

O ur next-door neighbors at the Friendship Hotel were Pakistanis working on the atom bomb, and I hoped they didn't hear our fights, especially the ones about sex. I'd snuck Maureen into China as my wife, the only way she would have been allowed to accompany me. That year she'd been appointed dancer-in-residence at the Performing Arts High School in San Francisco, but since I wasn't keen on living alone in Beijing, and she'd always wanted to see China, she gave up the position to accompany me. Despite our sometimes rocky circumstances in Florida, Guatemala, and Barcelona, we'd been getting along well lately, even in those unpromising times. Several of our friends were already falling ill with AIDS, greedy yuppies were taking over the city, and Ronald Reagan was president. When it came to politics, Maureen and I could finish each other's sentences. Yet something about the move to Beijing cracked our strong bond. Neither of us was used to being half of that cumbersome two-headed creature, the married couple.

"Where's Maureen?" people asked me whenever I was out on my own, as if a limb were missing. "Where's James?" they asked her. It was as though they wanted to know why in the world we were walking around wearing only one shoe. Of course, within the bugged echo chamber of China, we never dared tell anyone that we weren't legally hitched.

Funny, but all we had to do was pretend to be married, and there it was: instant bed death. It infuriated me to be denied sex for weeks at a time, and I blamed it not on the feigned marriage, our fishbowl home life, or the People's Republic of China, but on her damn vibrator.

One freezing winter night I threw off the satin comforter and leapt up to add water to the pan vaporizing on the radiator. Usually before turning in we emptied a bucket of water onto the concrete floor to add humidity to the parched air in the bedroom. My face was chapped raw, and brittle strands of hair were falling out in the cold, dry climate.

Maureen was turned away from me, coughing into a handkerchief that smelled of Tiger Balm. "Don't forget to latch the door," she mumbled into her pillow.

It had caused an uproar when I screwed an inside latch onto the front door to keep out the clamorous custodians in baggy blue Mao suits who barged into our apartment every morning at the crack of dawn slinging their filthy rag mops. We were sure they were spying on us. One morning Maureen came back from breakfast to find two women janitors trying on her new silk dress. Then I found long black hairs on our pillows.

I crawled back under the comforter and switched on the lamp. I was on volume two of *Sources of the Chinese Tradition*. Then I dog-eared the page, jumped up and went into the living room to smoke. I'd stopped lighting up in the bedroom after Maureen's second bout with bronchitis, when she started coughing up blood. Although private cars were still mercifully forbidden, since October Beijing had been blanketed by an impenetrable layer of bituminous coal smoke so thick that at eight in the morning we couldn't see across the street.

My university *danwei*, or work-unit, had issued us two white surgical masks to wear while riding bikes. They also gave me two condoms a month for birth control, and cautioned a single American colleague to beware: conniving Chinese women would only try to use him to obtain exit visas. The department promised this bachelor a list of "places to meet women in Hong Kong" during the New Year holiday. From the lace doilies draped over the overstuffed chairs that crowded their stuffy parlors to the frilly floral motifs everywhere, the Chinese struck me as essentially Victorian, not only in their sexual prudery but also in the hard, desperate lives they lived beneath a veneer of decorous formality and saccharine sentimentality.

I stubbed out the cigarette and stormed into the bedroom. "I don't know what to do."

"Do about what?" Maureen asked, rolling over and squinching up her freckled face. "The Four Modernizations?"

"About this," I said, grabbing my long johns at the crotch.

"Give me a break," she moaned, sitting up. "This is the People's Republic. Show a little respect, Comrade Nolan."

"We lived with 'the people' in India and Guatemala, where we screwed like bunnies. Look, I'm sorry I brought you here. But this was the last place we could see any hope for the future. For the duration, all we have is each other."

"For the tenth time, I fucking don't feel like making love," she screamed, loud enough to wake the Pakistani bomb-makers next door.

I thought I knew the reason.

The vibrator. I hated it.

"I've got to face an eight o'clock class tomorrow," I said, "and can't get to sleep."

"My body's not going to be your sleeping pill."

I struggled into my clothes and dragged the Timberland work boots from under the bed by their shoelaces. In the living room I gulped a tea cup of sugary plum brandy, then veered back into the bedroom. The lamp was out and Maureen was asleep, wheezing, her red mane spotlit by the streetlight streaming in through a crack between the curtains. I opened the drawer of her nightstand, slipped out the vibrator, then disappeared into the bathroom.

I kicked the door shut, slammed the vibrator against the tile floor until the white plastic cracked, and jumped up and down on it in my boots.

When the batteries and spring popped out, I gathered the pieces into the pocket of my vintage fireman's peacoat.

This Rumpelstiltskin tantrum played out, I then wondered what to do.

As I faced the deserted grounds of the Pound, I realized that in China there was no such thing as the garbage. The chunky gray buildings grouped around arc-lit quadrangles filled me with sudden panic. They squatted together in ominous rows like officers' housing on a military base, the last place I ever thought I'd wind up. Our phone was tapped, the mail read. The custodians went through our trash.

What would the Chinese make of a busted vibrator?

They'd think it was a bug, or a bomb. I imagined myself standing before the Central Committee of the Communist Party at Tiananmen Square, trying to explain what a vibrator was. I had little idea myself, except that it excluded me. Go ahead, condemn me for my male blindness to liberated women's sexuality. I've been down on my knees ever since.

The *da feng*, an icy wind from Mongolia, whistled through craggy tree limbs overhead. I pulled the black Catalan beret over my ears and twisted the wool muffler three times around my neck. It was one in the morning, and every window was darkened. I scurried toward a trash container plastered with a slogan about public neatness, and deposited a chunk of the vibrator.

Then I found another trash bin near the dining room, where I threw away a second piece. Circling the monolithic building, I tossed the rest of it into a third can. Then I looked up into the suspicious stares of two armed soldiers of the People's Liberation Army (P.L.A.). Their breath rose like puffs of smoke from rosy-cheeked, boyish faces framed by tall fur caps and ear muffs. As usual, they said nothing, but I could feel their stern eyes following me as I scurried back to our apartment, certain they were waiting for me to disappear before sorting through the trash cans.

At the moment, what I really wanted to stuff in the trash in China were years of leftist newsprint pamphlets and hand-lettered banners and petitions. Cuba. Chile. Nicaragua. I had entered the country as a committed Marxist, and now considered myself a political dyslexic, unable to distinguish between the left and right except by following the mole migrating across Chairman Mao's face.

At 5:30 in the morning, this square would be filled with yawning workers in Mao suits stepping through desultory exercises as the ever-present loudspeakers crackled about the "Campaign Against Cultural Pollution." I would hear the happy workers singing revolutionary songs as Comrade Nolan rolled over in bed with the pillow over his head.

Yes, soon would come the glorious new day.

In the meantime, everything smelled like coal dust and sour cabbage. It was November of 1983, and I was trapped inside the people's paradise with a sick woman who no longer loved or wanted me. And at eight in the morning, I'd be hunched over a desk whose chalky drawers were stuffed with abandoned little red books, facing a hundred and twenty blank young faces, trying to say something coherent about their favorite English poet, Robert Burns.

I began to suspect that Maureen was having an affair, and started spying on her. I'd never been the jealous boyfriend type, but every time I spotted her carefully making up her face or overdressing to go to lunch at the dining room, I knew those ministrations weren't meant for me.

Who could he be?

In the high-ceilinged gloom of the monumental dining room at the Friendship Hotel, the babble of languages rose and swirled with the cigarette smoke. A gigantic carved screen of ornate chinoiserie dominated the hall with its cranes and albino peacocks fluttering amid the stark branches of a mother-of-pearl landscape. Eternally stationed at the door, her fingers clicking over an abacus, sat the Eskimo-like cashier with the haircut and demeanor of a prison matron. Three times a day, past her hawkish eyes paraded a cast of characters that could have peopled an Agatha Christie mystery: the exiled Peruvian novelist who couldn't go home, vaguely linked as he was to the Sendero Luminoso guerrillas; the dwarfish Austrian aristocrat compiling a German-Chinese dictionary; the flushed tippler of a Scottish journalist; the preppy American postgrad in International Relations; the ex-junkie Sephardic Jew from Barcelona proofing government translations; the roly-poly atomic scientist from Karachi with his wool scarf wrapped into a turban; the Palestine Liberation Organization (P.L.O.) representative dressed like a London banker. This kennel of exotic, long-term guests was watched over by white-coated attendants stationed at the entrances to each of our buildings, clocking the arrivals and departures of any Chinese visitors, who first had to register with the soldiers guarding the front gate. Those

Helen Alice Partee, New Orleans, 1942 (photo: Leon Trice Sr.)

Joylynn, St. Petersburg, Florida, January 1968 (photo: Richard Waghorne)

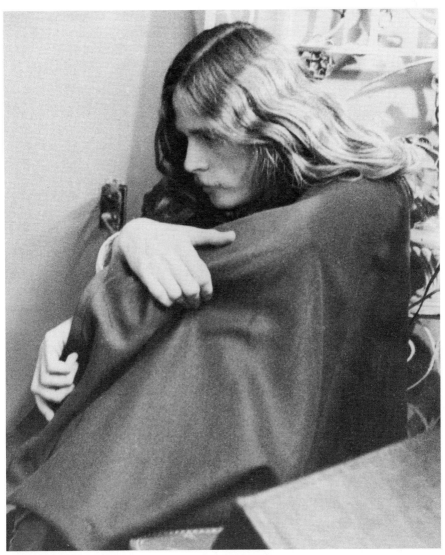
James Nolan at home, Joe Simon's house, Stony Brook, New York, 1969

Hibiscus, San Francisco, 1971
(photo: David Wise)

Rumi with Tina Turner,
San Francisco, 1971

James Nolan, New York City, 1978
(photo: Kinga Dessauer)

Tiananmen Square, Beijing, 1984

At home with Beat poet Philip Lamantia, Telegraph Hill, San Francisco, 1988

At home, Lavapies, Madrid, 1990

At home with Spanish writer Eduardo Lago, Malasaña, Madrid, 2002

At home with Lawrence Ferlinghetti, Barrio Gótico, Barcelona, 1991

At book launch for *Longing*, with Spain scholar Shirley Mangini, City Lights, San Francisco, 1994

At home with mother Helen Nolan, French Quarter, All Saints Day, 1999

red-starred members of the P.L.A. also kept an eye on our own movements in and out of the Pound.

At first I suspected Victor, a devilishly handsome Venezuelan who had just returned to Beijing, where his Communist parents raised him during the sixties. Although Victor, Maureen, and I spoke Spanish together, he was also fluent in Mandarin and English, effortlessly charming in any language. There was something about the ascot he often sported, along with his slight lisp, that made me think he might also be bisexual. Until recently, that would have been Maureen's type. Up until the AIDS crisis hit in 1981, a certain type of farouche woman couldn't get enough of bisexual men, although now we were considered Typhoid Marys.

I took to dropping by Victor's apartment at odd hours of the day or night to see if Maureen was there. Sometimes she was, along with Laura, the wife of Jaume, the ex-junkie from Barcelona, whose Sephardic family had shipped the couple off to China as a cure for his drug addiction. But no, the vibe wasn't right between Maureen and Victor. She didn't look at him in that unmistakable way. Victor had lots of clandestine visits from Chinese men, so in the seedy drama unfolding in my slowly darkening mind, something else was probably going on.

"Have you seen my, er, vibrator," Maureen finally asked me, after tearing apart the bedroom.

"Nope," I said, turning a page. I also had my secrets.

"I know who it was," she said, blaming the custodians who tried on her silk dress.

I was particularly miffed when she didn't come to the Halloween party I'd organized for my students at the university. They researched Halloween traditions and went to a great deal of trouble to stage a costume party in the spirit of the holiday. And they were most anxious to meet my wife, the lovely American dancer. I begged her to come, and although she claimed to be ill, some gut instinct made me suspect another scenario. In China, paranoia wasn't an illness but, as Chinese friends were teaching me, a survival tool.

And I was learning fast.

That afternoon I prepared my students for the party by turning off the lights and closing the curtains in the lecture hall to read Poe's "The Raven" by candlelight to a full house. Then the students set up tubs of water for apple-dunking, draped white bedsheet ghosts over poles, and put soft drinks on ice. They begged me to bring my boom box and disco tapes, since the only foreign dance music they were permitted was the tango. Then I went home to change into my costume.

Maureen wasn't there.

After suffering the intense scrutiny of my driver from the Pound's fleet of cars, I returned to the college dressed in a Moroccan djellabah, with a grey mop as hair and a red beard, of the stagey sort worn by foreign villains in Chinese operas. Many of the students were in drag, since the clothes of the opposite sex were the only costumes they could come up with. Girls in men's sports coats with penciled-on mustaches danced stiff-hipped tangos with boys in flowered kerchiefs, lipstick, and makeshift skirts. I felt as if I were back in San Francisco, especially when the monitors left the room and the students ditched their scratchy tango records to gyrate their hips with enthusiastic agility to the beat of my *Saturday Night Live* tape. One student, obviously more attuned to the politics of the Central Committee, told me that nobody should ever "move that way in public."

I learned that our classroom Disco Inferno, with its crepe-paper pumpkins, cardboard skeletons, and dangling apples, prompted severe self-criticism at that week's three-hour session of obligatory political study. As an antidote to my "cultural pollution," the students were forced to fashion crude posters of a student crawling into the pup tent of an opened yellow book bearing an English title (yellow signifies pornography in China, as blue does here) and coming out the other end as a Halloween skeleton. Yet, crazed as I was becoming, my students continued to view me as a cross between John Travolta and Edgar Allen Poe.

Why couldn't Maureen see that in me, unless she was busy with somebody else?

Wipe those red stars out of your eyes!" the man from the State Department had told me when I protested that since the public health care in China was so good, maybe we didn't need all the shots he recommended.

"If there's anyone the Communists will hate, it'd be you," huffed my Hungarian friend Kinga Dessaur. "And if there's anyone who will hate the Communists, it'd also be you." In 1956 Kinga's family snuck her out of

Budapest in a boxcar, and she was horrified that I was voluntarily going to live in another Communist country.

"You must spent 80 percent of your time helping your husband in his work," the severe Chinese consul informed Maureen when we went to apply for our residence visas in San Francisco. My feisty girlfriend laughed the whole way home on the Geary bus.

"Don't expect to find classes when you come back," the head of the English Department at the University of San Francisco warned me as I was cleaning out my desk.

"You'll never dance again in this town," the North Beach club owner told Maureen when she broke her contract with the show she was performing in.

"There's got to be a better way than this money-grubbing rat race, right?" One afternoon Maureen and I agreed about this over dim sum in Chinatown, after shopping among the Cantonese food stalls on Stockton Street. Along with many neighbors, our landlady was Chinese, and we pretty much lived in Hong Kong already. The way I saw it, I was practically Chinese: I threw the *I Ching*, drank ginseng tea, and ate with chopsticks and a rice bowl. While I studied Mandarin, I fantasized that in Beijing I'd be invited to discuss Marxist philosophy over tea with high-ranking planners of the revolution. Maureen packed her tap shoes, fuchsia leotard, and Afro-Caribbean tapes, hoping to trade classes in jazz for training with classical Chinese dancers.

We might stay for years, we decided. Goodbye, Ronald Reagan.

As it turned out, I wasn't even welcomed at the weekly indoctrination sessions at my university, much less invited to help plan the revolution. Maureen auditioned one of Martha Graham's choreographies for a government performing-arts fellowship, but was turned down in favor of somebody doing the Mexican hat dance. Although I'd hoped that the Chinese would embrace the best of the West while avoiding the worst, their cheesy taste didn't surprise me. They were as blind to our culture as we were to theirs, and after decades of isolation now seemed as baffled by the supermarket of Western values as we were on entering a Chinese herbalist's, unable to distinguish the beneficial from the toxic among those long rows of murky jars. The books of one of the great socialist writers of the century, Jean-Paul Sartre, were banned by the same leaders who in 1979 invited Bob Hope to televise a special from the Forbidden City, which he compared on the air to Jackie Gleason's patio. Then came the Muppets to dance along the Great Wall.

And I was informed that under no circumstances could I teach George Orwell's *Nineteen Eighty-Four* in 1984 in China. As I scratched the title off my spring syllabus, my students consoled me. They'd already read it, samizdat-style.

Maureen, ever the go-getter New Yorker, did land a job teaching dance to children at the International School, which helped with my measly salary of four hundred dollars a month in renminbi (then a closed currency, as opposed to open-market exchange bills). And for several sessions, she took the dangerous step of offering members of the Beijing Ballet Company classes in modern dance in the ballroom at the Pound. If these clandestine classes had been discovered, the participants never would have been issued another travel visa to tour outside of China again. Yet these cocky members of the cultural élite, probably the children of Communist Party leaders who could pass for Hong Kong Chinese, seemed to feel no fear.

Could one of them have been Maureen's romantic interest? It certainly wasn't the lead male dancer, who on meeting me grabbed my thighs from the rear, ostensibly to see if I were also a dancer, although the lusty grin on his face told me something else.

Our social life was limited to the bar at the Friendship Hotel. On weekend evenings, this musty watering hole was open until eleven, had no music, and was as stale and morose as one of Somerset Maugham's cobwebby colonial outposts. This was where the drinkers among us gathered in clusters to chew over our exiles around dirty white tablecloths lined with empty quart bottles of Tsingtao beer. The place wasn't even enlivened by the occasional groups of African bachelors, students shipped to China for seven-year technical educations and forbidden any entanglements with Chinese women. The young Africans kept to themselves, except during the shouting matches and fistfights with the Chinese waiters, who displayed a thinly veiled contempt for these lonely black men. They weren't getting any either, and whenever I felt sorry for myself, I considered their seven-year sentences, with no time off for good behavior in Hong Kong.

Since Maureen and I had recently spent two years in Barcelona, we gravitated toward the Spanish living in Beijing and the boozy parties at their Embassy. The Spaniards, who had emerged from under Franco's iron rule only a short time earlier, cast a seasoned eye on China's totalitarian police state. They were experts in how to live the good life underground in a dictatorship. On the other hand, our own compatriots, bouncy with international good will, followed the mind-boggling rules and limited themselves to exactly what the government wanted them to experience, as if waiting for an official ice cream social during which prizes would be awarded and the mysteries revealed. The other Americans didn't know how to sneak around, how to bribe a clerk at the Friendship Store to corner the market on imported wine for an upcoming dinner, or how to smuggle a Chinese friend into an Embassy cocktail party under a blanket in the backseat of a car. In short, they weren't much fun.

Or not as delightful as Lourdes and Gemma, from Madrid and Barcelona, respectively, who worked for the Spanish Embassy, had private apartments, and lived lives as free as anyone could imagine at that time in China: Pedro Almodóvar meets Chairman Mao. And it was at one of those late-night fetes at Gemma's elegant house near Wafujing Street when I finally found out who Maureen was stepping out with. Or who I thought he was.

At one point in the evening, I was drunk enough to think I was speaking Mandarin for half an hour with a Chinese guest. In any case, he spoke no foreign languages—that I do remember—so our conversation must have been in Mandarin. In the middle of a charade-like gesture to bolster my halting grammar, I knocked over a glass of wine and made a mess on the floor. I excused myself and headed to the kitchen for a rag to clean it up.

There stood Maureen in the dimly lit room, in the middle of a passionate kiss.

With Jaume, the ex-junkie from Barcelona.

"*Sinvergüenzas*," I shouted at the shameless lovers. They broke their embrace and stared at the floor as I stormed out.

I couldn't believe what I'd just seen. Was it really short, scrawny Jaume, who could have passed for Woody Allen's stunted kid brother? Victor told me that Jaume and Laura had just been released from confinement in a hotel room, where for two weeks they proofread the final draft of the Spanish translation of the collected works of Deng Xiaoping. The government editors didn't want the contents leaked during the process, so P.L.A. soldiers guarded their room day and night. And come to think of it, I'd seen a lot more of Maureen during those past two weeks.

Back at our apartment, I could tell that the Pakistani bomb-makers next door weren't going to get much sleep.

Maureen denied that she'd been seeing Jaume or anyone else. I apologized for the goddamn eyes in my head.

"Hasn't a drunk ever grabbed you at a party and kissed you?" she asked.

"No," I said, a bit enviously. "At least not like that."

We were at it all night.

"What about that time in Barcelona when you and Sebastián—"

"Well, if you're going to bring *that* up, what about when *you*—"

"I did not."

"You did."

"Liar."

"Cheater."

I didn't sleep that night, or many nights after. Maureen made herself scarce. Whenever I did run into her at the dining room, she was all dolled up. I started to buy pills from the Friendship Hotel pharmacy, some to get to sleep, others to stay awake. Unable to read the labels, I got them mixed up and didn't care. In a state of delirium one afternoon, too shaky to ride a bicycle, I was on my way back from class when I told the driver to stop the car. There, by the side of the dusty road, a donkey was munching on a huge bush of a strikingly familiar plant. I shooed the donkey away and broke off branches of the fragrant, budding leaves, then stuffed them in the trunk. Rubbing my stomach, I told the driver that this herb was good for indigestion, and he nodded approvingly.

And rolling up the donkey's lunch into fat joints with airmail stationery, I started getting high to survive the People's Republic.

We'd already planned our escape by the time Christmas came around.

Finally in December, five months after we arrived, with great solemnity I was offered a long-awaited contract to sign, one that stipulated that if I didn't accept the terms of said agreement, we'd have to pay our own way home, which would have taken every dime we had. Outraged, I read on. I was promised a two-week Asian New Year vacation in mid-February, with two months of salary as a holiday bonus. I calculated that if I converted my people's currency to international exchange notes on the black market, I could afford to fly us both to the Philippines one-way from Hong Kong. Of course, we'd also have to purchase round-trip air tickets from Beijing to Hong Kong, or the government wouldn't let us leave the country.

Forcing a smile, I signed my contract in thick red ink with the carved quartz seal of my Chinese name that the university had made for me. The ideogram of this name was pronounced *Noulan Jiamin* and meant "farmer promising orchids." I was honored that my friend Ziang had bestowed on me the calligrapher Ta Yin's first name, Jiamin. Yet this cagey Louisiana-bred farmer may have promised orchids, but coercive contract in hand, he wasn't about to deliver. What I had in my pickup was more like a load of live alligators.

No, we weren't coming back for the spring semester, and we didn't tell a single soul, not even Ziang. We planned to exit China in the same way that Eastern European intellectuals with temporary travel visas departed their countries, leaving our lives intact and simply never coming back. Except for a few articles of clothing, we decided to leave the apartment exactly as it was, not to arouse suspicion among the mop-wielding, vibrator-pilfering custodians on the morning of our flight. We were even going to abandon the boom box and most of the tapes. All I wanted to pack were Ta Yin's exquisite scrolls of calligraphy, the Moroccan djellabah, and my portable typewriter. Maybe I could bang out an article about China on a beach in the Philippines, but who knew where Chairman Mao's mole would be in a year. Where could I publish such an article without putting my Chinese friends in jeopardy? Should I use a pseudonym, as did many journalists writing about China at the time? A couple of years later, my essay did appear, but under the disguise of a Spanish translation as a cover story for *Quimera*, the cultural magazine from Barcelona.

Maureen's plan wasn't to recuperate on a beach in the Philippines but—how could I ever make this up?—to return to the tumultuous beehive of Hong Kong to conduct stress-reduction workshops.

Yet before we could get back to our real lives, first we had to make it through the holidays, which began with her students' Christmas dance pageant at the American Embassy. There in the dreary lecture hall, grade-school children from the International School, which included every continent on earth, wore matching leotards and pumped their tiny fists to our tape of the Weather Girls' 1982 gay anthem "It's Raining Men (Hallelujah!)" while their proud diplomat parents, garbed in everything from silk salwar kameez to brocade dashikis, beamed and applauded. Any minute I expected Sylvester from my Cockette days to prance up the aisle in full falsetto followed by the Two Tons of Fun, his hefty backup singers who later became the Weather Girls. The outrageousness of the Embassy spectacle made me homesick for San Francisco, and for the people Maureen and I used to be there together.

New Year's Eve didn't go as smoothly. Since nothing was happening for foreigners at the Pound, we decided to hijack the Friendship Hotel bar and invited every Westerner we knew. To mark the occasion, Maureen inaugurated her new fox-fur coat, one that matched her hair, a purchase so pricy and hush-hush that I was immediately suspicious. Was it as a gift from another man? She, of course, denied this. Ending this testy confrontation, she grabbed our boom box, sashayed out the door, and pranced across the wind-whipped quadrangle in her new fox coat with the Sony balanced on her shoulder, blasting at top volume a tape of "Every Breath You Take," that year's biggest hit: "Every move you make / Every vow you break / Every smile you fake . . . / I'll be watching you."

By the time I made it alone to the bar, wrecked on whatever I could find, the party was already in full swing. And by then I didn't care. It felt so good to dance again, with anyone, with everyone, to feel the freedom in my shivering, long-johned limbs that I so sorely missed. For the first time there was music in the bar, people were rocking out, and the Chinese waiters were beside themselves, on the phone every five minutes, probably to the Central Committee. *Comrade Noulan is at it again,* I imagined them reporting. *The Westerners have gone berserk, "moving that way in public."*

Yet we weren't the only group to take over the bar that evening.

Maureen and I spotted them at the same instant, the huddle of dark men in the shadows on the other side of the room. They were seated in a tight circle, intensely concentrating on praying, as if at a religious rally. Then I realized who they were, the members of the Palestine Liberation Organization living in Beijing, and I figured they were marking their high holy day, the anniversary of Fatah's first attack against Israel on December 31, 1964.

"I'm gonna invite them to come join us," Maureen slurred.

I placed myself between her and them. "Do not," I said, spitting out every word, "invite the P.L.O. to this disco party."

"Oh, don't be such an old stick-in-the-mud." She marched around me and headed toward the chanting men. Short of socking her one, my first impulse, I didn't know how to stop the disaster that was about to occur. Then there she was, the redheaded American lady in the new fox-fur coat chatting up the seething Fatah militants.

To my amazement, the Palestinians trooped over to our side of the room as if on a forced march from Mecca to Tel Aviv. Arms folded, they stood at the perimeter of the dance floor, glaring at the couples cutting up. I'd never witnessed longer faces on anyone. "Happy New Year," one of them finally intoned. "God is great." Then they turned on their heels and strode out of the bar.

To my further astonishment, China-veteran Victor managed to sweet-talk the wary waiters into keeping the bar open until midnight, when with sloppy hugs and kisses we staggering foreigners ushered in the ominous year of 1984 inside the Great Wall. With the boom-box cord trailing along the ground behind us, Maureen and I were soon crossing the planetary tundra of the Pound, hand-in-hand for the first time in ages, holding onto each other for dear life in the frigid enormity of the night, as if we were stranded together on an ice floe in the middle of the Arctic Ocean.

Twenty years after we escaped from China, I ran into Lourdes, one of my Spanish friends from Beijing, at a party in Madrid. She told me that after all this time, our Catalan friend Gemma was still living there, married to a Chinese man. I explained what a troubling time it had been for me. And, no, now that she mentioned it, I hadn't seen Maureen lately, not since 1987, during our last fight in a hotel room on the Rue des Arts in Paris.

"We really broke up in Beijing," I confessed, "although we did try to patch things up a couple of times after. We weren't legally married, you know." This was starting to feel like a class reunion. "Say, what ever happened to Jaume and Laura from Barcelona?"

"They're divorced," she said, moving closer to me on the balcony. She turned to see if anyone was listening. "You probably knew that in China Laura was having an affair with that Venezuelan, Victor."

"Funny," I said, slugging back my wine with a grimace, "but I suspected Maureen was."

"Oh no, it was Laura. Jaume was so broken up that he chased after everything in a skirt."

"You see, I was watching Maureen," I said, pointing a finger to my eye.

"Everyone was watching everyone, and being watched."

We edged even closer. Laughing, I confided what I'd witnessed in Gemma's kitchen, and she shook her head. "No, he wasn't seeing Maureen. Jaume was out of control. An ex-junkie, you know."

I nodded gravely, thinking back to those seven months at the Friendship Hotel. I wondered what that twisted tissue of lies, suspicions, and deceptions, both public and private, had really been about.

"Did you ever learn the big secret," I asked her, "what the government was trying to cover up?"

Lourdes winked. "I'll never tell."

I reached over as if to twist her arm.

"Just that everyone was so unhappy," she said with a shrug.

The wily leaders were so ashamed of China's misery that they tried to keep a billion people locked in the basement like embittered poor relations when foreign guests were invited over for dinner. Over the years, I'd lost track of the Central Committee's campaign slogans—the latest I'd heard was "To Get Rich Is Glorious"—but it seemed that by now Chairman Mao's mole had migrated far from his portrait in Tiananmen Square and deep into the heart of Houston. By 2004 the Chinese already had become the new Texans, and skyscrapers had long since replaced the alleys where I bicycled in Beijing, now a car-choked megalopolis that required not surgical but gas masks. Foreigners like us, who had helped with China's "Opening to the West," were among the last to glimpse the lingering shadows of its ancestral ghosts, so recently plowed under into a country where everything was newer, bigger, richer, and faster.

Not that life was much different at the moment in Spain, where things were looking up. A socialist government was in power, the economy was rolling in construction dough, and I was about to publish a book there. As Lourdes and I stood on the balcony, haunted by lives we'd led decades ago in an antique land, the sun was setting over the red tile rooftops of Malasaña, casting the neighborhood in richly striped hues of ochre and sienna. I glanced over the railing at a dreamy young couple holding hands as they ambled down the narrow cobblestone street below, and I waved to them, as you sometimes do when passing people you used to know.

14

THE DREAM ACT

A long with hundreds of other dreamers, I had to wait my turn. I was
standing in a line so long that it spilled out of the immigration office,
snaked down a curved second-story stairway, and spilled across the plaza,
where it ended in a jumble of confused foreigners paging through their
paperwork. This queue was so stalled that Latin American women were
walking its length peddling soft drinks and potato chips from baskets,
hawking their wares as if at a Mexican bus station.

"*¿Hola, guapo, quieres un chicle?*" one called out to me. No, I didn't
want any chewing gum but smiled. At least she spoke Spanish.

It was 10:30 on a sweltering July morning, and I was badly hung over
from hopping among Madrid's tapas bars the night before. My immigration lawyer couldn't make it, but she sent Pablo, a young partner from her
office, to help get me through the ordeal. In the merciless glare, we were
both wearing dark glasses, sighing, and trying to make jokes. The Moroc-
cans in front of us didn't speak Spanish, and neither did the Senegalese
behind us. I was the only fair-complexioned blond in sight, not that my
American passport provided me any advantages. We all were equally
considered "extra-communitarians," that is, part of an alien horde from
outside of the European Union clamoring to get in.

Why was I doing this?

I'd been standing in such lines for the past two years, trying to achieve
permanent residency in Spain. This was my first one-year renewal. I was
claiming *arraigo*—literally, rootedness—during an amnesty program for
the undocumented in a country where I'd lived and worked for eight years.
For four of those years, during which I taught North American graduate

studies at the Autonomous University of Barcelona, I'd paid into the social security system, a third of my monthly salary, if you're curious. But I still had to cross the Spanish border every six months into neighboring France, Morocco, or Portugal to renew my tourist visa, as I did for the four years while I taught at various universities as a Fulbright professor of American literature. The Fulbright Commission advised this unorthodox approach, explaining that my renewable one-year fellowship would be over by the time the temporary residency application was even looked at, a process even slower than the eternal line I was now standing in.

The Spanish have perfected the torturous art of bureaucracy, perhaps taught to them by their Arab rulers, one which the Iberians then exported to Latin America. Spanish bureaucrats are known as *chupatintas*, that is, "ink-suckers." And there's a tagline most commonly associated with them. After enduring hours in line, as the exasperated citizen finally reaches a bureaucrat's desk, the ink-sucker says "*Señor, vuelva usted mañana*": "Come back tomorrow, sir." Shuffling through the stacks of dusty folders on his desk, the ink-sucker will inevitably find some essential scrap of paper missing, misplaced, or—horror of horrors—unstamped with an official seal.

In my hand at the moment I held my temporary residency permit, about to expire, my Affiliation to Social Security card, my bank account passbook, a completed application, my passport and birth certificate, a form ascertaining that I had no rap sheet either in Spain or the United States, and four regulation-sized color photos of myself, taken the night before in a booth at the Atocha train station on my way home from the tapas bars. Pablo informed me that everything was in order, and now what we needed were *cojones*—the balls to persevere in the face of all odds.

I tugged at my own pair when, three hours later, we finally entered the actual immigration building to pass by the guard glaring at me like a prison matron.

"Are you European?" she barked.

"Yes," I lied. After all, I rationalized to myself, I'd lived here for years, my family originally came from France and Ireland, and New Orleans had not only been a French colony but an actual province of Spain, although more than two centuries ago. Of course I was European.

She waved Pablo and me over into a much shorter line, one in which I wasn't the only blond.

An hour later, when we finally reached the desk of an ink-sucker with his eyes glued to the clock—it was almost 3:00 p.m., closing time—he exploded when I handed him my passport.

"You're an extra-communitarian," he shouted. "This is the European Union line."

At this point Pablo took over, apologizing for our mistake and emphasizing how busy this American university professor was, even though at the moment I didn't have a job. I stood by sheepishly, head bobbing in agreement, marveling at Pablo's circuitous arguments. Finally the ink-sucker raised his eyebrows in resignation and held out an impatient hand for my paperwork.

Then he exploded again. It was almost lunchtime, and the poor guy was probably dreaming of a three-course meal and a bottle of Valdepeñas. Now it was the photos.

"*Tienes los ojos achinados*," he said. Evidently that was how you said slant-eyed in Spanish: Chinese-eyed. "Your eyes have to be wide open, to show their color."

True, I did look a bit squinty and flushed in the photos taken on my way home from the tapas bars last night. But Chinese-eyed?

"Sir, come back tomorrow," he said. There. He actually said it, the phrase I'd been dreading. "With new photos."

At that point Pablo grabbed my elbow, telling the ink-sucker, "Just a moment."

We raced across the plaza to a photo studio that served the immigrant trade, and just before the shop closed for the siesta, four new photos of me were taken, blue eyes blazing. Then we sprinted back into the immigration office, ignoring the lines, and confronted our ink-sucker friend just as he was packing up for the day.

"Will these photos do?" I asked, breathless.

The ink-sucker cursed, heaved himself to his feet, slipped the photos into my folder, and stamped the application receipt that he then handed me. Evidently the man didn't want to waste another goddamn moment arguing, especially since a roasted leg of lamb was probably waiting for him on the family lunch table.

"You'll receive notification by mail within six months to come pick up your residency renewal," he said.

That meant I'd have six whole months as a legal alien before I had to start the entire process over again.

"Let's go have a glass of wine," I said to Pablo, slapping him on the back. "Or two."

I'd received my first residency card the good, old-fashioned Spanish way: by *enchufre*, or nepotistic connection. My friend Felipe's brother, who worked at immigration in Barcelona, handed it to me at Felipe's birthday party, the paperwork evidently processed during a family dinner over a bottle or two of local Raimat wine. That was the least a brother could do for Felipe's girlfriend's former professor, a hippie-type poet from San Francisco. This backdoor maneuver reminded me of my mother's inevitable question whenever anyone in the family encountered an official difficulty in New Orleans: "Who do we know who works in that office?"

So that was how I entered the immigration labyrinth, began to fork over Social Security payments, and came to believe that I deserved legal residency in my adopted country. The easiest way would have been to marry a Spanish woman—this was before gay marriage was legalized—and I had several offers. But I didn't want to complicate my life with a paper wife, bogus bank accounts, and fake addresses because, you see, I suffered under the delusion that I actually merited residency on my own account. I was the English translator of one of the greatest Spanish poets since the Civil War, Jaime Gil de Biedma, and City Lights Books had just brought out *Longing*, a collection of my translations of his poetry. And I'd taught at Spanish universities for close to nine years, written for national magazines, would soon publish a collection of my essays translated into Spanish, and spoke the language fluently. I'd assimilated in every way.

"Listen, here's an unlikely American," my neighbor in Malasaña, Pilar Vázquez, used to tell her friends when introducing me, "one who, just like us, doesn't drive, smokes, and stays up half the night. Plus," she added, after I'd moved back to New Orleans, "like every Spaniard, in his own country he lives around the corner from where his grandmother was born."

My friend Pilar's introduction wasn't only a thumbnail description of me but of herself and her friends. I didn't migrate to Spain seeking the exotic, but so my singularly un-American eccentricities would finally blend into the woodwork around me, which I'd never managed to accomplish in the United States.

Why did I need a paper spouse? I didn't need to borrow an identity I'd already achieved on my own.

With my new legal status, I could open a resident bank account, lease an apartment, or even own property if I wanted to. And then the prize finally arrived: an actual work permit, good for one year. And it showed up at the right moment, just after 9/11, when the United States became hysterically paranoid and I was being evicted from my French Quarter apartment when the building changed hands. So I put my possessions in storage and bought a one-way ticket back to Madrid.

At last I was a legal resident with a work permit, yet an unemployed one whose mother was in and out of the hospital at home. As my mother's friend Miss Sarah told her when she learned of my plans: "Tell your son I feel sorry for his mother."

Yet after I moved back, Spanish as I felt, Sunday afternoons seemed lost and lonely. After lunch at a table for one in some bachelor restaurant I'd wander the streets of Madrid, wondering what I was doing there. I had friends, of course, but on those hollow afternoons they were busy with their own families, and while I lugged around the hefty Sunday edition of *El país*, I meditated on what the life of a permanent expatriate had to offer me. El Retiro park was filled with Chinese and Latin American immigrant families who were enjoying their day off, strolling in clusters and licking ice cream cones. I only had two well-assimilated American friends in Madrid, both of whom I'd met through the Fulbright Commission, but no such support from a similar immigrant community. Most Yanks and Brits did stick together in their own monolingual enclaves, but if I'd wanted to eat hot dogs or discuss the latest show at the Tate Gallery, what was I doing in Spain?

When not scouting for a university teaching position, I was trying to write. Mostly I was writing in English, learning how challenging it could be to write in one language while living in another. I found it tricky to transpose a snippet of dialogue, a reference, anecdote, or character from the linguistic context of one culture into another, almost as impossible as translating a joke. I had a tremendous admiration for expat writers such as Marvis Gallant and James Baldwin, yet noticed in their fiction that the experience of France was usually filtered through the points of view of foreign protagonists. I asked Pilar, a renowned translator, as well as her husband, Estebán Pujals, an erudite literature professor, if they could name one non-native speaker who had crossed over to become a success-ful writer in Spanish. Like the Irish Beckett in French, I stressed, or the Polish Conrad in British English, or the Russian Nabokov in American English. In the United States we seemed to produce such immigrant writers by the dozens.

No, they couldn't think of single one. So into the trash went my Spanish rough drafts.

All of my teaching jobs at Spanish universities had been as a visiting professor, only now I was no longer visiting. Supposedly I was in Ma-drid to stay. To get a permanent position, I would first have to become a civil servant, since almost all of the universities in the country were administered by the government. This would involve another mountain of ink-sucking paperwork, rising through the ranks, knowing the right people, state exams, and in Barcelona, mastering Catalan.

And I'd had it with nationalism, of the linguistic, ethnic, religious, or any other variety. Although I continued to admire Catalan culture, my relationship with the language had grown prickly during what in the early nineties was called the *normalización lingüística* in Catalonia, a statute that required all public discourse to be in Catalan, even though more than half of the population spoke only Spanish and the Catalans were bilingual. This law abruptly ended what initially attracted me to Barcelona, the stellar role the city had always played as a magnetic nexus of international Hispanic culture, a torch soon passed on to Madrid. Although, of course, I could continue to conduct my American literature seminars in English, when I went to confer with the dean at the university, I was forced to bring along an interpreter, who would translate what I said in Spanish into Catalan for the dean's benefit, and her Catalan remarks into Spanish for me, even though the dean spoke both languages fluently. And that awkwardness was the law.

I often swore that if I ever wanted to stick my head up the butt of some narrow provincialism, then thank you very much, but I'd just as soon move home for good to New Orleans, where the parochial island mentality was at least my own.

Okay, I did enthusiastically begin learning Catalan when I first arrived in Barcelona in those heady years after Franco's death, but have always been stubbornly perverse when *forced* to do something, especially if people insist it's for my own benefit. Although I understood most of what was being said in the language, it got to the point that when addressed in Catalan, I would answer in English, which would oblige the baffled Catalan to switch into Spanish, in which we then went on to have a conversation. I hadn't come to Spain to stand out as a foreign visitor but to fit in, and soon learned I'd never be allowed to feel like a Catalan. Being Catalan was like being born a redhead: either you were or you weren't. And I wasn't about to dye my hair. Every time I opened my mouth, the politics of language would pop up, and I would expose a second level of foreignness, that of not belonging to a regional tribal identity.

During the mid-nineties, toward the end of my years teaching in Barcelona, a Catalan colleague asked me over lunch if I would like to spend the rest of my life in Barcelona. Without thinking, I railed against the linguistic nationalism, and she lowered her eyes. That week I learned that a civil-service position teaching English-language poetry had opened up in the department, and I considered calling her to repent of my outburst.

That weekend I picked up a Brazilian in a bar and took him back to my place. Later in bed, as we lay around smoking hashish and commiserating about being immigrants, I explained how this very week I'd passed up the chance for a permanent civil-service job at the university.

"*¿Ser un funcionario catalán?*" he said, turning over in bed to expose his magnificent caramel-colored thighs. "*Qué futuro más gris.*" And the more I thought about it, the more I realized how right he was: what a gray future indeed to become a Catalan civil servant.

Eventually a grad student of mine landed the permanent poetry position. A Brit married to a local, they were raising their children in Catalan, and he didn't need a Catalan interpreter when he spoke with the dean. He was raising redheads, and had married one.

Several months before my mother's final trip to the Intensive Care Unit, I received a grim phone call about the prognosis from her friend Miss Sarah. I immediately slipped my hard-won resident work permit inside my passport, gave up my small apartment in the Malasaña neighborhood, said goodbye to Pilar, Esteban, and other friends there, and flew home.

Was it a dream? I often ask myself in New Orleans, thinking of the years I'd spent living in Spain. All that time, had I been walking around in a "fugue state," as psychiatrists call the manic delirium in which their amnesiac patients run away to invent new identities, often in foreign countries?

Yet during any of my recent visits back to Barcelona or Madrid, it only takes a single jetlagged day for me to jump alive, to feel that my American life is the dream and Spain the reality to which I've just joyfully awoken. I ask myself how I could possibly belong in a country whose signature feature is the gridlocked strip mall, not public transportation, where every lunatic is armed to the teeth, where people go to bed at ten p.m., where college students practically have to sign consent forms to have sex, where bars don't clatter until the wee hours with saucers of squid and octopus, where the national sport is brain-crushing football, not the balletic pageantry of the bullfight?

Then once back in the United States, I stumble about for weeks in a daze clutching my Styrofoam cup of watery coffee, wondering what I'm doing here?

Few immigrants to the United States ever told their butlers one bright morning, "Pack up the silver, Jeeves. I think I'll move to America." Like my own hardscrabble French and Irish ancestors, most immigrants uprooted themselves from where they belonged brimming with teary regret. They left because of wars, famines, poverty, politics, or ethnic strife, not as an adventure but as a necessity. So perhaps my relationship to Spain was more that of an expatriate, not an immigrant, my boxes of stamped paperwork to the contrary. After all, I'm already bilingual and bisexual, so why couldn't I be bi-national? In *Paris France*, Gertrude Stein insists that "writers have to have two countries, the one where they belong and the one in which they really live."

I suppose first-generation immigrants everywhere walk around in the same dream, half here, half there. Why else would President Obama call his bill to grant residency to rooted, undocumented immigrants the Dream Act? As they say, you never belong to a place until somebody you love has died there, cementing your investment in the past. By the same token, perhaps first-generation immigrants can never claim their new countries as home until they give birth to a child there, putting a down payment on the future.

Belonging is the one thing in life you can't buy (I'm no longer so sure about love). And belonging is a generationally vertical relation to place, more about bones in tombs and children in schools than about paper-work. And although over the years I'd lost several close friends in Spain, my only child there remained a box filled with expired immigration forms, one I'd stored for several years on the uninhabited third floor of Pilar's mother's house in the staid Argüelles neighborhood. Frail Doña Vázquez was 102 years old, and never even knew my name or that my boxes were there.

During a visit to Madrid just after Pilar's mother passed away and her house was put up for sale, I realized the time had come to reclaim whatever I'd saved from my last residency during 2002. I'd been in the process of my permanent five-year residency renewal when Hurricane Katrina struck New Orleans in August of 2005. Only three weeks earlier I'd been traveling through Spain on a book tour. Except for a month's visit that November after the hurricane, when I had nowhere to go and friends in Barcelona rescued me by inventing a series of paid lectures I could give, once home again I couldn't escape the devastation surround-ing me and didn't get back to Spain for a whole year. In December of the following year, when the immigration official examined my passport with a magnifying glass, he noted with a scowl that I hadn't entered the country for twelve months and stamped my application "denied." My lawyer's protests about an "Acts of God" clause in the immigration law did no good. She advised me to pretend to lose my passport, get a new one with no stamped entries and departures, and then reapply. Simple.

What I did was return to New Orleans to rebuild the city and my life.

And there in Argüelles, as the sun set through the terrace window on the third floor of Pilar's mother's empty house, now I was deciding what to save from another ruin. This pile of debris consisted of a Chinese rug I'd rescued from a dumpster, a few boxes of clothes, lecture notes and syllabi, books, and immigration paperwork. Miraculously, I found my grandfather's robe, wondering when I'd brought that over, and a ceramic pot that I particularly loved, along with a wooden spatula. Here was correspondence from the Carmen Balcell's Literary Agency in Barcelona about my translations of books by Neruda and Gil de Biedma. University contracts. Years of electricity and telephone bills that proved my "rooted-ness." Earlier letters from my mother, who had died several years ago. Drafts of essays and stories and translations I'd published. An out-of-date printer. A striped blue sock with no mate. My father's tweed sport coat that no longer fit.

Watery-eyed, Pilar was staring through the terrace window at the splotches of purple and scarlet streaking over the treetops, while in my own bleary haze I was sorting through what was left of my Spanish life. I looked up from my boxes just as she turned toward me. The small cobwebby bedroom was soaked in crepuscular grief. She told me this was the first time she'd visited her childhood home since the funeral. We both burst out crying.

Her mother was gone, along with childhood. And so was this creature I'd invented, a Spaniard called Jimi.

We hugged, and then did what needed to be done, as sensible people do at such crossroads. Pilar began closing the terrace shutters as I lugged down to the street everything I needed to throw away.

First into the dumpster went the box of immigration paperwork. Then the box of university contracts and syllabi. Then the box of drafts. I saved the translation correspondence—after all, my books were still in print— my grandfather's bathrobe, and the ceramic pot and wooden spatula. Three thousand miles away, I'd use them to cook the Spanish food I loved.

On the darkening street next to the dumpster, ordinary Spaniards scurried from shop to shop buying bread, wine, and sausage for their evening meal before the stores closed. In a hurry, they didn't seem to notice the blond foreigner tossing boxes into the trash or suspect what it meant to him. I tried not to get in their way. Unlike me, the street where they walked was no doubt around the corner from where their grandmothers were born. They belonged.

With a wan smile, Pilar joined me on the sidewalk, and without saying a single word we took a taxi back to her apartment on Calle Pez in Malasaña.

It wasn't until we plopped down in front of a recuperative bottle of Rioja at the kitchen table that I realized what I'd really just lost. My glasses. I'd probably forgotten them in the bedroom on the third floor of Pilar's mother's house, and they were the only pair I had with me in Madrid.

Obviously, I couldn't let go. Now, like it or not, I had to return to where I'd thrown my life away.

As far back as I could, to every immutable mistake I'd ever made in my long, twisting journey toward becoming Spanish.

"I can't possibly go back to Mama's house tonight," Pilar told me, hands trembling.

"I understand." I couldn't go back to my own mother's house, ever.

We waited for her husband Esteban to roar home on his motorcycle, on the back of which I then took an exhilarating ride through Madrid's rush-hour traffic toward the shadowy twilight of that abandoned bedroom, where both Pilar and I had buried so much of our pasts.

I spotted them right away. My glasses were perched on top of a dusty bureau.

I grabbed them, put them on, and raced down the stairs. Now I could see with startling clarity what was real and what wasn't. Even though my official Spanish identity lay moldering at the bottom of a dumpster, Spain was still there, much as Gertrude Stein described that other country expatriate writers inhabit: "The second one is romantic. It is separate from themselves. It is not real but it is really there." And so it wasn't a dream that by the time Esteban and I made it home to the kitchen table, there was still wine to drink from the Rioja we'd opened, and Pilar's lamb stew was almost ready.

III. ABOUT TO STORM

Like one who's long prepared, like someone brave,
as befits a man who's been blessed with a city like this,
go without faltering to the window . . .
and say goodbye to her, the Alexandria you are losing.
—C. P. Cavafy, "The God Abandons Antony"

15

OUR HELL IN HIGH WATER

The real nightmare began last Wednesday morning, when the city cut off the water supply two days after Hurricane Katrina slammed into New Orleans and the levees breached. Until then, I hadn't regretted the decision not to evacuate my second-story French Quarter apartment, even when the electricity flicked off in the middle of the storm, plunging the city into darkness and ending most outside communication.

I still had hope.

I'm not particularly brave, but I am a fifth-generation New Orleans native raised in a culture that knows how to deal with hurricanes. As a matter of fact, I was a storm baby, delivered at the hospital Hôtel Dieu as an unnamed hurricane swirled across the waters to devastate New Orleans two weeks later in September of 1947. Amid the flooding from that disastrous storm, my first glimpses of life occurred in a kerosene-lit house in the Tremé, where howling wind and rising water no doubt seemed a natural part of the world into which I'd been born.

So as clouds darkened on Sunday afternoon, generations of storm folklore—sheer instinct by now—sprang into action. I filled the bathtub with water, cut the wick on the hurricane lamp, froze water in plastic jugs to keep the refrigerator cool, secured the dilapidated wooden shutters on the front gallery, stocked up on batteries, food, and drinking water, and got out the portable radio and the plug-in white Princess phone. Then I opened a bottle of wine. By the time my friends José Torres Tama and Claudia Copeland arrived to weather the storm with me, I'd cooked a three-course meal, which we topped off with a bottle of Spanish cognac.

"Here's to Katrina," we toasted, "the Russian spy," even as the TV broadcast its unrelenting instructions to *evacuate, evacuate, evacuate.*

After Katrina began to pound us at seven Monday morning, the only moment of panic took hold when a storm shutter tore open and a buckling set of French doors threatened to usher the hurricane into my study. While José and Claudia wired the doors shut, I held them in place with a wooden cooking spoon wedged inside the handles. Then we retired to the back gallery to watch the howling wrath of the storm whip through the brick courtyard. My building dates back to 1810, and has survived two centuries of storms from the Gulf. It knew what to do.

Or rather, the original architects of the city knew just what to expect, and designed houses on brick pilings, windows and doors with jalousie shutters, thick plaster walls, and enclosed courtyards. Most of the buildings constructed before 1910 have been waiting during centuries for a storm of Katrina's magnitude, and survived her with iron-lace grace, as did my place. Houses with concrete slab foundations poured on reclaimed swampland, and towering plate-glass hotels and office buildings, were chewed up and spat out. As my mother complained after her suburban home was flooded several years ago, "Honey, things like this aren't supposed to happen anymore. These are modren times."

Nature hasn't changed, but the city certainly has.

Summer camp by kerosene lamp didn't last long. By Tuesday afternoon I was already beginning to hear about martial law, widespread looting, and the city's mandate that everyone leave and nobody return. "You have nothing to come home to," the lone local radio station announced to the evacuated. "New Orleans as we know it has ended." Friends from both coasts called me on my non-electric Princess phone to report that the French Quarter was under water, even as I was peering down from my balcony into a bone-dry street. When we took a walk around, the Quarter resembled a cross between the morning after Mardi Gras and a grade-B war movie. Choppers swooped overhead, sirens wailed, and army trucks rumbled through the streets. At night, for the first time in my life, I could see the stars in the sky over the French Quarter, and all I could hear were tree frogs and the crash of shattering glass in the distance.

I began to notice groups of residents lugging water bottles and suitcases, heading for the Convention Center. Hours later they straggled back. At this point my chief means of communication was shouting from the balcony, and I learned there were no evacuation buses. The city had ordered us to leave, but was allowing nobody in to rescue us and providing no transportation out. On Tuesday evening, my skeletal neighbor Kip Michaels, a kidney-transplant patient, waded home alone by flashlight from the Convention Center, where there were neither dialysis machines nor buses to get him to one. His last treatment had been four days earlier, and he was bloating.

"I hate to bring this up," my neighbor Tede Sinker said, "but what are we going to do with Kip's body when he dies?"

We had to get him out.

By Wednesday morning, when the water was cut off, the city was already descending into mayhem. A looter had shot a policeman in the head, a car was hijacked by someone wielding a machete, gas was being siphoned from parked cars, mail trucks and school buses were being stolen, and armed gangs of kids from the projects were circling the streets on bikes. The social problems in this impoverished city had been simmering for decades; now the lid was off, and the pot was boiling over.

Despite orders to evacuate, roadblocks had been set up, and nobody was being permitted either to enter or leave the city. Molly's, a local bar, opened by candlelight and the rumor spread like wildfire: they have ice. If evacuated residents and proprietors had been allowed to return, to take a stand, some public order would have gradually prevailed. Yet the only advice from the city was to head for the Convention Center and not to drink the water.

We all knew the water wasn't potable, and seldom drink it anyway. If I learned anything growing up here, it was never to buy a dead crab or to drink the tap water after a hurricane, the two most sacred writs of the Creole catechism. The water was turned off to force us out, and the city's heavy-handed tactics made me bristle. "We got too many chiefs and not enough Indians," the mayor complained. I knew what *that* meant: nobody was in charge. The Homeland Security police-state had collided with Caribbean inefficiency, and the result was disaster. I took action. I latched the shutters, kissed my deceased mother's rabbit-foot and cat's-tail ferns goodbye, and in five minutes had packed a bag. In a daze, I was acting out a recurring nightmare: the borders are closing, the Nazis on their way, grab my grandfather's diamond question mark and gold Swiss watch.

And run.

I'd heard that hotels might be busing their guests out, and the place to head was the Monteleone Hotel on Royal Street, a Quarter institution. So at 5:30 p.m. José, Claudia, Kip, and I arrived trailing luggage and low expectations. But it turned out that the Monteleone had gotten together with several other hotels to charter ten buses to the Houston airport for $25,000, to do privately what the authorities should be doing publicly. We bought a few of the remaining tickets at $45 each. The sweltering lobby was littered with fainting bodies, grandmothers fanning themselves, and children seated in shadowy stairways, a scene straight out of *Hotel Rwanda*. The last bus out of New Orleans was set to leave at 6:05, the Austrian hotel clerk informed me. I had my doubts.

We weren't the only locals in line. I spotted the legendary jazz musician Allen Toussaint. "Allen," I said, "where did you hear about this?" He shot me a broad grin and walked on, as if we shouldn't talk about such things. By 9:30 that evening the buses still hadn't arrived. Five hundred people were milling around in front of the hotel, guarded by a hotel-hired security force of teenagers in "New Orleans Police" T-shirts with shotguns slung over their shoulders, the pitch-dark street illuminated by the beams from a lone squad car. An obscenely obese man was hauled in on a beeping forklift, and a row of passengers in wheelchairs formed at the corner. A run on the buses was expected, and we were warned that only those with tickets would be allowed to board. Anyone else would be dealt with by the kids with rifles.

Bus headlights appeared at last. A cheer went up. And then a single yellow Jefferson Parish school bus rattled up, bearing the news that the state police had commandeered the ten chartered buses to evacuate Parish Prison. We heard on the sly that this bus was offering passage to the Baton Rouge airport at $100 a seat. Allen Toussaint was the first to jump on, and after negotiating the price down with the driver, we crouched on the floor and held our breath. Ours was the only vehicle sailing along a dry, unlit highway. Why, we wondered, isn't the city providing hundreds of these vehicles to carry people out by the same route? The authorities may fix the electrical grid one day, but who is going to fix the authorities?

Later my neighbor Tede, who stayed behind, told me that the ten chartered buses never did show up. The five hundred waiting passengers were sent to the Convention Center, and then attempted to march across the river on the Crescent City Connection Bridge, where they were shot at by the Gretna police. "You mean you all escaped on *that stolen school bus*?" Tede shrieked. The news, she said, was all over town. As in the Battle of New Orleans, the pirates were better organized than the soldiers, and saved our day.

We're now luxuriating in my friend Andrei Codrescu's air-conditioned house in Baton Rouge, taking hot showers and sucking on ice cubes. I'm safe and dry, but however comfortable, this isn't New Orleans. The minute the lights flash back on, I'll be back home, unlatching my shutters and staring down a French Quarter street that I hope stretches as far into the future as it does into the past. As Stella says to her sister Blanche in *A Streetcar Named Desire*, "I wish you'd stop taking it for granted that I'm in something I want to get out of."

16

CINDERELLA SWEEPING UP ON DESOLATION ROW

They're selling postcards of the hanging,
They're painting the passports brown,
The beauty parlor's filled with sailors,
The circus is in town

—Bob Dylan, "Desolation Row"

Today I'm flying on a bankrupt airline into a bankrupt city powered by a bankrupt energy company. New Orleans has become a metaphor for the ecological, economic, and moral collapse we've all been dreading since the turn of the millennium. What the sinking of the Titanic meant for the early twentieth century, Hurricane Katrina has become for the start of the twenty-first: an assault on our hubris, the smug assumption that in these civilized times the authorities know what they're doing and everything is under control.

In my carry-on, I come armed with rubber gloves, face masks, a hot plate, dried food, and a flashlight purchased at a Florida K-Mart with my Red Cross debit card. My heart is in my stomach, wondering what pieces of my life Hurricane Katrina has left intact a month later. I know the second-story French Quarter apartment that I evacuated two days after the storm is dry and still standing, but little else.

Beginning at six this morning, I had to fly to New Orleans from Tampa by way of Detroit to arrive here before the six p.m. curfew in Orleans

Parish. No taxis or shuttles are operating from the airport, so for the first time since I was a spoiled college student, someone comes to meet me. My friends Jules and Joanna Côté are waiting for me when I step past the security gate, just as my parents would have been thirty years earlier. The airport shops haven't reopened yet, but at least I'm not slipping on any blood from the triage center that the National Guard maintained here until a week ago.

"I'm sitting in my air conditioned bar," poet Dave Brinks had shouted to me over the cell phone two days earlier. I'd been riding a bicycle in circles around the pier in St. Petersburg, hanging out with the pelicans that lined up to be fed every time a tourist appeared at the pelican-feeding concession. I could relate. It was like FEMA.

"Air conditioned?" I swerved to the side of the road.

"Yeah, and I'm listening to Santana. Hear?" He must have swooped the receiver around the Gold Mine, the bar he runs on Dauphine Street, because I could hear the familiar intro *oye como va*. "And I'm drinking a cold beer."

I almost fell off my bicycle. "The lights are on in the Quarter?"

"Came on this afternoon."

"What's the city like?"

"Three days ago I went by boat to check on our house in Mid-City. The first floor is gone, but the second is salvageable. A coffin was rocking against the fence of the cemetery across the street. Another coffin had floated through the gates up onto the railroad tracks, as if it were waiting for a train. The neutral ground was full of cemetery vases and plastic flowers and shit. But," he said, taking a deep breath, and repeating words I'd hear over and over during the coming weeks, "the city's coming back."

The mayor wasn't letting people into the neighborhood, not just yet, but I couldn't have cared less about his timetable. *The lights are on in the French Quarter*: I'd been waiting for weeks to hear those words. I booked my flight immediately. The reservations clerk thought I was mad to forgo an easy connection in Memphis for one that detoured me through Detroit. That is, until I explained about the curfew.

"But there's no ground transportation," she said. "Or food or water in New Orleans."

"You don't understand." I could have shaken her shoulders with joy. "The lights are on in the French Quarter."

From the window of my friends' van, I glance down from the Interstate over a ghost town with an ashen aura, boarded up, abandoned. For the first time I witness the ominous X's spray-painted by the side of each door, as if the angel of death had left its biblical seal in passing over each house, indicating how many among the living and dead remained inside. The streets are piled six feet high with debris, and are lined with refrigerators secured with duct tape. We pass trucks filled with camouflaged soldiers, their assault rifles pointing straight up in the air. Once-bustling Canal Street is empty.

It isn't raining frogs—not yet—but my mouth is hanging open.

This is my home. Was. Is. I go back and forth.

The French Quarter is more recognizable. A couple of faded balloons bounce from the doorway of a gay bar, where a hand-lettered sign invites "Come on in for some long-awaited hurricane relief." As long as we still have our sense of humor, I console myself, passing balcony after balcony of brittle brown ferns hanging in baskets and curbside refrigerators scrawled with an ominous voodoo logo. I wonder if the battery-operated watering system on my balcony kicked on when the water came back.

Yes and no. I look up to the iron-lace balcony at 624 Dumaine Street filled with green hibiscus and desiccated jasmine vines. Jules and Joanna drop me off and go for a drink at Molly's before the curfew falls.

I drop my bags in a courtyard filled with toppled trees, roofing shingles, and brick chimney shards. I take the flashlight out of the carry-on and flip the breakers for my apartment, walk up to the second floor, and unlock the door.

Everything is much as I left it.

The Secret History by Donna Tartt is still opened on the twisted sheets that cover the chaise, where I had left it a month ago, clipped to a portable reading lamp that came with my subscription to *The New Yorker*. For nights I lay there sweating, trying to read, listening to tree frogs croak in the courtyard next door. The battery-powered boom box is next to a river of melted candle wax, and the bathtub still half-filled with my hurricane water supply. The restless nights and frantic days of a hurricane holdout seem far away. I flick on a lamp switch.

Nothing.

I try all of the lights, walking through the late afternoon gloom of a shuttered Creole townhouse.

Nothing.

I race down to the fuse box. All the breakers are on.

Did I come back for this? There is no one to call. I try the bankrupt energy company. *For English, press one.*

I sprint around the corner to find Jules, a Québecois contractor and trapper's son who knows what to do with a screwdriver and Bowie knife. He makes a seat for me at Molly's.

I don't want a seat at the bar. I want my life back.

"I wonder if this is the master fuse switch," he says a few moments later, rummaging around in the dark carriageway with my flashlight. The lantern in the carriageway pops on, a delicate flicker of light under the grime of dust and cobwebs. Here in the French Quarter we're used to discerning life beneath this patina of time.

When we walk into my apartment, the lamp is on and the refrigerator humming. I'm humming Santana. *Oye como va.* Then I swing open the refrigerator door, and we both reel back and run gagging onto the back gallery.

Opening the refrigerator door is the defining moment in any evacuee's return. This is when we first smell the death that has overtaken the city. And it infests our chicken salad and red beans, a month later. Our own death. "The worms crawl in, the worms crawl out," goes that cemetery ditty we learned as children, the one left over from the nineteenth-century yellow fever epidemic, "in your nose and out your mouth." Only opening the family tomb a month after a burial could evoke similar horror.

What gets me isn't the live maggots swarming on the walls blackened with mold, or the stench of exploding eggs, or the colorful fungi sprouting everywhere. It's that finally I recognize what the entire city smells like, every nook and cranny of it, here where garbage hasn't been collected for a month and the streets are lined with reeking refrigerators and restaurant freezers.

The five pounds of frozen calamari or the shrimp stock in my freezer don't help.

No problem is insolvable, I decide, given a large enough plastic bag. I fill bag after bag, carrying them down to the trash heap on the street.

Then I set the freezer on high, and send the wiggling little fuckers inside the refrigerator to Siberia. I wait on the balcony, where below an empty tourist surrey clops by. A message for either God or helicopter pilots is painted in stark red on the surrey's fringed top: HELP US SAVE OUR MULES.

Two hours later I still don't feel hungry, and can barely keep down the airline pretzels.

I fish out the yellow rubber gloves and the face masks from my carry-on, spill a mixture of bleach and vinegar into a pan of cold water, and get to work on the refrigerator. Down on my knees, as I wipe and squeeze, wipe and squeeze, I feel joined by ancestral ghosts in the neighborhood, scrubbing away for dear life.

White boxes filled with decay all in a row. Tombs and refrigerators.

This is how we used to wash down the family tomb on All Saints Day. As that blues song goes, "One last favor I'll ask of you / see that my grave is kept clean."

I keep the sepia studio photograph of Sylver Landry propped on my living-room mantle, the one taken by Adams & Simon at 111 Royal Street in the early 1880s. Next to it is a black-and-white photograph of his sister, Alice Marie Glaudot, my great-grandmother, cradling me just after I was born. Sylver is a dark, devilishly handsome teenager with a wide, ill-fitting collar and flowing silk cravat. There is the trace of a wispy moustache above lips so full they suggest the African: the Landrys were probably Creoles of color.

Their father, Numa Landry, was a French Quarter banker, and his family lived in the Creole mansion at 915 Bourbon Street, next to what is now the rowdy gay bar Lafitte's-in-Exile, a block from my own apartment. In the twenty-five months between June 29, 1882, and July 18, 1884, this is where Sylver and his three teenaged siblings died of yellow fever. An ornate L still appears on the house's wrought-iron gate.

My great-grandmother wore her hair pulled straight up into a topknot, and every evening at bedtime would perch at the oval mirror of her vanity to back brush the long yellowish-white mane over her face into her lap. With hair cascading in front of her eyes, this was the perfect moment for a game of peek-a-boo, or so thought her great-grandson. Grande Mémère died when I was six, and over the interminable checker games in our Seventh Ward shotgun house, she rocked and reminisced. But she never confided in me what it was like to lose her four older brothers and sisters when she was my age.

Clippings saved from the French- and English-language newspapers of the day are more eloquent. "Some twenty months ago, sorrowing friends followed to an early grave the oldest son of our well known citizen. . . . Last Sunday, the insatiable monster—death—still seeking fair victims— again enters the sorrow stricken household, and this time carries off the oldest of his daughters." The article recounts that after strewing flowers on Sylver's and Amanda's double tomb in St. Louis Cemetery Number Two, the Landry family brought flowers to the double tomb of the two children they had buried the previous year, Rosalie and Numa.

The Creoles are often portrayed as lavish and sensual, filled with an irrepressible *joie de vivre*. That was exactly what they wanted people to think. To them, carefree meant wealthy. Only *les américains* and other poor people fussed in public. But in private, the Creoles' homes were austere, their attitude frugal and stoic. They did what they had to do to survive in these harsh climes, chins held high with steely determination.

In the early twentieth century the summers in New Orleans were so pestilent that families were divided into the "can leaves" and "can't leaves." Even though my family was a "can leave," and for many years rented a summer place in Bay St. Louis on the Gulf, one summer my mother fell violently ill with scarlet fever. The doctor in Bay St. Louis advised my grandmother to make funeral arrangements. But Mémère scooped up her dying ten-year old daughter and took her on the train back to New Orleans. There she found a specialist named Dr. Rateau who cured her child. Twelve years later her daughter married Dr. Rateau's nephew, my father.

Once when Mémère was trying to teach her unruly blond grandson some manners, I asked why the gentleman has to walk on the outside of the sidewalk when accompanying a lady. It didn't make any sense.

"Why, so if somebody empties their slop jar off the balcony into the gutter," she responded, "the lady won't be soiled."

That was a perfect nineteenth-century French Quarter answer, even if it confused me in the 1960s.

Yet now it's not difficult for me to imagine that ghostly world of slop jars, smudged kerosene lamps, tattered mosquito netting, and vats of laundry boiling in brick courtyards. Turn off the electricity and running water, and there we are again, just like after Katrina. Successive hurricanes, floods, fires, and epidemics have decimated the city over and over again. Once the stench was so terrible and airborne disease so prevalent that people crossed the muddy streets holding handkerchiefs over their noses. Death and destruction were constant companions to these displaced Francophones who lived in a neighborhood floating on top of cypress logs lashed together over a tropical swamp. Once a year they did put on Mardi Gras masks, but only to forget the creased faces of the priest, doctor, and undertaker they knew so well.

Also on my black marble mantle is the Landry family clock, ticking since the 1860s. In a winged helmet and Roman toga, a tarnished Mercury sits contemplating the passage of time, an elbow on his knee and two fingers raised thoughtfully to his cheek. Despite everything that Mercury has witnessed in New Orleans during the past hundred and fifty years, his features remain boyish. He hasn't lost his baby fat. The clock's mechanical *tick-tock* and chiming always have been the comforting heartbeat of the house. Now, as I survey the mantle after the month-long evacuation, I find the key to the silent clock and wind it.

Tick-tock, tick-tock, tick-tock.

It's still keeping perfect time.

Mercury has seen even worse days in this town. He's not about to give up the ghost.

People from the Quarter don't have any right to be angry," the red-faced librarian tells me. We're at a neighborhood meeting in Molly's bar to discuss the future of the French Quarter. "You have lights and your house is dry. I live in the Lower Ninth Ward and lost everything."

It will be months before she and other residents are allowed to tour their neighborhood from behind the windows of Gray Line buses. Still nobody is allowed in, and she isn't exactly sure what she no longer has. Large sections of the neighborhood are still under water.

Uptown, the Central Business District, the Quarter, and the Faubourg Marigny, all located on that crescent of higher ground that follows the intestinal turns of the Mississippi, are the only neighborhoods to which we're allowed to return. These are the same dry areas that soldiers ordered us out of at gunpoint only a month ago. Even unflooded portions of

Mid-City are closed to residents. Dave Brinks tells me about driving past an old man wheezing on the stoop of a badly damaged shotgun house in an abandoned neighborhood.

"Can I help you?" Dave called out.

It turned out that this grandfather with a pacemaker had hoofed it all the way to Mid-City from suburban Metairie, where National Guardsmen had blocked his car from entering Orleans Parish. All he wanted to do was see his home.

"Just got a little water," he told Dave on the long drive back to his car. "Sure, we can fix it up. Fixed it up after the last storm, and the one before that."

Like most hurricanes, Katrina did damage randomly, flattening this house but sparing the one next to it, flooding this block but leaving the next one dry. The National Guard and city authorities aren't allowing for these distinctions, cordoning off enormous expanses of the city "for your own safety."

"Feel guilty because the Quarter was spared?" the homeless librarian asks me.

"Not on your life," I tell her. "Residents put up with a lot to live here, noise, trash, gentrified prices, and nonstop waves of drunken tourists." As a matter of fact, we carry the entire economic engine of the city on our backs, an enormous price for our several feet of higher ground. In spite of the nightly vampire tours that congregate under my balcony, I entertained no doubts when I chose to live in the second-floor apartment of a building constructed in 1810 with plaster walls thicker than I am.

This meeting consists of a ragtag collection of hurricane holdouts and one-issue activists ranting into a microphone about garbage, abandoned pets, and team spirit. The wildest rumor is that the city plans to close the strip clubs on Bourbon Street. That draws a boozy hoot from the crowd.

I'm well into sobering day three of sanitizing my refrigerator and, still without gas, of taking cold showers, line-drying clothes, and cooking on a single hot plate. Everybody at this meeting to decide the future of the French Quarter is already drunk.

And that, I realize, is the future of the French Quarter.

My friend Toni Christopher and I are the first disaster tourists. We're driving through devastated Lakeview, tracing the water lines on the sides of houses.

"Look, this block got it up to the roof," we comment, or "Here the water only came up three feet."

We keep the air on and the windows rolled up, at far remove from the acrid atmosphere outside that stings the eyes and makes us itch. Toxic mold.

The brackish floodwaters have turned everything an unsightly shade of brown: houses, lawns, flowerbeds, trees, cars parked in driveways, and tricycles abandoned at curbs. It's as though we're floating in a submarine through the ochre shadows of some submerged civilization. Mounds of sodden carpeting line the streets, topped by warped furniture and wrinkled books. Every once in a while we spot someone in a face mask squatting over a plastic bucket, washing some beloved object next to a bottle of Clorox. It has only been two days since people were allowed into these neighborhoods to assess the damage and to pick through their homes like *glaneurs*, gleaning whatever grain has been left by the Grim Reaper.

We spot a family outside of their house, and roll down the window.

"Y'all planning on staying?" Toni asks.

"We'd love to," says a red-faced man approaching the curb. "But we have to wait on what the insurance adjuster says. And the government."

"Holy Jesus," I say. "The government."

"Yeah, the government." The man squints his weary eyes. "We're really a strong community, and have had a bunch of meetings with FEMA, but they haven't made up their minds."

If these residents had been allowed back in directly after the flooding subsided, they could have had a three-week head start on battling the corrosive effects of mold and mildew, which by now have climbed the walls and blackened the ceilings. Rumors are spreading that the government has intentionally kept the residents out of their homes so they *would* rot. The Halliburton plan, I hear, is to declare eminent domain, bulldoze the neighborhood, add landfill and build expensive condos, offering the neighbors pennies on the dollar for their homes.

Keeping people out, they say, is for their own safety. So was ordering us out of the city at gunpoint in the first place. "For your own safety" has become the mantra repeated to justify any level of manipulative control. Like Huck Finn, I was born on the banks of the Mississippi River, and would rather have the freedom to take risks and make mistakes. As one of Ellen Gilchrist's characters comments, "Americans have become such pussies."

"We think you should stay and fight for your houses," I say. I can't imagine waiting for government paperwork to decide if I could come or go or live in my own house. After all of the careless, wrongheaded decisions the government has made during the past month, how can anyone still trust the authorities to direct their fate? I shudder to think that the reconstruction of these neighborhoods remains in the same hands as those responsible for the botched levee system that caused the flooding in the first place.

New Orleans needs the white middle-class professionals from Lakeview and Lake Vista as well as the black middle-class professionals from Gentilly and New Orleans East. They are our dentists, doctors, lawyers, teachers, engineers, and small business owners. Now if I need to have a tooth filled or get a haircut, I have to go eighty miles to Baton Rouge, where 250,000 former New Orleanians are hanging on in motel rooms and efficiencies, screaming into cell phones.

Everywhere we drive, we encounter roadblocks of National Guardsmen, state and local police. When we try to use an off-ramp to turn around on the freeway, a city cop gives us a piece of her mind.

"If I let y'all through and they find y'all," she says, leaning out of the squad car blocking the road, "I could lose my job. Already done lost my house, and my family all over the country. I was on duty at the Superdome and seen what people is like."

Toni describes earlier that morning, when she was stopped at a roadblock behind a car driven by a matronly woman with perfectly coiffed blue hair who was trying to get back to her house in Lakeview. The matron's voice rose to a shriek when the National Guard told her that, for her own safety, she couldn't go home. Finally she gunned the car and sped past the roadblock, shouting out of the window at the Guardsmen, "So shoot me."

Our next stop is Alex's, Toni's brother's house in Lake Vista. It is a cloudless Sunday afternoon in early fall, and I can't help but be wafted back to the Sunday afternoon drives of my childhood. After lunch, which we called dinner, the whole family would often pile into my great-aunt's new turquoise Plymouth. A favorite destination was "the new sub-divisions out by the lakefront" featured in the *Dixie Roto* magazine that came with the Sunday *Times-Picayune*. We would pull up in front of some snazzy, split-level brick ranch house and stare out of the window.

"It's so modren," my Aunt Mercedez would say.

"They call it 'ultra-modern,'" my school-teacher aunt Marguerite would enunciate, pursing her lips at her sister-in-law's mispronunciation.

The subdivision looked like *Ozzie and Harriet* or *Father Knows Best*. I was brought up in raised shotgun houses with green storm shutters, separated by narrow weedy alleys from the houses next door, where we could hear the neighbors snore and pee. As a boy, I spent a lot of time in the cool darkness between the brick pilings under the floorboards, look-ing for lizards. Yet squeezed into the car on those Sunday afternoons, no doubt remained that these boxy manors built flat on the ground, these plate-glass picture windows showcasing some oversized artificial flower arrangement were the modernity to which we were meant to aspire.

We sat staring in awe at the future.

The dilapidated wooden houses I grew up in downtown have survived the hurricane. We're now taking a Sunday drive through the phantasmal ruins of what was supposed to be the future. In New Orleans we have much better luck with the past.

Alex's story is typical of the breathless plots in the tales I've been hear-ing. A week before the hurricane, taking advantage of the hot real estate market, he sold the house in Lake Vista and, two days before Katrina hit, moved all of his family's possessions into a newly purchased house in Lakeview. The day before the hurricane, the financing on the Lake Vista house fell through. The hurricane not only flooded the new house stacked with all his possessions, but carried it away: the house is no longer there. His family had spent one night there before the storm. Unpacking.

Stepping through Alex's opulent palace in Lake Vista is like touring the ruins of Pompeii. A child's green inner-tube lies deflated next to the cracked oval swimming pool filled with fetid sludge. The pool house stands grey and empty except for a bicycle. Inside the main house, a woman named Cookie has ripped out the flooded Sheetrock on the lower walls, so that only the skeletal wooden braces are left standing.

"Is that art or Katrina?" I ask, pointing at a twisted bronze chandelier in the family room.

She studies the asymmetrical loops for a moment, and then laughs. "That's art."

This is Cookie's job, cleaning out houses that owners cannot bear to re-enter. She's plump and rosy-cheeked, evidently in good spirits as she lugs armload after armload to dump into a heap in the street. Business is booming.

The air makes my skin itch and I'm beginning to cough.

"I feel like a grasshopper visiting a devastated ant hill," I whisper to Toni. The whole scene before me turns Aesop's fable on its head. Alex and his wife both worked so hard, meticulously paying their mortgage, insurance, and credit card bills every month. They hired decorators to faux-antique the walls and commissioned landscapers and sculptors to design their space. Like me, Toni lives on a shoestring in a rental, and spends all day painting and writing. Neither of us even have health insurance. Our houses are fine, our lives unchanged. Those Sunday afternoon drives into the futuristic "new subdivisions" backfired on me: I was never convinced of the need to own all this or to be "modern."

As we are leaving, I notice a sign done in a child's crayoned block letters above what used to be the kitchen garbage: "Remember to take out the trash every day." We make our way to the curb past a shoulder-high mound of soggy velvet drapes topped by a mateless high heel.

Maggie Beal, who runs an antique shop on Chartres Street, was so delighted on the first day people were welcomed back into the Quarter that she called every returning resident she knew to make plans to meet at Muriel's on Jackson Square, one of the few restaurants open. Gas service hadn't been restored yet, so the cooking was done on hot plates and food served on paper and plastic. It didn't matter.

The whole neighborhood was there that evening at Muriel's, table-hopping, exchanging hugs, and relating breathless hurricane sagas. Wine glasses were raised, and toasts flew across the glittering dining room. Waves of applause, hoots and hollers, greeted returning friends as they made their entrances. Every face beamed *we're home again*.

Suddenly an army Humvee pulled in front of the restaurant and four soldiers in battle fatigues stepped inside.

The diners put down their wine glasses. The room fell silent.

The soldiers didn't utter a word but froze stone-faced into sentry positions alongside the four walls with M16s across their chests. Diners exchanged glances and attempted some muffled conversation. After twenty minutes, the soldiers exited and climbed back into their Humvee. Then the baffled neighbors returned to their revelry.

"Make us feel safe?" Maggie laughed derisively, recounting the dinner. "They scared the bejesus out of us."

This scene was played out countless times at the same Place d'Armes location during the fifteen years of the previous Reconstruction. Major General Butler, whose Union troops took over the city in the spring of 1862, was known as "Silver Spoons" Butler because of the enormous quantity of confiscated local property he acquired at ten percent of its value. He described the city's residents as "hostile, bitter, defiant, explosive," words that accurately illustrate our present attitude toward the new invasion. These days, mention FEMA to a New Orleanian and—as if thrusting a lit match into an old gas heater—stand back.

Once again New Orleans is an occupied city for sale, cheap.

And once again, a thinly veiled distrust separates the occupying army and the native population. Sauntering down the street with my groceries, I can't imagine what, in these Caribbean surroundings, could possibly inspire such terrified condescension in the soldiers' corn-blue Midwestern eyes.

"Silver Spoons" Butler's solution to friction with civilians was General Order No. 28, which prohibited Creole women ("calling themselves ladies") from looking at or speaking to Union soldiers, or the offender would "be treated as a woman of the town plying her avocation." Butler claimed that the women's defiant words and gazes provoked the soldiers. Women now tell me that they lower their eyes when they pass National Guardsmen in the street, shrinking from the sexual aggression in their glares.

These young soldiers are clean-cut, unmistakably horny, and probably delighted that a hurricane hit Louisiana. After all, it got them out of Iraq, even if it didn't get them laid by the Creoles. Not by the ladies, in any case.

"I'm so horny I'm about to go gay," I heard one shout in a Bywater bar.

"Come here, honey," the swishy bartender said in an audible whisper. "Let me show you the broom closet."

A pair of Guardsmen approached two gay friends of mine walking to a dinner party in the Marigny. "We're here to protect you with our *muscle*," the soldiers told them, without prelude. They repeated this phrase several times, employing body language, until the mystified gay men understood what the soldiers meant by their "muscle." Word has it that these friends "plied their avocation" and arrived late at the dinner party.

From their trucks and Humvees the friendly soldiers wave at us, as if they were royalty on Mardi Gras floats. Yet few of us wave back. We sense what a general in Iraq instructed his grunts: "Wave, but have a plan to kill them."

These friendly soldiers with a plan to kill remind the painter Vidho Lorville of home. When he was a child during the U.S. occupation in Port-au-Prince, Haiti, he would hang out with the Marines, who would hand out candy and chewing gum to children in the street.

"Now New Orleans really feels like Haiti," he tells me, wide-eyed with disbelief that this could be happening in the United States.

I'm not the only returning New Orleanian mystified by this military response to a markedly humanitarian situation. Bivouacs of National Guardsmen have been set up in the most unlikely places: along the tourist mall of upper Decatur Street, inside the performing arts high school, on the lawn of the old Dominican College. In a city that hasn't experienced a single murder since the day before the hurricane hit, we're confronted everywhere by buzz-cut jarheads cradling M16s with their pelvises stuck out.

Our tragedy is about lost jobs, moldy Sheetrock, missing relatives, and closed schools. Yet the sole response has been to impose what suspiciously looks like the Baghdad Plan. Just as in Iraq, we have a curfew, and the National Guard to enforce it. And as in Iraq, Halliburton is in charge, the no-bid contractor for FEMA's reconstruction of the city. The government has suspended the Davis-Bacon minimum-wage law, and Halliburton has shipped in busloads of cut-rate Mexican workers, making it difficult for local contractors to find jobs. And Halliburton's sinister security goons from Blackwater are here. You remember who these privately hired mercenaries are: four Blackwater agents were burned and hung from the bridge in Fallujah, another empty city in which 80 percent of the population evacuated before the American occupation. Now a thousand Blackwater agents are in New Orleans in their black uniforms, stationed everywhere from the public library to the Jewish Community Center, making a thousand dollars a day to maintain order among the 60,000 mostly middle-class evacuees cleaning their refrigerators and filling out insurance forms.

This isn't the first time that the military has practiced on New Orleans. Only last year the city hosted Marine war-game maneuvers on how to deal with the Iraqi insurgency. From January 21 through February 17, 2004, from early morning until late at night, earsplitting choppers flew so low over New Orleans rooftops that a Marine hotline was set up to answer residents' complaints about structural damage to their homes. Camouflaged soldiers took up sniper positions behind parked cars, frightening motorists to death, and pointed guns at pedestrians. A convoy of trucks mounted with weapons entered the Ninth Ward announcing through megaphones, "We're friends of the Iraqi people. Stay in your houses." Petrified neighbors peered between the lattices of their shutters at armed soldiers scurrying in and out of alleys.

This being New Orleans, people weren't sure if a war movie was being filmed, Mardi Gras was starting early, or the mayor had declared war on Washington. I called the Base Operations headquarters several times to complain, as did dozens of friends. Yet, when the Marines departed, the *Times-Picayune* ran an article headlined "City Welcomes Marine Maneuvers with Southern Hospitality."

One Pentagon official explained that New Orleans had been chosen for practice in urban warfare because "it is our most foreign city."

The plot thickens. FEMA is now part of the Department of Homeland Security, which has been complaining since 9/11 that it has no practice in evacuating an American city in the event of a biochemical terrorist attack. So Hurricane Katrina has given occasion for a second set of maneuvers in New Orleans. The devastating monthlong evacuation, when for the first time in world history a major city was completely emptied by force, and the continuing military occupation long after any threat has passed make little sense to most New Orleanians. Unless, of course, New Orleans has been serving as a guinea pig for ill-conceived plans in urban control.

And these plans have worked no better here than in Iraq.

If there should be a biochemical terrorist attack on an American city, its residents should remember New Orleans during Katrina and make plans accordingly. Steal a school bus, if you have to, but don't wait for the

National Guard, Halliburton, and Blackwater to rescue you. These guys are now in New Orleans rehearsing a madcap action flick that, I promise you, you'd rather not see up close.

Toni is the kind of New Orleans woman for whom "Silver Spoons" Butler designed General Order No. 28. At 6:30 this morning she was nursing a latté at the leisurely Rue de la Course coffee shop on Magazine Street. She looked up from her *New York Times* to spot a National Guardsman done up in a bulletproof vest and matching assault rifle next to her café table, adjusting his combat helmet in a mirrored wall.

"Feeling a little overdressed?" she asked.

The first thing I notice climbing the stairs to the party is the sea of unstrung violins gleaming in the moonlight on the rooftop.

"We were driving through Lakeview, and saw a mountain of violins on the curb," explains Andy Young, the poet hosting this party of returning Quarter denizens. "There must have been at least five hundred, all bent and soggy. So we loaded some of the least damaged ones into the car, and now they're drying on the roof."

A sepulchral silence reigns in a city in which all of the violins are warped and only an eighth of the residents are back testing the waters, perhaps just for a few days. Because no schools are open, I see few children, and because most hospitals are closed, the elderly are staying away. Most of those who have returned resemble the people at this party, youngish to middle-aged with few attachments, no children or major expenses. Our jobs are gone, but we are scraping by. Our month as evacuees in Texas or Florida, California or Arizona, has taught us a lesson: there is nowhere else in this whole wide country where we feel at home. We're ex-pats at heart, and belong either here or abroad. For many of us, this is abroad.

Khaled Hegazzi, an Egyptian writer in a flowing djellabah, has roasted a lamb in honor of our homecoming, its paws pointing toward Mecca. He is from Alexandria and has adopted New Orleans as a sister port city. I'm wondering how it felt in Alexandria, many centuries ago, a month after the library burned down. With that symbol of their flowering civilization suddenly gone, did people stumble around in the same shock we feel now? Did they bid goodbye, as Cavafy does in his poem, to "the Alexandria you are losing"?

Through the window opened over the moonlit pools of warped violins, I spot flames on the horizon. They are licking up into a pitch-black sky from a part of the city where streetlights are still out. Rumors fly. Is it close to the Quarter? Are firemen back on the job? Everywhere there are fires or reports of fires. We listen for sirens, and hear none.

What we hear is Herbie Kearny, an Irish painter with a long braided beard who looks like a Blakean angel. He is standing in the middle of the room, knees doubled in a half-squat, howling from the center of his being like a dog. He howls like the wolves who prowl forests after a fire searching for their mates, like the skeletal mutts in forsaken Mexican plazas after the harvest has failed, like the strays who keep watch under the windows of the sick, foretelling death.

"Care for another glass of wine, Herbie?" somebody asks when he has finished. Exhausted by the tension, we crack up and gulp wine with him, glass after glass, while a slinky black cat twines between our feet.

On the way home, carrying my foil-wrapped plate of leftover lamb, I encounter soldiers in battle fatigues standing guard next to their Humvee on all four corners of my intersection. I mumble a civil "good evening," and their eyes drop unsmiling to meet mine, heads held erect. The night air smells caustic as tarpaper, sweet as decay, and tastes like the figs of Fallujah.

For blocks around, not one sound.

Not a soul is walking on Royal or Dumaine, nothing is moving far into the darkened, refrigerator-lined ruins of Lake Vista and Lakeview, Mid-City and the Lower Ninth Ward. Inside the musty contagion of a tomb in St. Louis Cemetery, my mother is sinking down into the bony arms of my grandmother, who is resting on the shoulder of her father, who has collapsed into the chalky remains of his own mother. In the flaking gold lettering above their names, a silent prayer floats across the flooded, feverish centuries we have survived: *Parce que le temps passé, je prie pour vous.*

Mémère, Pepère, who is left to speak for you?

Upstairs, Mercury in winged helmet is still at his post on the mantle, ticking. I push my speakers onto the balcony and put a prized piece of vinyl onto the turntable, blasting Bob Dylan's raspy, lonesome moan into the ghost-town streets: "And the only sound that's left / after the ambulances go / is Cinderella sweeping up on Desolation Row." I'm not sure if the soldiers below understand these words. I'd like to imagine they do. No boots stomp up the stairs, nobody pounds at the door. Perhaps their war games are over for the evening or they're needed in another forlorn corner of the empire. Before the song has ended, they're gone.

17

BLACK AND WHITE, WITH BROWN WATER ALL OVER

The summer before Katrina, New Orleans was spinning out of control in a boozy maelstrom of guns and drugs, murder and corruption. Flush with tourist dollars, the sweltering city felt overripe and frantic, like some blowzy hooker who, late into besotted middle-age, sinks to new depths because she hasn't got much longer to live. In July, after my gentle dog-groomer friend was shot to death in a demented crime of passion, I wanted to run onto Canal Street, hold up my hands, and scream *stop, New Orleans, just stop.*

A month later, the hurricane took care of that.

Toward the end of the summer, the city had been plagued with three or four murders a day, so common that most went unreported. Every evening I'd scan the faces in the obituary columns of the *Times-Picayune.* Inevitably, all of the young black men pictured there had died of gunshot wounds. Although predominantly centered in the drab brick housing projects, turf wars over the crack trade extended into almost every neighborhood. Children playing on their front porches were slaughtered in drive-by shootings; a grandmother was shot in the head while unloading groceries from her car in the driveway; an esteemed Carnival seamstress was gunned down along with her daughter, then the house was torched. The most violent gangtsa scenarios were being acted out in real life on the city streets, and the lives of a whole generation of young black men were written off as obituary boilerplate.

Lavelle, gunshot wound. Tyronne, gunshot wound. Jamal, gunshot wound.

And tomorrow looked even grimmer, if the future of a city can be predicted by the health of its public schools. Tony Amato, the fifth school board superintendent in seven years, had just resigned, the board was paralyzed by petty quarrels, and the school system had gone bankrupt. Over the veto of the school board president, the state had sent in the New York accounting firm of Alvarez & Marsal to untangle the system's financial mess, and the accountants reported what everyone already knew: during the past twenty years, the school system had become an open cookie jar for the greedy hands of every tinhorn politico, shyster bureaucrat, and hack educator on payroll, and of their numerous family members. The middle class no longer wanted their rising property taxes to support a 117-school system with 102 failing schools, one in which girls were raped in the bathrooms, boys machine-gunned during general assemblies, students couldn't bring home textbooks, and metal detectors were installed in doorways to guard what essentially had become penitentiary preps.

Kindergarten through high school, I was educated in this same school system, as were my parents. Then the schools had been racially segregated, and in my parents' day segregated by sex. The lavender-scented Creole spinsters who taught there marched us through a blackboard boot camp that today would rate as college preparatory. Many of us had hoped that the social injustices of the city would be addressed when the schools were integrated, but they never actually were integrated. During the sixties, the middle class, both white and black, abandoned the public school system wholesale for private education, leaving behind schools made up 95 percent of kids from poor black families. The few integrated schools that worked, ones that could count a minority enrollment of forty to fifty percent, were lambasted as "racist" and "elitist." Despite the overwhelming black majority, every issue was about race, and nothing about effective education. When the school board elected Superintendent Amato, a Hispanic who had turned around several failing school districts in other cities, a contingent of black ministers marched around the room in protest, singing "We Shall Overcome." The entrenched civil rights establishment, which had made its heroic mark during the sixties, didn't know any other song.

Most New Orleanians knew the school system was a boondoggle for the well-connected, a Tammany Hall of squabbling factions, and a tragic joke for the kids who suffered through it. What we also saw was the direct relationship between the crumbling schools and the exploding violence on the streets. The dazzling future that the public schools guaranteed their inmates was, for a girl, to get pregnant at fifteen and then become a hotel maid, and for a boy, to lead a glamorous life as a gangsta dealer until gunned down at eighteen.

For the enormous population of poor blacks, New Orleans had become a town without pity or hope. Every day brought news photos of mothers wailing behind the yellow caution tape at the crime scene where their sons had been murdered. And the mothers all said the same thing: "He was a good boy." I would see their sons singing in the church choir, carrying their grandmothers' grocery bags, playing ball among the weedy potholes in the street. This was what I did as a child, and in the same neighborhoods. I had studied in the same classrooms, as had my parents before me and, believe me, those classrooms haven't been painted since. These kids' aunties or grandmothers worked as housekeepers for ladies I knew, their uncles and grandfathers fixed my pipes and plastered my walls.

And it's possible they all were good boys—Lavelle, Tyronne, and Jamal—both the murdered and the murderers.

Maybe the city itself was killing them.

When I was growing up here in the fifties," Father Ulysses D'Aquila told me, "St. Francisville used to be about 80 percent black. The sharecroppers would come buy their seeds and tools on credit at Mimi and PawPaw's dry goods store. The town is a different place now, all white and gussied up."

We were standing on the main drag in St. Francisville, in front of what used to be Jimmie D'Aquila & Son Groceries and Dry Goods. The battered sign was still there, but the funky storefront had become a slimming salon called Uniquely You. The town bank had been turned into an antique button shop, and several turn-of-the-century homes into quaint restaurants. This gentrified bedroom community twenty-seven miles from Baton Rouge, with its moss-draped live oaks and genteel Anglican aura, is a success story, as far as small Louisiana towns go. People still live and shop here, even if the new residents work in Baton Rouge office towers and don't sharecrop on the large estates, as the inhabitants did a couple of generations ago. The Saturday night honky-tonks and Sunday morning revival churches have long closed, and the town has completely changed its complexion. We could be in Marin County, California, for all you see of an African-American presence.

Father Ulysses, one of my oldest friends, is now a priest in San Francisco, and only returns here during the summers, when his mother drives down from Oklahoma to air out her parents' house. His cousin Billy D'Aquila is mayor, one of the few residents remaining from the Sicilian family that immigrated here a century ago. After a meal of meatballs, pasta, and cush-cush at his mother's traditional table, Ulysses and I set out in a rented car to New Orleans so he could catch a flight back to San Francisco the next day.

Walking down teeming Canal Street from the Budget car rental agency to my French Quarter apartment, we passed nothing but black faces on the sidewalks.

"You know, that's funny," I observed. "When I was a little boy in the fifties, Canal Street was mostly white. My mother and aunts wore their hats, gloves, and pearls to come shopping here. Look at it now." The people were mostly young and surprisingly obese, dressed in frayed running outfits and tunic-length white T-shirts.

It was as if the main streets of St. Francisville and New Orleans, over the past half century, had changed places.

The downtown neighborhoods where I grew up were racially checkerboarded yet predominantly composed of Catholics with French last names. The black families were mostly light-complexioned Creoles of color headed by tradesmen—bricklayers, plasterers, and carpenters—and their extended clans were as numerous as our own. Now these neighborhoods are exclusively black, historically so, if you believe contemporary chronicles written about the faubourgs. Vivid memories tell me otherwise.

What is not in doubt is that by mid-century, a massive migration brought rural blacks pouring into the city, as the farming areas of small-town Louisiana were taken over by factories and the modern Sun Belt was born. Many of these rural migrants were moved into housing projects, where they lived for generations. They were looked down on not only by whites but by the long-established Creoles of color. Most of these country people were dark-skinned, Protestant, and didn't have French last names. Unlike the sophisticated Creoles of color, they lacked any urban job skills. They were bumpkins.

This is a story as old as New Orleans.

In *Old Creole Days* (1882), George Washington Cable devotes one of his local-colorist tales to portraying these city/country differences in the nineteenth century. In "Posson Jone'," a down-on-his-luck Creole named Jules St.-Ange, an "elegant little heathen," and Baptiste, "his yellow body-servant," hustle two country bumpkins in the French Quarter. Their marks are blond Parson Jones and his "very black" servant, the squat Colossus of Rhodes, visiting from the area around St. Francisville. This rollicking tale introduces for the first time that eternal New Orleans prototype, the Quarter con man. The two broke, smooth-talking Francophones use their city wiles and Catholic mumbo-jumbo to outfox the God-fearing Anglophone hayseeds, getting them to drink and gamble, almost making off with all of their money.

As in the Cable story, the differences that marked the mid-twentieth-century migrants to New Orleans weren't racial or economic, but ones of color and origin. These were country people slow to get the hang of city living. I'm not sure why, but my parents' and grandparents' generations entertained a marked prejudice against anything or anyone that came from the Louisiana countryside. We may have been backward and Southern, but we were undeniably urban. When I was a hippie teenager with hair curling around the collar of my army surplus jackets, blue jeans rolled up into stiff cuffs, the worst insult my father could pronounce was that I looked like a "hick."

As a matter of fact, I didn't grow up eating the crawfish now so closely identified with New Orleans. Back then they were considered "filthy mud bugs" that only poor country people ate. When I first came up with the novel idea of boiling a sack of live crawfish, my great-aunt Marguerite was so squeamish that first she made me give each one a little bath. Dozens of mud bugs squirmed from the sink and scuttled around her house for days until they died a slow death under the armoires and sideboard, far from the reach of my aunt's broom.

When I was growing up, I once asked her if the aunts on Bayou Road with the old-timey French accents were Cajuns. She screwed up her face and turned on me in a way I'd never seen before. "Don't you *ever* say that," she hissed.

Now New Orleanians have come to embrace country culture, and have enshrined Cajun food and Zydeco music to the point that many visitors confuse it with our own. But there was a time when city people resisted anything that smacked of the country. Darker-skinned sharecroppers were not well received by New Orleanians of mixed African and French descent. This is why in a city now dominated by a class of light-skinned professionals anchored in Gentilly and New Orleans East, for decades an enormous percentage of the black population has moldered jobless in the violent housing projects and derelict downtown neighborhoods. The distinction here is not about race, or even about class (in the American sense of mere money), but about background. Black Catholics with French last names educated in parochial schools, those with a long history of family in the city, are a people apart from the descendants of sharecroppers who arrived here a generation or two ago. These two groups came together during the civil rights era in marches, meetings, and voter-registration drives, but have had little to do with each other since, except during elections. This is why New Orleans is home both to Xavier University, an African-American Catholic university with premier pharmaceutical and pre-med curricula, and to the worst public schools in the United States. There is little crossover between these two worlds.

During the sixties, as the rural black population was moving into New Orleans, white New Orleanians were migrating in droves to the suburbs and exurbs, a white flight that hasn't slowed during the past decades. Now some of these ex–New Orleanians, moving farther and farther from urban hubs, have reached bedroom communities like St. Francisville. They are turning storefronts where sharecroppers once shopped into sleek fitness centers while the descendants of these sharecroppers occupy the dilapidated historic neighborhoods where these white people's parents once lived. Mayor Moon Landrieu, while in office during the 1970s, speculated that in the past few decades "New Orleans lost 125,000 people—mostly white and affluent—moving out to the suburbs, and in their place, 90,000, mostly poor and black, moved in." During this era, New Orleans once again became a black-majority city for the first time since the 1840s, when Irish and German immigrants flooded into the city, tipping the racial balance.

I grew up during this transition, unaware that the world had ever been any different. The countrified people who worked for us fascinated me. Mildred, my great-aunts' housekeeper on Bayou Road, was from Assumption Parish, and kept live turtles in the kitchen's *garde manger* to "draw the misery" out of her. Nana, my Irish grandmother, would ask me to help her yard woman Irene, also from the country. Irene didn't know how to use a lawnmower or shears, and cut everything back by swooping a razor-sharp sickle, as if she were harvesting sugarcane. Both were towering and ebony. Neither trusted New Orleans people, whom they called "high-yella city slickas." And they let me know right away, cutting their eyes at the blond pipsqueak in their way, that they didn't have much use for white men.

I'm afraid that Mildred and Irene's children and grandchildren haven't done well in New Orleans. Nobody has ever taught them how to read, ply a trade, or open a bank account. These were the people whom the world watched huddled in the Superdome and Convention Center in the aftermath of Katrina, with their numerous children and few plastic bags of humble possessions. They were the refugees of a botched social transformation from country to city long before they were orphans of the storm. Finally, after a week of degrading privations, they were bused out of a city that never understood them, that seems pleased to be rid of them, carrying little more than the worn Bibles their grandparents brought from the countryside years ago, wrapped in kerchiefs inside of hampers.

This month the Preservation Resource Center gathered together a group of college-aged African-American volunteers from outside of the state with a group of young African-American volunteers from the city. The object was to restore a house in the Lower Ninth Ward flooded during Katrina, a home where generations of the same black family had lived since 1884. The coordinator explained the history of the house, which a white Creole had deeded to his octoroon mistress and their descendants, along with his name.

The volunteers "from away"—as we say of anyone not from here—were indignant. "We're not going to work on the house of any white man who raped a black woman," they protested.

"Who says it was rape?" the local volunteers asked. "This was a system called *plaçage*. In all of our family trees a Frenchman shacked up with a free woman of color. This is our history, our Creole culture."

The volunteers from away put down their hammers and walked out. The situation didn't fit the either/or paradigms they had learned in the rest of the United States about race relationships. Like many, they wanted to help New Orleans, but just couldn't understand us.

In New Orleans, this thing called race has served as a legal punishment, a political cause and, at present, an ongoing family argument. But it has never been an easy matter of black and white.

More than a decade ago, a city councilwoman named Dorothy Mae Taylor introduced an ordinance that banned all-white Mardi Gras krewes from parading on city streets during Carnival. The injunction put the city into an uproar. Mardi Gras, many argued, is a liminal celebration in which men dress as women, women as men, whites as blacks, and blacks as Indians. A politically correct Mardi Gras is a contradiction in terms. At one point a city official called one of the offending krewe captains to demand if their organization included any black members.

"Damned if I can tell," the krewe captain replied.

It is rumored that in 1921, Creoles of color burned down the warehouse in which birth certificates from the late nineteenth century were stored, documents that specified their race. These public records dated from the Jim Crow era of the "one drop" law, in which one drop of African blood would identify someone as "Negro." Ever since this alleged arson, it has proven difficult to ascertain who is really black and who is really white in New Orleans. Many of those descended from the *plaçage* system have *passé en blanc*, or passed for white, for generations. It is generally assumed that most native French families have a black-identified and a white-identified side, so that many old-line New Orleanians, across the racial divide, are cousins.

Until the Civil War, what divided New Orleans was not race but language.

The term Creole originally was used to refer to French people born in Louisiana, and provided a practical distinction: this gentlemen was *français* from Paris, that one *belge* from Brussels, and the other one *créole*, born of French-speaking parents in New Orleans. This term, of course, eventually came to include the descendents of racially mixed unions. To-gether with the foreign-born and native-born French, the Creoles of color, produced by the Gallic propensity for horizontal integration, formed a unified culture. Both French and African elements were creolized into something entirely different, a New World French mentality.

Speaking French was the defining principle of Creole, as opposed to the English-speaking *américains* of both races who lived on the other side of Canal Street, the "neutral ground" that separated the rival worlds. Re-cently, Creole has gained usage as a polite euphemism for the demeaning word "mulatto," with its roots in animal husbandry (a *mulato* is a young mule in Spanish). In fact, many so-called mulattos are Creoles, but not all Creoles are mulattos. This term is further complicated by its meaning in the country, where Creole is used to distinguish Francophone blacks with origins in Saint Domingue (Haiti) from the Francophone Cajuns, those white descendants of eighteenth-century Acadian refugees from Canada. In short, no matter what the racial identification may be, anyone born into a New Orleans family with French-speaking ancestors is Creole.

When New Orleans was Americanized after the Civil War, the cul-tural dividing line switched from language to race. This was a deep historical wound for Creoles of color, one that has festered for genera-tions. The American system would have segregated the Francophone servant Baptiste (from the George Washington Cable story) together with the Anglophone servant Colossus of Rhodes, although the two did not share a common language, religion, or culture. The Jim Crow laws of the 1890s exacerbated the situation, often to the breaking point for Creoles of color. Many decided to *passe en blanc*, if only so they could attend Mass in French, send their children to convent schools, or legally marry their spouses. Today in New Orleans it is not uncommon for their black-identified and white-identified descendants to meet, unaware they are related.

I thought there was something strikingly familiar about Kichea Burt when we first became friends. When I found out that she was born a Landry, and this Landry family was originally from Ascension Parish, I began to suspect what I recognized in her. My great-grandmother was a Landry, also from a family with origins in Ascension Parish. Kichea, who is black-identified, is *café au lait*–colored, from a prosperous family, was educated by nuns, and is a graduate of Xavier University. Although both of my great-grandparents were born and raised in the French Quarter, during their declining years, when I knew them, they lived in the Seventh Ward, the neighborhood most associated with Creoles of color. They had that latté-hued, traditional Seventh Ward look, one in which the men dressed all in white and the women wore their long, straight hair pulled back tightly from their foreheads. My family was white-identified, something I never questioned until I began showing the crumbling nineteenth-century Landry photo album to black friends. They inevitably did a double-take and assured me that "honey, you mixed."

"I know these people," Kichea told me, flipping through the faded portraits in the same album. "I mean, they look just like the old photographs in my family's album."

This revelation brought to mind unspoken things about my family that I never could figure out. They carefully enunciated the word "Negro," quick to correct anyone who uttered the N-word in their presence. Yet my great-grandmother had a white housekeeper, a Cajun woman named Amelia from the country, during a time when every family I knew had black housekeepers. Those who *passe en blanc* must have lived in daily fear of being outed by one of their own. Their daughter, my great-aunt Marguerite, who was christened at St. Augustine Church, was a volunteer at Charity Hospital during World War II, "the only white woman who ever worked on the colored ward," as my mother told it. I doubt that, in the 1940s, she worked there out of integrationist zeal. In certain circumstances people passed, and in others they didn't.

In her later years, my mother received with stoic amusement what she called "your little theory" about her family's origins. She never quite identified with them anyway, their dark, heavy furniture, their Catholicism, and the language they spoke that she never learned. Like a second-generation immigrant, she rebelled, and Americanized herself with all due haste. These concerns—who had passed, or who hadn't, in the nineteenth century—were Old Country distinctions that didn't fit into her modern perspective. During the fifties, she had known where to sit on the segregated streetcars, and that was what mattered.

Doubts linger, but not heavily. This is something for Kichea and me to joke about. Certainly nothing about my life has changed, except that on questionnaires I sometimes check the "other" box and write in the blank next to it: "New Orleans." I don't know how else to describe what I am. The racial stock of the urban middle class is so mixed, and had been for so long before Kichea and I were born, that "damned if I can tell" has become the only response to questions of who may be what. Governor Huey Long once commented that "you can feed all the pure-bred white people in New Orleans with one pot of red beans." Or as *Washington Post* columnist Eugene Robinson observes, New Orleans is the only place in the United States with "so many black people who look white and so many white people who sound black."

Marc Morial, the city's mayor during two terms, comes from such a racially ambiguous Creole family. It always amused New Orleanians that his face on campaign billboards in poor, black neighborhoods appeared several shades darker than it is. Once at a party I met a man who looked somewhat like him, and after a few drinks together, we decided to go to Frenchmen Street to check out the live music at the clubs. When I asked him his name, he told me Jacques Morial. I wasn't at all surprised to be having a drink with the mayor's brother. What shocked me was that this light-complexioned man, who I'd assumed was white, was, by self-definition, black. After all, I had been visiting from California, where people wear their ethnic identities like name badges.

The signature strength of the city has always sprung from its *café au lait* mingling of races and cultures, not from the warring factions of its racial purists. And now our chief problem is not black vs. white but brown, as in the nasty brown flood waters that threaten to engulf us all. One day New Orleans may well become what former Mayor Ray Nagin called, in his campaign rhetoric, a "chocolate city," when the gumbo-colored waters of the Mississippi meet the dun salt-waters of Lake Pontchartrain several feet above the rooftops of what we now call home. When my time comes, I've considered being buried in a swimsuit and flippers, because I'll probably have to swim toward the light.

At the Madison Square Garden benefit several weeks after Katrina, the musician Cyril Neville sported a T-shirt onstage that read ETHNIC CLEANSING IN NEW ORLEANS. This is a perception shared by a number of Americans: that New Orleans has used the hurricane to get rid of its black population. It is also believed that all white people, obviously rich, inhabited higher ground and were spared the destruction of the hurricane and flooding, and that all black people, assumed to be poor, live in low-lying areas and were either drowned or driven out. This Marxist dollhouse suggests a seductive dichotomy, providing a moral high ground from which to view the sheer irrationality of the devastation.

But hurricane Katrina was an equal-opportunity destroyer.

The hurricane and subsequent flooding didn't only devastate the working-class black neighborhood of the Lower Ninth Ward, that heart-rending poster child of New Orleans ruins. The middle-class white neighborhoods of Lakeview and Lake Vista, as well as the middle-class black neighborhoods of Gentilly and New Orleans East, were also wiped out. The economically and racially mixed Mid-City and Broadmoor areas were also hit hard, along with the middle-class white enclave of Old Metairie. I want to insert the adverb "largely" in front of these convenient demographic tags, because I know people of varied races and colors and classes displaced from these neighborhoods. My friend Ken Fontenot, a Cajun poet, is from the Lower Ninth Ward, and my friend Gina Ferrara, an Italian-American poet, lived in Gentilly. If I could simplify this for you, I would.

But life in New Orleans is too layered with nuances. Once the gumbo is cooked, you can't separate it back into the ingredients.

In the face of such random mayhem, the instinct is to reach for the cherished old verities, whether of a political or religious stripe. And the universal struggles of the poor vs. the rich and of black vs. white are comforting dichotomies, much like the catechismal good vs. evil that the fundamentalist right trades in. But they just don't fit. An equal number of black and white bodies wound up in the St. Gabriel morgue. The tribulations I hear are in similar proportions at the deli counter from white people living in FEMA trailers and in the unemployment line from black people staying with relatives.

What unites us is our anger at authorities.

Within an Aristotelian twenty-four hours, and with all of the tragic inevitability of a Greek tragedy, the hurricane landed, the levees breached, and the city flooded. Yet the inhuman conditions that prevailed in the Superdome and Convention Center, and the violent chaos unleashed in the streets in the wake of the hurricane, did not need to occur. I doubt that a largely black city administration specifically discriminated against black hurricane victims. But it certainly was blind to the problems of the elderly, the poor, and the infirm.

For three days before Katrina hit, television screens were glowing with evacuation routes out of the city, according to a new contra-flow plan of streamlined highway access. It never occurred to those in City Hall that a third of New Orleanians don't have cars, myself included. The TV maps of evacuation routes could have been a video game or a Japanese science fiction movie, for what they mattered to me. No provisions were made for those in nursing homes, hospitals, and prisons, or for those who didn't have the credit cards in their back pockets to sail off on a three-day evacu-vacation. Remember, this was at the end of the month in a city where a majority of the people live from paycheck to paycheck.

The city had at its disposal a fleet of public-transport and school buses, which should have been parked on dry over-rise highways to carry people out of the city in the event of flooding. I grow impatient with city officials' excuses about the lack of bonded drivers with chauffeur's licenses, a cover-up, according to historian Douglas Brinkley in *The Great Deluge*, to the unpardonable bungling that actually occurred: these officials couldn't find the bus keys. Impoverished Cuban and Mexican authorities routinely execute a bused evacuation of their populations whenever a dangerous hurricane approaches. But in the city of New Orleans, the needs of those who fall outside of the able-bodied middle class remained invisible.

Urging all New Orleanians to evacuate in their cars was akin to passing out FEMA website addresses to evacuees in the Houston Astrodome. What could these myopic bureaucrats possibly have been thinking? Perhaps they hallucinate that we live in a city in which everyone can toss the Mac laptop into the S.U.V. and zoom off to lounge by a Holiday Inn pool for three days.

That is not the city where I live, not where most of us live.

A humpbacked legless man with powerful forearms wheels himself every day from the projects through the streets of the French Quarter to beg on Canal Street. I'm thinking of him, and of the bobbing gray perms of the disoriented ladies slouched in lobby armchairs at the assisted living center where I used to visit my mother. And of the uniformed housekeepers and Walgreens clerks seated beside me on the buses and streetcars, so tired at the end of the day they can barely hold up their heads to watch out of the windows for their stop.

Where was the contra-flow for these citizens?

The people who wound up in the ill-conceived shelters set up in the Superdome and Convention Center were not there because they were black, but because they were poor and forgotten. A wide cross-section of other poor and forgotten New Orleanians couldn't get there, or wouldn't have dared set foot inside. New Orleans was not "ethnically cleansed" of the black but of the weak. Across the board, the sector most affected by the hurricane has been the elderly. New Orleanians sixty years and older account for only 15 percent of the city's population, but comprised 74 percent of the dead left by the hurricane, nearly half of whom were over seventy-five years old. An entire generation of our parents and grand-parents has been wiped out, if not by the storm itself and subsequent flooding, then by the ardors of the chaotic evacuation that lost them in nursing homes all over the country, where most still linger. Those in their late seventies and eighties who, before the storm, were defiantly hanging on to their independence have given up, and are now dying in states located light years from everything they once called home. The effects of the hurricane represent not genocide but geronticide.

Not since the Third Reich has any Western nation demonstrated such cruel public disregard for the weak.

For a week no buses arrived to rescue the panicked crowds stranded here without transportation. Gang members, not the city, provided food and water to those trapped in the Convention Center. While young men were looting TVs, with nowhere to plug them in, their grandmothers lay dying on rooftops. And those of us who wanted to stay, to maintain some modicum of civic presence, were forced out at gunpoint.

Yet New Orleans is still a city of extended families, tight neighbor-hoods, and caring church communities. How could our leaders have allowed such a callous free-for-all to happen?

We weren't raised that way.

For black and white, rich and poor, old and young—and most New Orleanians fall somewhere in between—the effects of the hurricane pro-voke an overwhelming question: who have we let ourselves become?

"The hurricane blew America's dress up for all the world to see," a preacher recently said, "and her drawers were dirty."

IV. AT THE END OF THE OPEN ROAD

At the end of the open road we come to ourselves.

Though mad Columbus follows the sun
Into the sea we cannot follow.
We must remain, to serve the returning sun,

And to set tables for death.

—Louis Simpson, "Lines Written Near San Francisco"

18

HOPE CHEST

Two weeks before she moves, my mother is after me to phone the fire department.

"I'm telling you," she insists, "firemen move widows for free into the old folks' home."

At least she calls the place what it is, like those fast-talking dames in the thirties movies she grew up on. But the ritzy "assisted-living facility" where she has reserved a room, built on reclaimed swampland near Louis Armstrong International Airport, has a gazebo, and Tudor towers covered with aluminum siding. It's at the end of the strip mall where she and my father moved thirty-eight years ago. At the time she didn't realize it, but the highway to modernity inevitably leads to the old folks' home.

"Can I ride there on the hook-and-ladder?" I ask. Keep it upbeat, I remind myself. My mother straightens her frail frame with dignity. She's shriveled to the size of a fifth-grader sticking out of a baggy lavender pantsuit. Her body has taken on the shape of her will, all gristle, pared down to bony essentials. I call her "the incredible shrinking mother" as I try to fatten her up with the stuffed crabs and gumbo she eyes suspiciously.

"I hate to eat," she says, as if complaining about mosquitoes or nasal spray.

"You have to. Try this garlic bread. Uhmmm good." The role reversal is lost on neither of us. Spinach is inseparable in my mind from the story of the goblin changed into a doorknocker. As a finicky little boy, Mother coaxed me into eating forkfuls of the stringy vegetable by reading aloud the enchanting tale over and over, until the book's pages were stained green.

I wonder if the same technique would work for her with garlic bread and "Dear Abby."

What my mother does approach with relish is her sectioned pill tray: blue for blood pressure, yellow for cholesterol, red for the heart, green for arthritis. And that's just the first course. I'm sure there's also a little white one to make her larger, and a pink one to make her small. Now they're known as mood-modifiers.

I call her condition MIS, for Medically-Induced Immunodeficiency Syndrome. MIS is how Miss Gladys and Miss Norma and Miss Yvonne—most little old ladies in the United States—end up these days. The medication that doctors prescribe for one condition causes another, for which doctors give them another drug, which results in another ailment, until the patient becomes a walking pharmacopoeia of antagonistic medicines and side effects. The immune system breaks down and, like people with AIDS, they get everything.

My friend Kinga tells me that every night she snuck into her mother's pill supply, gradually emptying the granules out of the capsules until she weaned her off of medications completely. Her mother bounced back from a mummified state of MIS to her former self, a holy terror of a Hungarian ex–beauty queen.

I live far from my mother's house, and am not as headstrong as Kinga. I do encourage my mother to question her doctors. But challenging authority is the greatest taboo of her generation, although one of the virtues of my own. We ended an unjust war and dismantled Southern apartheid by asking "why?" and saying "no." Her generation made it through the Depression and World War II by trust, sacrifice, and following orders. I've never known a ration-book; she's never been to a demonstration. She is sure her HMO doctor has her best interests at heart. Whatever he says, goes.

As it turns out, firemen haven't moved people into old-age homes since the Depression. That was when firemen and cops were the only social services people could count on, outside of the church. Then it was with enormous reluctance that relatives were packed off to grim charitable institutions with names like Home for the Incurables, Crippled Children's Hospital, and Home for Wayward Girls.

When I was growing up, putting someone in such a "home" was as secret and shameful as divorce. Families still prided themselves that they could take care of their own, no matter what the circumstances: mental illness, deformity, retardation, illegitimate births. And certainly the infirmities of old age.

Yet it is my mother's decision to sell her tidy brick bungalow on the circle, a cul-de-sac where she devotes herself to polishing furniture and tending azaleas. Since retirement, her life has become a battle against stubborn stains and unruly twigs. My idea has been that as long as she could crawl to the back door to let a nurse in, she should stay put, there on the front line against disorder. Yet at seventy-seven, after surviving a host of conditions with unpronounceable names, she has developed a terminal one: she no longer drives.

Selling her car was, in effect, a double amputation at the knees. For the past few years she's depended upon the kindness of neighbors, but most older people in the suburbs who no longer drive are ready for the warehouse. It's not as if they can hobble to the corner for bread and milk, or catch the bus or even a cab to a doctor's appointment. No matter who you are—or how much money you have—the strip mall ends at the assisted-living facility, right next to the used-car lot.

Vast distances, subdivisions, the nuclear family as-seen-on-TV: that was the promise of the automobile, and of the mobility and prosperity of the fifties. This was the social experiment of my mother's generation, as radical a break from their past as the free love and communes of the sixties were from our own upbringing. Their dream was to disentangle themselves from the tentacles of the ethnic family in the inner city, with its cacophony of slamming screen doors in rented houses where relatives crowded around enameled kitchen tables in flowered aprons and shirtsleeves, quarreling in two languages under creaking ceiling fans.

That, in any case, is how I grew up, spoiled by the attentions of three generations of Creoles in downtown New Orleans. Childcare? Mémère around the corner, an aunt down the block. Nursing homes? I've just excavated from my mother's wash shed a pink wicker commode, a dainty piece of furniture that I remember parked in the shadows of my great-grandparents' bedroom. Tucked inside is a white porcelain slop jar.

Funny, but you don't see old people moving around much anymore. The images of old age that haunt me from childhood, or that are seared in memory from the foreign cities where I've lived, are of an unrelenting activity that dominates the landscape. In most cultures, they run the show. They are the venerable oaks in which we starlings nest.

My neighbors in the fifth-floor walkups where I lived in Barcelona always turned out to be ninety year-old widows who bumped their collapsible shopping carts down the stairs every morning with infernal racket. Later I would spot them at the market arguing over the price of tomatoes, or yakking in the plaza with their cronies. After a bracing aperitif of sherry at the corner café, they would lug the bulging contraptions back up five flights of steps, stopping at each landing to wheeze and gossip. Doors would open and slam up and down the stairwell as the air began to sizzle and smell of onions and garlic. At two o'clock, the others would straggle in from work or class, then three or four generations would sit down to eat.

And afternoons in Beijing, the wizened grandfathers in blue Mao suits would walk their canaries in bamboo cages, then hang them from overhead tree limbs as they'd squat in the shade to gamble, smoke, and spit. I can still see the toothless grins of Indian sadhus, those emaciated old holy men who wash out their loincloths at dawn on the banks of the Ganges. In San Francisco, I was never a match for the gangs of Cantonese grandmothers with pink plastic shopping bags elbowing their way onto the packed 30-Stockton bus that I took to work.

Here comes my grandfather at ninety, trudging home from the streetcar stop, mopping the back of his neck with a handkerchief, muttering about which jeweler on Canal Street is Jesse James. And my Creole grandmother at my mother's age, clomping down the back stairs every day in black orthopedic oxfords with a heaping basket of laundry to hang on the clothesline. Not to mention Nana, my Irish grandmother, who at eighty-five married a gentleman she met on an Arthur Murray ballroom dance tour of Mexico. Frankly, I'd always looked forward to becoming old, to stomping my cane and bullying the young, acting out whatever eccentricities I've managed to suppress so far.

Something has changed.

I tour the assisted-living facility with my mother. It's college without the hormones, a geriatric dorm. Instead of posters announcing the fave rock groups, each resident's door is done up with a wreath of artificial flowers that reflects her taste. Posted is a syllabus of activities: Rosary, Kick the Can (Activity Room), Bingo (Parlor), Rosary, Ice-Cream Social, Fan Tan (Activity Room). In arts and crafts, they make plant holders out of Mardi Gras beads. We take the elevator between floors, then step along spongy blue carpeting to the library, the white-wicker room, the chapel, the ice-cream parlor, the activity room, the TV room. Behind us a woman is clanking along on a walker.

"The doctor told me to do this," she complains. "Gotta walk every day for exercise." A game show is blaring from her room.

In the dining room, it's cloth napkins and china. But we're having fish sticks, unseasoned frozen vegetables, and pudding, college cafeteria fare. One bite and I'm in the mood for a food fight. Young black women bustle through the subdued murmur, addressing everyone as "Miss." The lady across from us is buttering the cellophane of an unwrapped package of crackers. Another leans on a cane, chatting with my mother, then shakes her turkey-wattle at me.

"Don't look so shocked," snaps the mind reader. "This is where you're coming when you get old."

I nod in agreement, dying for a cigarette. Longevity has never been my first priority.

Excusing myself from the table, I wander the labyrinth of pastel corridors. Walking along, I imagine this bubble of silence split by the joyous shrieks of children, each one carrying a drawing or construction-paper daisy for a lonely old lady. I picture a long file of them snaking through the halls, looking for old folks so they can be useless together. The children want to be read to, to hear stories, to ask foolish questions, to look at photographs of old-fashioned people in funny clothes. They have come here for the one thing their parents can't afford to give them, attention, and to provide the only amenity these residents can't buy: hope. Why are daycare centers so far from old folks' homes? Why are they separate at all?

"Here everyone is old," said a friend's father, surrendering to the assisted-living director the pistol he was planning to shoot himself with. "And there's no future."

I arrive by taxi several afternoons to help my mother pack.

"Leave that there," she orders as I start to take family pictures off the wall. "Don't touch anything in here," she says, rattling the door to the china cabinet.

I try to convince her that my high-school graduation photo and her demitasse collection won't help attract buyers to the house, but she wants "people to see things." She plans to move, but can't quite bring herself to dismantle her home.

"Look," I say, "we don't have to sell the house right away. Let's leave everything just the way it is. You can take the essentials with you and in a few months, if you decide you don't like the assisted-living place, move back home."

"Oh no," my mother counters, crossing her arms. "I'm not like you young people who think 'why not get married, I can always get divorced.' When I make a commitment," she says, lifting her chin, "I stick to it."

Allowing other people their cozy self-contradictions is the thorniest part of helping them. From the outside, what needs to be done seems so obvious. I could pack up this house in twenty-four hours and have her in her new room by this time tomorrow, if that's what she really wants. But my mother is determined to make every step of this move a veritable Station of the Cross. This afternoon our task is to go through a box of old greeting cards to see if I want to keep any. I take several deep breaths.

"Isn't this one pretty?" she asks, handing me a yellowed Mother's Day card. I glance at it, then hand it back. "You didn't even read the message," she says, her voice trailing off.

"The movers are coming in seven days," I explode, gesturing at the jam-packed house, "and look at all we have to get rid of."

She picks up another greeting card, opens it, and begins to read the message, silently moving her lips.

Her impatient son becomes time, the enemy. I only have room for one piece of her furniture, but she won't let me take it.

"Not today," she says. "Not yet."

In the forties, it was still the custom for girls from Creole families to be given a hope chest for their bridal trousseau. The chests were made of Louisiana cedar, which warded off the moths that ate holes in woolens during the long, unairconditioned summers. Like door and window screens, they don't make them anymore. Ours is a world in which windows don't even open.

Eventually, I hauled my mother's hope chest to my French Quarter apartment. Because my windows still open, the cedar chest is useful. And because my mother buried her hopes there, it feels important.

I've stripped off the dull mahogany finish that disguised the wood to match the bedroom set my parents bought when they were married. The reddish tiger-stripes that emerged from beneath the tar-like varnish were considered vulgar at the time. Cedar was a utilitarian wood that needed to be gussied up. I am pleased by the nakedness of the blond wood, and by the label I discover inside the chest. It was made in 1946 by Mr. Pukoff, at 329 Dauphine Street, six blocks from where I live. Hope has come home.

Inside she kept our baby booties and report cards, sheets of newsprint covered with the crayoned zigzags of her toddler Picassos, my father's World War II souvenirs, elbow-length gloves and veiled hats in musty boxes from long-disappeared Canal Street department stores, the house title and bank papers, her first U.S.O. dance corsage wrapped in tissue paper, her first pair of glasses.

"What's this?" my sister asks, as we help my mother unpack her hope chest. She holds up an elastic harness by one of its dangling straps. "Your first girdle?"

I wonder if my mother's hopes have been fulfilled. She has her victory bungalow, where she has lived in peace and prosperity for four decades. She has two slightly nutty single children with advanced degrees. She has one grandchild, my sister's part-time daughter from a shared-custody divorce. She has three TVs, a dishwasher, freezer, a kitchen full of gadgets, and an empty carport.

She perches on the edge of the bed like a fragile doll, her past scattered in heaps around her, tired from packing for the old folks' home. But she can't rest. Her bony hand dives into a box.

"I promised this to your aunt," she says, holding up a swan figurine. "But I know you asked for it," she tells my sister, who rolls her eyes. My mother is confused about who wants what. The truth is nobody wants anything. Our houses are brimming over. There's no room anywhere for her keepsakes.

And her hopes? I suspect they are like her Glenn Miller and Lawrence Welk LPs. They're still here, but she can't find a hi-fi to play them on.

Every American generation sets out to be modern—that's what it means to be American—until the next generation comes along to redefine the terms of modernity. Thoroughly Modern Millie is soon sitting on the shelf with other antique dolls. We begin to grow old when the world no longer recognizes how young we still are.

What will I keep in my mother's hope chest? I will store papers, boxes and boxes of papers—the manuscripts I hope to turn someday into books—at the very moment when books and the world of paper seem about to disappear. American hopes never go unfulfilled; they simply become obsolete, like this lovingly frayed *Mantovani Strings* album on top of the record rack in my mother's den. "Old Uncle Jimmy and his papers," I can hear my cyber-obsessed niece complain, as one day in the not-too-distant future she empties the brittle manuscripts from this cedar chest into the trash, and prepares to bury her own hopes here.

GERMANY SURRENDERS," announces the wall-sized headline from the New Orleans *States-Item*. I am wheeling my mother through the D-Day Museum, which has just opened. More than a museum of World War II memorabilia, it is a monument to the Greatest Generation, now that they're almost gone.

I have made previous visits to donate my father's war souvenirs: the bridal edition of *Mein Kampf*, the heavy Luger in its stiff leather holster, the blurry snapshots of barracks life and of the concentration camps his unit liberated. We have also sent them my mother's pictures as a U.S.O. belle, and her paltry pay stubs as a war-effort clerk for the navy.

"I used to take three buses to get to work at the Port of Embarkation," she tells me from her wheelchair, dwarfed by an amphibian boat that landed on the beach at Normandy. "And after that we'd go roll bandages at Charity Hospital. Nobody complained. We all just did what we had to do." Churchill is sputtering from a newsreel in the video room. I look down at my mother's huge milky-blue eyes in her withered face, stopping a moment to memorize the modesty of real heroism, in case I should ever come across it again.

The military dioramas with their camouflaged tanks and soundtrack explosions attract mostly ten-year-old boys. I worry that they'll leave thinking war is some glorious affair, and grow up to start one. My mother is fascinated by the displays of civilian sacrifice: the grainy black-and-white photos of paper drives, scrap-metal and cooking-oil collections, people using ration cards. Everyone is wearing a hat, and smiling.

Now I understand why she is incapable of throwing anything away. Every mayonnaise jar and broken pot handle must be hoarded to contribute to the Greater Good. All week I've been squatting on her kitchen floor, holding up everything I find on cabinet shelves for the inevitable verdict: "Somebody can use that."

Just who, she's never sure, as the boxes pile up throughout the house, awaiting a Greater Good to charge every bent percolator lid and chipped gravy boat with purpose. But there is no Greater Good at the moment. And even the Salvation Army has gotten picky.

Asian social security is having a son. For both Chinese and Indians, parents move in with their eldest son and daughter-in-law. This daughter-in-law's duties are to care for her husband's parents in their old age and to produce a son of her own, with whom she will live in her declining years.

Creole social security was having an ugly daughter. Or if they were all beautiful, as was often the case, it was scaring off the suitors of the smartest one, educating her as a teacher, secretary, or nurse, and depending on her to care for aged parents. I was taught in the public schools by a generation of Creole spinsters, all of whom lived with their elderly parents. A few were ugly, but almost all of them were smart. Until the sixties, teachers in New Orleans public schools weren't allowed to marry.

All of my teachers were friends with my great-aunt Marguerite, another unmarried schoolteacher. She and my grandparents took in the budding little beatnik when my parents moved to the suburbs in my junior year of high school and I refused to follow. She nursed both of my great-grandparents and later both of my grandparents to the grave, a real saint: Our Lady of the Pink Portable Commode. My mother inherited the commode, but not the role. When Marguerite became demented, she put her in a nursing home next to a trailer park.

That was when the late-night calls to San Francisco started. When I'd pick up the phone, my mother would be in mid-thought.

"She spent her life doing for other people," she'd say. "It's not right. We moved in with her, Mémère, and Pepère during the Depression, when

Daddy couldn't find a job. She practically raised me, and now . . . I could keep her in the back room."

"And when you're at work?"

"I could hire someone. And put bars on the windows. She wanders at night." During this time my mother first began to develop her serial symptoms. She crashed her car and repeatedly needed to be hospitalized. Now she was too sick to put bars on the windows and take in her aunt. It made perfect sense.

Europeans claim that Americans have no sense of shame. Yet I watched my mother sicken and almost die of shame. For the first time in her family, the matriarch was in a "home."

Lugging my mother's boxes into her new room, I avoid the eyes of the black women working here. I read their glances as accusatory, disgusted. They are the only Southerners left who understand the family betrayal that this move really means. Most of them are working at minimum wage to care for grandchildren and their own mothers at home. White friends mumble sympathetically when I tell them about my mother. Their parents, they assure me, are in the same boat. Only these Southern black women, working two or three jobs to support the extended families that live with them, are able to recognize, in averted eyes, my own shame.

Many argue that traditional cultures, such as the Asian, Creole, and Southern black, create tragic roles for women: the daughter-in-law as servant, the spinster on perpetual bedpan duty, the forty-year-old grandmother who slaves away to care for her mother and grandchildren.

I look around at the faces of these modern white women in the assisted-living dining room. Almost all have raised families, held jobs, welcomed grandchildren, buried husbands. And I wonder if this is not an even more tragic fate, to be abandoned at the first signs of uselessness, thrown away because an addled mind can no longer balance a bankbook, a palsied foot can no longer work a brake pedal.

Yet I know of only one alternative to the old folks' home: to wait for an angel of death to appear.

He probably killed her and buried her under the house. Who would know?" My mother is trying to locate Wanda, a lifelong friend who hasn't returned her calls for a month.

"Don't let your imagination run away with you," I warn.

"Look who's talking." She arches an eyebrow at her son, the poet.

She and Wanda Siegel graduated from John McDonogh High in the same class, went to church, and dated boys together. Wanda was going out with a GI whose brother turned into my father. That was how my parents met. The crumbling black pages of a photo album tell the story of my mother's violet-scented friendship with Wanda. There are Wanda and Helen posed on a W.P.A. bench in City Park, dressed up for the opera, in gypsy blouses on Mardi Gras, feeding the swans from a rowboat.

Wanda was an intellectual girl from a German Jewish family who also went to the Presbyterian church on Esplanade Avenue. My mother was from a Creole Catholic family. Everyone in their downtown neighborhood, it seems, no matter what their background, went to the church that served as a community center during the Depression and war. Wanda made my mother read Hölderlin and Goethe, and listen to Brahms and Schubert, when she was pregnant with me. It worked. Out popped six pounds and five ounces of hopeless romantic.

After my mother wed, Wanda settled into a lesbian marriage with another classmate of theirs, a dwarfish, steel-jawed military nurse named Tiny. I confess, at one point, this aroused certain suspicions about my mother, but I never brought them up. Look who's talking, as she would say.

Owl-eyed Wanda ballooned to a gargantuan size, a circus-tent of a woman with elephantine legs, and was already beginning to suffer from diabetes and cancer when Tiny died. She became helpless and morose, and eventually took up with a coarse younger man from Chalmette, a handyman referred by social services to help her maintain her dilapidated house. He fixed the leaks, stole her heart, moved in, then took over her finances.

"He says he's in love with me," she confided to my mother.

"Go look in the mirror, Wanda Siegel," my mother commanded. "Who could fall in love with that?"

My mother did some sleuthing, and found out that lover boy had served two terms in Angola State Prison. She is convinced he poisoned his first two wives. Wanda put a fifty-thousand-dollar CD in his name, then bought him a brick house in roughneck Chalmette. They both moved in last year, and for the last month there's been no word.

When the angel of death is needed, he appears, in a puff of smoke from around the corner: the last resort. Much the same happened among certain friends in San Francisco with terminal AIDS. Just as Wanda, the cultured lesbian, has wound up with a gigolo ex-con from Chalmette, the angel of death is invariably the most unlikely person. But he is courted as a passive mirror for the needs of the dying. In spite of the downy halo, the angel is a hustler, and takes whatever he can. But in exchange, he allows people to die enveloped in their own worlds, a final act of self-delusion for those who refuse to enter old folks' homes, those of us whom you might call hopeless romantics.

The black-and-white snapshot of my great-grandparents in their late eighties stares down from the wall of my mother's new Valium-blue room. They are cradling me, a newborn, on the side porch of a peeling shotgun house in the Seventh Ward. They spoke French *en famille*, and kept turtles in barrels to make into soup.

"At first I didn't want to put it up," my mother confesses. "They look so old." And poor, I want to add. She is surrounded by old, but the real statement of the reproduction antiques and Victorian drapes, of the luxurious hush of the assisted-living facility is that old is not poor anymore. It's posh.

When my mother was young, the money her in family was so old it wasn't even there anymore. She grew up in linoleum-floored rentals crammed with beveled mirrors, marble-topped tables, and tarnished silver, not unusual circumstances for a Southern lady. And like many in the modern Sunbelt, her life has been a flight from old and poor, from cracked plaster, ominous crucifixes, and pink wicker commodes.

A dining room table with folded side-leaves dominates her room. On it is her grandmother's sterling coffee service, polished to a gleam, and above it an oil painting, rimmed in black velvet, of Oak Alley plantation. Were we to extend the table as far as it goes, including the two leaves stored in my closet, it would seat ten, an unlikely event in a bed-sitter with a stoveless Pullman kitchen.

But in my mother's imagination, the old world that failed and fell into ruins is restored. She reigns at the head of the table in the Oak Alley dining room, an extended family of the living and dead gathered around her as she pours coffee from the silver service into demitasses. Nephews, nieces, and grandchildren clamor for sweets, and somebody is telling the old stories—the ones we love to tell on evenings like this—when everyone is at his place at the table. And, for better or worse, we belong to each other.

And this is how, with the TV at a murmur, she lies on her brocade bedspread and, as the gospel song goes, walks around heaven all day.

After dinner, my mother and I are rocking with other residents on the porch of the old folks' home. Here they are—survivors of the first generation to use the power of the gas pedal to move out of the city, away from poverty, family, and history—watching the cars whiz by on Jefferson Highway.

"What a shame," I comment, "the gallery isn't in the back facing the grounds, where the azaleas and gazebo are." Across from the fake Tudor towers are po'boy joints and muffler shops.

"Oh no," my mother says, "we love to sit here watching the cars go by. It makes us think we're going somewhere."

19

ALONE IN THE URBAN MUSEUM

Royal Street is deserted under an alligator sun. I stop in the shade under a balcony to mop my face with a white handkerchief. An empty tour buggy clops by as I carry two bags of groceries from Rouses. Today I was able to shop without standing in a checkout line behind drunks with balloons on their heads, each buying a quart of beer. And to my relief, the street performers weren't stationed in front of my bank as usual, clapping and harmonizing on "Under the Boardwalk," the only song they know. Jazz Fest and Essence Festival crowds have come and gone. It's August and, for a while, the French Quarter is ours.

The humid air hangs heavy with intimacy and the scent of jasmine. Neighbors walking their dogs greet each other, lingering to chat. It's as if I'm stranded in some remote tropical colony after the colonists have left. Without the throngs of tourists, I realize how few we are, the people who actually live here full time. All afternoon we laze in courtyards like alley cats, wondering if summer will ever end.

"How can you stand to live in the Quarter?" friends asked when I first moved home several years ago from Barcelona. "It's so touristy. And there's no parking."

"But I don't drive," I'd explain, enunciating the words loudly and clearly, as if talking to the deaf. "I need to live where I can do everything on foot. Besides, my family's from this neighborhood."

In the minds of the Creoles who raised me, the "old neighborhood" took the place of the Old Country, even after they moved away. In those days the Quarter was chock-a-block with family-run businesses, like my great-grandfather's corner tobacco shop. Sicilians ran the French Market, heaped with fruits and vegetables trucked in every morning from the country. Everyone dressed up to take the streetcar to Canal Street to shop, see the doctor, go to the bank, have something repaired. At night burlesque clubs opened, naughty but refined, and families dined at restaurants with checkered oilcloth on the tables.

This hardscrabble warren of merchants seems glamorous, perhaps, only in its passing. That was long ago, when I was a child, and people still came to cities to make money, not to spend it. Now there's only one business: mass tourism. And without the French Quarter, the engine room of this industry, downtown New Orleans would be as boarded up as Detroit, the first ex-city.

So with the instinct of a homing pigeon, I returned to live here, unpacking boxes marked SPAIN, CHINA, INDIA, and LATIN AMERICA, in this dilapidated slave-quarter apartment situated toward the rear of a lush pink courtyard. Inside the brick walls I only hear the gurgling of a fountain, birds in an overhead live oak, cats in heat, and screaming matches between a couple next door I call Stanley and Stella.

If I let memory and imagination wander, it almost seems real. I could be in an Andalusian patio, or a hutong apartment in Beijing, or a crumbling palace overlooking the ghats in Benares, or a colonial courtyard in Guadalajara. But when I walk out my front gate, I don't find sidewalks bustling with native commerce and street-life. I meet only the empty gaze of video eyes that have come to watch. There they stand, tourists with go-cups in hand, trying to soak up an authenticity that their very presence precludes. Whatever they've come looking for has long since vanished, to make way for them.

Real travel, of course, changes the traveler, who conforms to the contours of a new location. Tourism, on the other hand, modifies the place visited, which must adapt to the tourist expectation that every experience be translated into familiar terms. Like a factory, tourism depends on the endless repetition of a successful formula, with few variations. The tourist experience has become homogenized on an international scale, much like airports. Wherever the tourist goes is a differently themed nowhere.

For residents, tourism becomes a funhouse mirror. We see our image distorted, made garish and childish, simple enough to grasp for those who can't be bothered with complexities. It's as if, day after day, you were forced to watch a bad made-for-TV movie about where you live. Tourism empties local culture of meaning, freezing it at a certain moment in history until it's no longer free to grow. New Orleans is stuck with that dubious concoction, Creole-Cajun, just as San Francisco will forever be beatnik, and Manhattan, the Broadway musical.

Residents retreat indoors into private social lives, far from the klieg-lit hard-sell of public spaces. We won't participate in the hoax—for free. To survive, we may work as musicians, waiters, tour guides, desk clerks, or hire ourselves out as convention psychics or carnival revelers, but the culture we're selling is no longer our own.

When I was growing up, New Orleans was still a functioning port, and the Quarter bars along the river attracted foreign sailors together with an underworld of pimps, prostitutes, and card sharks. But when the antiquated wharves no longer could accommodate modern freighters, along came waterfront redevelopment to convert the decaying port and the adjacent brick factories into quaint malls. This design is international. Decatur Street in New Orleans has been refashioned by the same vision that created Fisherman's Wharf in San Francisco, South Street Seaport in Manhattan, Viejo San Juan in Puerto Rico, and the Villa Olímpica in Barcelona.

But New Orleans has more to sell than an intersection of water with history: we have sex. A block from my front door is what taxi-drivers call the "fruit loop," several blocks of gay bars where the come-on question is: "Where are you from?" My get-lost response: "around the corner." Beyond these bars churns the 24-hours-a-day sex-mall that Bourbon Street has become. I've mapped out elaborate paths through the neighborhood to avoid crossing that carnie midway of titty bars and corndogs.

New Orleans has taken the place of her Communist stepsister, Havana, to become the brothel of the United States. This is where overworked, overweight Americans come to let their hair down. It's like the sale aisle at Walmart, except everyone is drunk: not a pretty sight. The party is as seasonless as that casino bar in Las Vegas where New Year's Eve is celebrated 365 nights a year. None of the subtleties of the Catholic calendar apply: the travel package includes Mardi Gras in October. Whether it's Halloween, Christmas, Carnival, or Jazz Fest, for dental surgeons or real estate agents who attend conventions here, there is one formula only: eat spicy food, listen to Dixieland, put on Mardi Gras beads and a funny hat, and get sloshed. Sex is the theme. History is the backdrop.

But the wrought-iron balconies and colonial convents might as well be made of papier-mâché. The real historical fascination is that this is still a pedestrian neighborhood. Not only can you walk from place to place, but here architecture assures that people connect. Front porches, balconies, and courtyards are ways of making private space public. Suburbanites come to see how people used to live, before the isolation of the freeway and subdivision. It's that legendary land of small shops, streetcars, and lively sidewalks, of leisurely strolls and outdoor cafés, of seeing and being seen: what the malls pretend to be but aren't.

The truth is that most Americans lived this way until well after World War II. But what my family called "going to town" has already acquired the sepia patina of the Civil War.

Everything before the car is the olden days.

On my daily rounds, I lug groceries or dry cleaning or packages through the Ghost Walking Tour or the Vampire Walking Tour. Clumps of people are gathered around a tour guide done up in a top hat or preposterous cravat. Reciting the script, his stentorian voice rises in pitch: "There she stood naked on the balcony, blood dripping into the street!"

But the tourists aren't staring at the balcony where the bloody ghost supposedly appeared. Mystified, they are watching me at my gate, juggling a coat on a hanger, a bottle of wine, a bag of tomatoes, mail, and house keys. I am the real ghost, of how urban Americans used to live.

I am a living exhibition in the urban museum. I've often considered asking the mayor's office for a monthly stipend to walk the streets wearing a beret with a baguette under my arm. But I doubt they would understand. City Hall is doing everything possible to discourage permanent Quarter residents. Regulations about the amplified street performers and mushrooming walking tours go unenforced, and apartments are being converted on a grand scale into corporate condos, illegal short-term rentals, and time-shares. Soon most of my neighbors will be virtual: holiday visitors wheeling suitcases, trying to find the right door.

The last of the downtown department stores, office supply shops, and bakeries that I remember from childhood have closed, and in their place are chain hotels and restaurants. If I need a zipper or a stapler, I have to bum a ride to America—the suburbs where real commerce takes place. But if I should ever happen to need a vulgar t-shirt, a feather mask made in China, or an overpriced bottle of hot sauce, I'm in luck.

Only once have I come close to murdering a tourist. For the third time that day, I was on my way to Mary's on Bourbon Street, the only hardware store left in the neighborhood, to find the right-sized screw to fix the bathroom light.

Two-hundred-year-old houses molder in the tropics. Everything is always breaking, crashing down like the bathroom light fixture had that afternoon. You fix the light, the shelf under it falls. You put the shelf back up, a hole opens in the wall. It's a way of life: Managed Decay.

I was unable to pass two gargantuan tourists lumbering in front of me. And as if their sheer size weren't enough of a roadblock, they were holding hands. Cursing to myself, I realized that Americans have forgotten how to walk down a city sidewalk. They think they're at the mall, lords of infinite space.

At the door to Mary's the tourists stopped and peered in the window. "What in the world is this?" one asked the other in a nasal Midwestern whine.

"A hardware store!"

"What's *that* doing here?"

I reached for the screwdriver in my back pocket, ready to lunge, then checked myself. My attack would only put Mary's on the Violent Crime Walking Tour.

My friend Kim Sunée has just moved home from Paris, and has rented an apartment on Royal Street. We meet at the outdoor café in Pirate's Alley, where I'm trying to convince her that it's still possible to lead a European-style life in the Quarter.

"It's a long way from Baudelaire's *boulevardier*," I say, "but at least it's not the burbs. You can take the streetcar to work, later join friends at a café like this, then walk to a restaurant, stopping along the way to shop for daily groceries."

"I suppose you can," she agrees, weary from trying. "But you'd be the only one doing it."

In 1980 there were 10,000 full-time residents in the French Quarter. Now there are fewer than 2,500. Although more than nine million tourists pass through the neighborhood every year, it's lonely in the urban museum. Even at the height of the season, surrounded by throngs of visitors, permanent residents feel as if we belong to an almost extinct species.

Often I think of Ishi, the last Californian "wild Indian," who spent the final seven years of his life living in the University of California anthropological museum on Parnassus Heights in San Francisco. I imagine him circulating among the crowded exhibition rooms as a living exhibit, the last member of the Yahi tribe, speaking a language only professors understood. I picture him at night walking the empty corridors, coming across Yahi sandals or a bow-and-arrow in a glass case. In the end, Ishi was so lonely that he made friends with the janitors, helping to dust the artifacts of his lost world.

One place Ishi avoided was the room where the bones of his family were kept catalogued in boxes. In New Orleans, where we make a ritual fetish of our relationship with the dead, even our bones are on display. Whenever I visit our family tomb in St. Louis Cemetery, scenic-cruisers are disgorging groups of tourists. One All Saints Day, a tourist edged his way between the rows of crypts, then popped his head around the corner just as my mother was placing flowers at our tomb. He almost startled her to death. What he wanted to ask, on this day of communion with lost loved ones, was "how many corpses can fit inside this white box?"

Venice was the first urban museum, residents fleeing as tourists poured in. Later Venice was followed by Florence, the center of which is now almost uninhabitable. April is the month when the first excursions of French schoolchildren appear on Las Ramblas in Barcelona. Like the return of the sparrows, this is a signal for locals to avoid downtown, to which they don't return until mid-October, when once again the miracle occurs: streets are filled with Spaniards going about their business.

Visiting friends there during the summer, I often feel as if I have taken a wrong turn and wound up back in the French Quarter. Las Ramblas has become Bourbon Street without the tits. This ancient Mediterranean promenade is now lined with fast-food restaurants, souvenir shops, and sidewalk acts from some universal central casting of street performers. At times I do a double take, certain that I recognize the same Tarot readers, mimes, spray-painted statue people, or Pakistani souvenir vendors from the Quarter. And as at home, you can barely walk down the Ramblas for the gangs of people gathered around a juggler or break-dancer with blasting boom box. Kiosks that used to sell Spanish and Catalan literature now display guidebooks in ten tongues, porn magazines, and phallic doodads to enliven destination bachelorette parties.

All of my friends in the Barrio Gótico have been evicted from their apartments and artist studios, which are being restored and sold as corporate pied-à-terres. Neighborhood shops I long frequented have disappeared. I stand staring up at my old apartment on Calle Marlet. Geraniums are blooming in the balconies, but I wonder how anyone can stand living there. Walking along the waterfront brings a stronger sense of déjà vu: it's a quick trip to Decatur Street, to Fisherman's Wharf.

I suspect that among the dusty archives of that nefarious sixties-era architect of "urban renewal," Robert Moses, are the original blueprints for the city as urban museum. This same model has been superimposed on various unique cities to turn them into generic tourist towns. These radical reorganizations of public space are usually ushered in, with great civic fanfare, by heavily financed international events. For New Orleans, this was the World's Fair of 1984, and for Barcelona, the Olympic Games of 1992. In both cases, local businesses that offered support and hoped to make a killing lost their shirts. Meanwhile, global corporations had moved in to impose The Plan.

Why, you might ask, would people visit a place that is a copy of where they were last year? This is the genius of marketing. Recently I shared a train compartment with a young Spanish couple from Valencia on their way to Disney World outside of Paris. They hoped it would be as thrilling as Port Aventura, another theme park south of Barcelona where Moroccan immigrants are hired to impersonate wild American Indians. The couple had no interest in actually visiting Paris, but only the virtual Versailles that Disney had created. They preferred the image to the reality. My ten-year-old cousin summed it up when I took her to the San Francisco Zoo: "The animals on TV are better."

People who travel from one theme park to another, I suppose, are the same as those who travel from one urban museum to another. They want an identical experience: the same cartoon but a different episode. The question that remains is how long it will be before Disney purchases the entire French Quarter or Barrio Gótico, walls it off, and charges admission. Then perhaps I could get that job walking down the street in a beret with a baguette under my arm.

A friend in New Orleans tells me of a marvelous discovery: downtown Naples. He's ready to move there tomorrow.

"There's the most stunning old quarter," he says, "no tourists, and cheap real estate."

"And crime?" I ask, waiting for the catch.

"Well, locals don't go there anymore because they feel it's too dangerous. But it's not like here. No shootings or rapes but, you know, stabbings, break-ins, and muggings, the usual sort of crime related to heroin." He's a death-penalty lawyer, and takes a sanguine view of such shenanigans.

For the twenty-first century, these seem to be only two models available for that relic of industrial capitalism, the center city: either deserted and crime-ridden, or the urban museum. When New Yorkers complain about the Disneyfication of Times Square, they ask each other with resigned shrugs, "So which one do you want already, the mugger or the tourist?"

Everywhere the city is in crisis. Major Latin American metropolises such as Mexico City, Bogotá, Caracas, and Lima have become so violent that no one dares go out after dark. In most of the United States, and increasingly in Europe, business has been transplanted to industrial parks in the outskirts, and manufacturing shipped to the Third World. The city has outlived its function: wealth is no longer produced here, only consumed. So like a nineteenth-century scythe hung as décor in the breakfast nook, the city can recycle its lost purpose into charm to become a showcase of gentrified real estate, or it can rust in the fields, abandoned by the middle class to the poor and desperate.

Neither is good news for walkers in cities. We form a hard-core of urban veterans, people who grew up on foot in the city when streets were still vibrant with economic life, before crime and before tourism. We can't—or just won't—participate in the cultural amnesia of "development," and give up the only way of life we know. While walking, we remember. And like aboriginal song lines, our paths of remembering keep ancestral landscapes alive.

Downtown is encoded in my genes. Every day my retired grandfather dressed in a suit, loud tie, fedora, and every piece of flashy jewelry he owned to catch the streetcar downtown to buy a cigar, mail a letter, and have a cup of coffee. As a boy he took me with him on his rounds, and I met every doorman, counter waitress, and newspaper vendor on Canal Street. As we pushed through the brass revolving door at the Roosevelt Hotel, I was so dazzled that I wanted to keep going around and around in the door forever. So did my grandfather. He died at ninety-two, three months after the doctor told him he couldn't go to town anymore.

Walking the streets has become bittersweet for the surviving inhabitants of the urban museum. We spend a lot of time cowering indoors, hiding from booming street festivals cooked up to attract tourism, or from the crush of suburban weekenders who come here to try out their car alarms and vomit on our doorsteps. "VISITORS," pleads a sign taped to many windows here, "THE FRENCH QUARTER IS A RESIDENTIAL NEIGHBORHOOD. PLEASE RESPECT OUR HOMES." Occasionally, between parted curtains or blinds, I've spotted a face peering out from behind such a sign, like the defeated surveying the occupying army. The eyes are hesitant, almost ghostly, and whether they are staring out at the street or looking back in time is hard to tell.

20

PARCHMENT AND LAPTOP

I was sorting through a shabby shoebox of family papers a few months after moving home to New Orleans when I came across a parchment document in French that turned out to be the birth certificate of my great-great-grandmother. As George Washington Cable observes in *The Grandissimes*, "Those Creoles have such a shocking way of filing their family relics and records in rat-holes." The elegant calligraphy on the parchment attests that Marie-Josephe Dieudonné was born in 1829 in Alsace-Lorraine on an agricultural commune. My Mémère had told me about her own Mémère, a severe, bony old lady who presided over the family until she died in 1905. The Creole furniture I've inherited probably was bought during the period of 1893–1907, when my great-great-grandparents, great-grandparents, and young grandmother lived in a courtyard double masionette at 825 Royal Street, around the corner from where I do now. I often imagine old Marie-Josephe kneeling bolt upright on the prie-dieu I just rescued from the rat-hole of storage. That birth certificate, along with her faded daguerreotype, is all that's left of a fascinating life. And so I've framed it, perhaps because it still amazes me that an American living during the twenty-first century could have such a visceral kinship to the French Revolution.

Before moving back here from San Francisco, I set out on the dreaded mission to upgrade my computer, suspecting what humiliation lay in store for me. For several years, publishers and typesetters had been confounded by my floppy disks and word-processing program, complaining that my texts needed to be "translated," as if they were trying to listen to a 78 rpm Victrola record on an iPod. They were amused when I revealed that the computer dated back to the Stone Age of computer technology, 1986. I confess to what is considered a major heresy in California: I'm interested in technology not as an ever-expanding way of life but only as a tool that makes the specific tasks I do easier. I want to plug in a computer and, as with a toaster, expect the bread to keep browning and popping up in the same way for the next twenty years. I'm relieved that my breakfast doesn't depend on incessant updates or downloads: toast.2 and toast.3. I'm not a toast techie. I already have a life, and digital technology should better serve it, not devour it.

"What are your computer needs?" Fred Flintstone was asked at the Jetson-styled computer shop on Geary Boulevard.

"Well, I want to turn the damned machine on, write immortal words, save and print them. Period. No, I don't care about rams, ROMs, bytes, icons, streaming, social media, tweeting from jets or skyping with people in Australia, thank you."

I escaped with a simple laptop, the cheapest and lightest I could find, feeling that I was the one who had been born on a peasant commune after the French Revolution.

The longer I live, the less I believe in the myth of chronological time, and the more I consider the possibility of Einsteinian time-space pockets for which there is no universal measure. In California, the pace of time wears me out. Within months, not only technologies but events, writers, artists, music, food, hair styles, and people are out of date. Each generation reinvents itself every five years as if there were no yesterday or tomorrow. And there isn't. A twenty-year-old and a fifty-year-old are dubiously of the same species. A ten-year-old and sixty-year-old stare at each other across an abyss measurable only in light years.

In California, it's not that I feel old but obsolete. The whirligig of living in the future soon becomes exhausting, especially since the snazzy promises of tomorrow have a sneaky way of turning into the messy snafus and disappointments of today. Living in the past, as we do in New Orleans, is less stressful. Here, as in Europe, everything of major significance is already over, which is relaxing, unlike California, where everything life-changing is just about to happen, only a download away.

Recently I tried to interest my fifteen-year-old Californian cousin in my collection of vintage LPs. "Who's Donovan?" she wanted to know. "What's a record?"

M y fifties childhood in New Orleans was shattered by previous inva-
sions of so-called "disruptive" Californian technology: the car and
television. At first, the car seemed a miraculous machine to make life
easier. When my father bought the '56 Studebaker, we could transport an
ailing aunt across town, or bring home a ten-pound sack of potatoes and
a case of soft drinks at once. Sundays, instead of walking to City Park,
we would drive there, then spend the afternoon picnicking under live
oaks while we polished the car to a sheen with a shimmy and scrubbed
whitewall tires with Brillo pads. At home the Studebaker was an extension
of the front gallery. When people wanted to escape the hubbub inside for
a private chat, they'd say, "Let's go sit in the car." At first the car was an
appendage to the life we were already living: it didn't change it.

And I'll never forget the moment my parents uncrated the Motorola
console in the living room on the afternoon of Queen Elizabeth's corona-
tion. They turned it on, and there in fuzzy black-and-white was the future
queen of England marching into a tent. When she stepped out, she had a
diamond crown on her head. Then we turned off the TV. The show was
over. And we went about our day. That was how we related to this inven-
tion: it was like going to a show at the Saenger Theater, newsreel and all,
only you didn't have to catch the streetcar. We paraded in, watched the
show on TV, then left. Nana, my Irish grandmother, didn't understand
you weren't supposed to talk, so she would gab away as if rocking on the
gallery gossiping about people walking down the street.

"Look at the way she's treating that man!" she'd blurt out, shaking her
red head at brash Ida Lupino. "She's going to get in trouble."

"Shush, Nana," we'd whisper. "It's the show."

Soon Claiborne Avenue, one of the most walkable boulevards in our
neighborhood, was torn up to build a freeway overpass, and those of us
still on foot darted around like small forest animals in the cement shadow
of progress. The petroleum and automobile industries contributed to the
campaigns of politicians who voted to build these freeways and cut back
the public transportation system, eventually succeeding in taking off
Canal Street our beloved streetcars. And TV was no longer a free show
once in awhile but began to tyrannize the house. We bought folding
plastic TV trays so we could eat frozen TV dinners in front of the screen,
mesmerized by bouncy suburban families jumping in and out of station
wagons. And many began to follow that elevated concrete rainbow out

to the developers' TV dreamscapes, where the car was a necessity of life. So was the TV, which confirmed the reality of a Martian landscape of tract housing. There the set was on eighteen hours a day, since there was nobody to talk to, nothing else to do.

What began as tools became the contours of our lives.

Now in California, they are trying to undo the way of life created by the disruptive technologies of the fifties. Smog-besieged Los Angeles is attempting to rebuild a public transportation system. In San Francisco, antique streetcars are back on Market Street, and a downtown freeway overpass damaged in the 1989 earthquake was demolished, to everyone's delight. Washington is debating a V-chip to control the content of television, which is now raising its third generation with devastating results. And Chambers of Commerce are in overdrive to lure the middle class back downtown, where the selling point for pricey condos is that you can walk to work, to shop, or to party. "I hardly ever have to take my car out of the garage," brag these downtown converts, many of whom don't own TVs and ride everywhere on bicycles. The consensus on the cutting edge is that the effects of fifties technology are a mistake.

How can we undo them?

At the same time, Silicon Valley's new technologies are galloping hell-bent in other uncharted directions. When I first encountered comput-ers, I was told how much easier, as a writer, they would make my work. And they have, in the limited tasks of typing, editing, and printing. Yet twenty-five years later, letters are sneered at as "snail mail" and books as the "dead-tree editions." Friends abandon communication if you're not on Facebook, or abuse it if you are. And whatever doesn't make it onto the Internet simply doesn't exist. Microsoft has donated a billion dollars to public libraries to replace books with computers, much in the way that car and oil companies did away with public transportation. The new San Francisco Public Library is a Pharaonic temple to online technology, but where are the books?

Once again the tool has not only become a way of life but has been eroticized into a love-object. I've been told that, as a result of what is called "one-handed typing," a major problem in computer repair shops is unsticking keyboards gummed with semen. Recent generations were conceived in the backseats of cars or in front of TVs. Future generations, bless them, won't be conceived in chat rooms. Yet wherever they are conceived, they'll grow up within the confines of a virtual neighborhood determined by the triangle of car windshield, TV image, and electronic screen.

I grew up in a family, in a real neighborhood. I walk places, know how to converse with people, how to read and write letters, and even books. But every few decades a box appeared, and we unwrapped the new machine with trembling hands. How much easier it made things, at first.

Then the rest of the package arrived, new lives we hadn't purchased or foreseen. Our tools changed, and so did we.

Yesterday I sat on the St. Charles Avenue streetcar reading a letter from a friend, the poet Mario Lucarda in Barcelona. The crinkly onionskin of the airmail stationery was fluttering in a breeze from the open window next to me. Occasionally I'd glance out at the canopy of overhead oak branches dappled with afternoon sunlight. What pure pleasure this is, I thought, lingering over the loops of Mario's courtly scrawl, lulled by the *clackety-clack* of the streetcar swaying down the avenue. I was in no more of a hurry than the pokey streetcar, or than the letter had been to reach me, or than the two-hundred-year-old live oaks to grow. How relieved I felt not to be speeding home through rush-hour traffic on an expressway to glance at Mario's message on a computer screen, or to scan it as a transitory tweet or text on an iPhone.

New Orleans has been called backward and its citizens Luddites, but I prefer to think of ours as "the Venetian solution." Like Venetians, we don't go out of our way to reject modernity but live our lives as if it simply didn't exist. The past exerts a greater gravity on us than the accelerating demands of the future. So much of the historic city remains intact not because we are preservationists but because, in a deeply philosophical sense, we distrust haste, effort, and above all else, any sort of improvement. Ben Franklin's self-help axioms are lost on us. If the rotting beams of the back porch collapse during dinner, we lock the back door and get on with the rice pudding, pretending for as long as possible that we never had a back porch.

Here my sense of time is cumulative. Today isn't a disconnected race but an accrescence, a drop of liquid sediment turning into the rock I'm standing on. As Faulkner put it in *Requiem for a Nun*, "The past is never dead. It's not even past." After all, I was raised here by grandparents who discussed the "War Between the States" as if it were current events, what my grandfather referred to as "that recent unpleasantness." They were brought up by parents whose lives were as determined by Civil War mythology as mine has been by Vietnam. And my grandparents' grandparents, who in turn raised them as they raised me, were born in France in the wake of the French Revolution. Down the line, they taught each other how to speak, sit, cook, and pray. Family mannerisms and superstitions were handed down like a stained soup pot, directly from the French Revolution to me. Somehow, I am more the residue at the bottom of that soup pot than I am the infinite megabytes of the voracious Californian capacity for an unimaginable future.

Yet in my world, the parchment birth certificate and my laptop peacefully coexist. As a matter of fact, I'm now using one to write about the other. In my sixties, however, my focus is on continuity rather than change. "Away at sea," I lived in California long enough, reinvented myself in liberating ways, and now is the time to put these weightlessly free *mes* in perspective with the more ponderous soup pot handed down through the generations. A future without history—not as an operatic backdrop but rather as the accumulation of daily actions that brings one generation into another—is death-in-life. The parchment returns to me a submerged part of myself, and the computer, like everything else in California, is portable. Whatever I may need from the future, I can bring back home with me.

- 21 -

THE MIDDLE OF NOWHERE

At the moment, I'm nowhere, trapped inside the intestinal coils of an airport security line, trying to remember why I ever loved traveling.

I'm surrounded by passengers panicked that they're about to miss their flights. People are pawing the ground like stunned livestock in a pen awaiting the abattoir. A uniformed woman with a clipboard is walking through the line, pulling out those who have less than fifteen minutes to catch their planes. Inching forward, the rest of us are checking our watches and stomping in place, wondering why we are actually forking over money—lots of money—to undergo this experience. The traveler, by definition, wants to be somewhere else, but we are stranded in the limbo of nowhere.

I'm already sedated. That Vicodin, hoarded from the stash prescribed for oral surgery, has come in handy. Spitting blood, I halved the pills to save them for the real suffering ahead: flying. Passing through an American airport now is like those other liminal experiences, being booked in jail or admitted to a hospital. Take my belt, shoes, keys, and wallet. Here are my volition, my dignity, and my body cavities: do with me as you will.

But first let me swallow this little white pill.

The airport turns me into the perfect zombie. Arms outstretched and pupils dilated, I float through uniform concourses of chain stores and TV monitors chanting in a monotone the recorded warnings about unattended baggage, smoking, and accepting packages from strangers. Friends assure me that they prefer one airport over another—Miami over JFK, Dallas/Fort Worth over Phoenix—but I don't see why. Outside is neither day nor night, summer nor winter, coastal nor mountainous. Outside, in fact, is the enemy, with its storms and blizzards, its atmospheres we never breathe, its planetary landscapes we never touch. Emblematic tokens of the outside are prepackaged inside in kitschy food courts with cartoonish local themes—New York is bagels, Philadelphia is cheese steaks, and some city, I can't remember which, is waffles—but this is as far as we get. We cling to the processed climate of nowhere against the threatening contingencies of time and place.

Several decades ago, the airport was someplace so fascinating that people would drive here to have a drink and watch the planes land. Passengers dressed to the nines, celebrities waltzed in to the pop of flashbulbs, and families staged tearful reunions. Flying then was a cocktail party in the sky rather than a concentration camp. Although the architecture was modern, airports were imbued with a celebratory feel that reflected the nineteenth-century attitude of traveling as a grand adventure into the unknown.

Then prices dropped, the airport turned into a bus station, and the wealthy bought their own planes. These days the airport has become the ideal security state, a model for the controlled atmosphere in which we are destined to spend timeless, placeless, and bodiless lives, everywhere at once and nowhere really at all. Its design combines aspects of the mall, the gated community, the TV lounge and, of course, prison. This Orwellian blueprint for herding hypnotized consumers behind bars was already in process long before 9/11.

Seated behind a sheet of plate glass staring at a TV screen, I'm reminded of the paperback science fiction I read as a teenager and of the dystopian novels I studied in college. I close my eyes and picture the hive-like city as space station, with its landing strips shooting out jet-propelled spores into other galaxies. I see bald drones in unisex jumpsuits lined up like insects, tuned in to the electronic instructions they receive from wireless antennae fixed to their ears.

I open my eyes, glance around in the fluorescent glare of Concourse B, and don't see much difference. Yes, I am afraid, not of terrorists or their bombs, but of the airport itself, of this degree of control we have come to accept, how rapidly it's spreading into every other aspect of our lives, and of how we've gradually learned to call nowhere home.

Given the choice, on entering the airport I'd prefer to play hospital rather than jail: cram my street clothes into a carry-on, be issued one of those backless paper gowns, and then line up to gulp tranquilizers out of paper cups proffered on trays by stewardesses in surgical scrubs. I need chemical help to get through this, if only to master the telltale facial muscles of my antiheroic perversity while airline security agents grill me.

"Who packed your suitcase?"

My Palestinian roommate.

"Have you accepted any gifts or packages to carry?"

Yeah, from that bearded cabdriver in a turban.

Medicate. Bite your tongue. Become dour and bovine. You might as well get used to it.

Just remember, the worst is yet to come: the flight itself, where I'll be secreted into a cubbyhole like a larva in a wasp's nest, then later the airport shuttle, seat-belted between eight strangers on cell phones mouthing in chorus "I just arrived," and then the labyrinthine corridors of the chain hotel, where I can never get the computerized door lock and light cards to work.

It may take a lifetime to get out of nowhere. And my pill is already wearing off.

I live in the center of New Orleans and don't drive, which is why I have particular trouble getting used to the suspended animation of nowhere. I'm accustomed to every space I happen to occupy being someplace. As a matter of fact, even as a passenger I don't like visiting friends who live in the suburbs. I find the ugliness depressing. I shouldn't tell them this, but often I'm forced to out of self-defense when they insist that I *must* come visit.

"But my house is beautiful," they protest. "It has a patio, a landscaped yard, and is surrounded by trees."

"I'm sure once you're there it's gorgeous. What's ugly is the forty minutes in a car to get there."

"It is?" They sound perplexed.

They just don't see it.

How could they? These friends spend hours a day in a road trance, driving back and forth along the strip malls that line the way home, and no longer notice the visual assault offered by one parking lot after another surrounding the big-box stores, fast-food outlets, and used-car lots. To them, this Martian landscape of cloverleaves, billboards, and exhaust fumes is a TV commercial they have to endure to get back to the movie, a segment of nowhere they have to traverse to get home from the somewhere they just left. Real life resumes when they pull into their driveways.

Walking around my neighborhood, catching a bus or streetcar, I'm immersed in the experience of being where I am. I don't turn myself off to get somewhere else. I study the people I pass on the street, or the faces of those next to me in the streetcar. Often I strike up conversations, and sometimes wish I hadn't. But whatever the experience, however sublime or annoying it may be, there I am, all of me. I don't share with my driving friends the disorienting luxury of stepping in and out of a bubble of nowhere to get where I'm going.

Nowhere used to be what came in between. Now it has taken over and become where we live.

As a child growing up in New Orleans, everywhere was somewhere unique, particular, permeated by identifiable smells, textures, accents, tastes. The lakefront tasted like syrupy snowballs. The river smelled of the hops brewing at the Jax beer plant. Walking to school was tripping on a loose brick in the banquette. Shabby shotgun doubles were downtown and white pillared mansions uptown. Canal Street was the candy counter at Maison Blanche department store, Bayou Road was my aunts' French accents and chicken coops, and sketchy Washington Avenue was where I waited in front of the drugstore at a bus stop littered with empty bottles of codeine cough syrup.

It wasn't always pretty, but I knew where I was. Someplace.

I'd never been nowhere, so to speak, until my father bought a car and drove us to visit his relatives in the suburbs. My parents informed me that this area was called Metairie, or that development River Ridge, or the other subdivision Lakeview. But I couldn't tell the difference. All the houses looked like the ones on TV, identical squat brick boxes with carports. Walking around, as this antsy kid was wont to do, I'd get lost in a minute. There were no landmarks, no corner grocery stores or bars or churches. Nor was there any sense of history. Everything looked like it had been built yesterday. The endless highways that led back home also had names—Jefferson or Veterans or Airline—but rolling down the window and staring out, I couldn't tell the difference. I didn't see any blocks or buses or trees or people walking down the street.

Even today, as a passenger en route to the burbs, I have no idea where I am, except for the large green signs that whizz by too quickly to read. Sometimes I fall into a memory hole of temporary Alzheimer's and think I'm in Florida or California. Then I remember that the person we're going to visit doesn't live in Florida or California. By the time I spot somewhere familiar, we've already passed it. Our scribbled map will indicate "take a right at the second stoplight after Burger King, across from Home Depot."

This must be the directions to everyone's house in the country.

My first experiences with nowhere genuinely spooked me. I was raised among identifiable places marked by generations of architectural decay and restoration, and wasn't used to everything always looking the same. I took my first steps under the shade of three-hundred-year-old live oaks along streets where my great-great-grandparents had walked, following in their tracks, although I didn't mean to. Driving along anonymous highways or careening through indistinguishable suburbs made me feel like an astronaut, slippery-footed and lightheaded, disconnected from both history and geography.

The airport is simply the supreme distillation of this timelessness and placelessness. It's not much, but for many of us, it's what we're used to calling home.

Time and space. Minutes and miles.

These coordinates no longer determine the contours of our lives but have been commoditized into units of exchange: anytime minutes and bonus miles. Minutes and miles are now translatable into dollars as the universal measure of exchange. Time is money, and now so is space. No matter how much we may owe on credit cards, we feel rich if we have 100,000 frequent flier miles and free weekend minutes on the cell phone. Time and space: we're just rolling in the virtual stuff.

A cell phone rings, and the first thing the caller wants to know is "where are you?"

The cell phone connects us at every moment to everywhere we're not, negating where we are. Why am I talking to this person, here and now, when I'd much rather be speaking with her or him, somewhere else? We see it every day: a couple is walking down the street, and both are talking on their cells. Their feet may be on Royal Street, but each maintains a connection to the infinite possibilities of nowhere. "Where are you?" the caller wants to know. The finite hereness of somewhere can be frightening, overwhelming, or what is worse, boring. Thank you for calling.

With the Internet, we can work anywhere, and with the cell phone, can be anywhere. And with an iPhone camera, we're able to capture somewhere like a lightning bug in a jar and email it to nowhere. But where are we?

I do go to the Internet to send or receive messages. A few years ago I published a book in Madrid, which would have been impossible without email. When I send an email, I entertain an image of a paper airplane sailing through the air, from here to there. But I am never tempted to go to the Internet to lollygag around in cyberspace, to chat with people I don't know, much less to have sex with them. The Internet reminds me of a cross between the Airline Highway and *Reader's Digest*, garish and commercial, a mental extension of the airport and the cloverleaf. Give me Molly's, our corner bar, as a way to while away time with strangers. At least there someone might buy me a drink.

"There is something you just don't get," people tell me, growing indignant.

"Be gentle," I say. "I'm from New Orleans."

We New Orleanians pride ourselves on our intractable European charm, but even the Old World can seem too new. Last year I was talking with a Spanish friend at a bustling outdoor café in Barcelona filled with attractive college students. Carmen, a forty-year-old divorced mother, was telling me that she'd been picking up hot twenty-something-year-old guys on the Internet.

"Do you bring them here?" I ask, somewhat envious.

"Oh no," she says. "We never meet."

"How do you have sex, may I inquire?"

"By chatting."

I try hard to imagine this. Finally I blurt out, "So you're talking about masturbation?"

"Well, not really." Now she looks embarrassed. "We exchange photos."

I'm at a loss. What is this bedroom game called: Let's Pretend You Have a Body? Carmen lives four blocks from this sexy café filled with horny young people. Why would this good-looking woman spend hours alone, typing to God knows whom (say, some geezer with his nephew's photo) and imagining she's making love?

The Internet and iPhone have become eroticized because we humans are capable of eroticizing anything, even corsets and bound feet. But they continually undermine the singularity of time and space. Why am I here when I could be there, why am I with you when I could be with him or her? A touch to a keyboard makes anything possible—almost. Yet these infinite possibilities lead to nowhere, define nowhere. The mantra of my generation, taken from the title of Baba Ram Dass's popular book, was *Be Here Now*, reminding us that enlightened perception could only be realized through full participation in the particularities of a time and place, interacting with the propinquities of that moment. What's the mantra now: *Click, Tap, and Scroll: Be Anywhere, Anytime, with Anyone*? No wonder people are flocking to yoga classes or to trendy retreats in Northern California where they can unplug themselves for a whole weekend to practice "mindfulness."

Look around. As the cell phone caller wants to know: "Where are you?" Let's pretend you have a body.

When my sister flew to visit me in San Francisco during the mid-seventies, she lugged with her an ice chest packed with Gulf Coast shrimp and on the homebound flight filled it with Dungeness crabs, if only to demonstrate, in a culinary way, that she was traveling between two unique places. Now most of the shrimp sold in New Orleans are no longer local, Dungeness crabs don't come from San Francisco Bay, and I can't imagine what alarms an ice chest of seafood would set off at airport security. During an orange-coded high alert, a package wrapped in brown paper was discovered in an airport lavatory in New Orleans, and security blew it to smithereens, splattering somebody's mama's gumbo all over the men's room walls.

A campaign is afoot in the state to demand Louisiana shrimp in stores and restaurants. All you could find, until a few years ago, was local seafood. Now most of the once indigenous products we consume come from elsewhere: shrimp from Venezuela and Brazil, catfish from Vietnam, crawfish tails from China, sugar from Mexico. Native industries are dying, and every day we are less who we were. Surrounded by bayous once crawling with edible critters, we sit down to family recipes concocted from frozen exports. *Lapin Sauvage* is made with cottontails from Canton.

The global economy undermines place in the most traditional reaches of our lives, erasing century-old identities from the ground up. Christmas decorations are made in atheist China, ski gear in tropical El Salvador. Native crafts disappear, local economies flounder, and we never taste anything that comes from the patch of earth where we walk. Fruits and vegetables are waxy, pumped up, and unseasonal. Unripe one day, they are rotten the next.

Now we know what nowhere tastes like: the airport.

The reaction, of course, is to fetishize any remaining sense of place. Horticultural purists in California want to uproot any plant that wasn't growing there when Balboa landed. In Santa Cruz you can get sticker shock in a produce store, where price is determined by how far an organic eggplant had to travel to reach you. Someplace is for sale, and in certain regions, is all we have left to sell. Visit your travel website to book a week-end getaway to San Francisco's exotic Chinatown, or fly to New Orleans to celebrate Mardi Gras any time of year. Unfortunately, all you'll see when you get to Chinatown or the French Quarter are mobs of tourists videoing each other as barkers hawk two-fers in front of glitzy replicas of what used to be there before the likes of you arrived.

Mass tourism brings nowhere with it, as I can attest from the second-floor balcony of my French Quarter apartment. At certain times of year my street is more like happy hour in an airport concourse than a neigh-borhood thoroughfare. The city has lost cotton, the port, shipbuilding, and petroleum, the industries that once defined it, and now our only business is to freeze-dry and package somewhere to sell to people from nowhere.

Yet we natives live in a perpetual state of nostalgia for the vanished city of our childhoods. "Ain't dere no more" is our wry refrain as we catalog the local businesses replaced by chain stores. We pepper our speech with an argot called Yat (from the Ninth Ward greeting, "Where y'at?," the dialect immortalized in *A Confederacy of Dunces*), the same working-class accents we were ashamed of in our youth. Now we speak it to each other in comic defiance, to distinguish ourselves from the TV accents of transplants to the city, those who will never get the gist of where we're from.

It is still 1958 and we're rocking on the front gallery with MawMaw in her flowered housedress, or so goes the illusion under which we labor.

"Went by my mama and dem's on Monday to have me some red beans and rice," says my friend Toni Christopher, the financial consultant.

"For true?" asks this Ph.D in comparative literature, chewing on the mint sprig in my iced tea. "Where she stayin' by, dawlin?"

"Over by Mata Delarosa catlick choich."

Then the cell phone bleats.

"I emailed you this afternoon," I bark into the receiver, "right after I received the fax from Barcelona. Where are you?"

And this is how we keep nowhere at bay, like the members of some historical society that meets to stage tableaux from the Civil War, another battle we lost long ago.

I'm at Louis Armstrong International Airport, this time on my way to spend a few months in Madrid. I made the mistake of buying a one-way ticket, not sure when I might want to return, so my name is tagged in the airline computer as a suspicious character. Evidently the Al Qaeda members who flew planes into the World Trade Center traveled on one-way tickets. Why buy a round trip if you're going to crash the plane mid-flight?

The frugal terrorist.

Two smiling young men in uniforms, probably just out of high school, take me aside and instruct me to open my suitcase. I groan. It took me days to pack for such a long stay abroad. They lackadaisically pat my belongings, sleepy eyes lowered and dark hands eerie inside of white latex gloves.

"Where you going?" one asks. *Pat, pat, pat.*

"Madrid, Spain."

"What the ladies like over there?" *Pat, pat.*

"Really beautiful."

"You know, I mean, they easy?" They stop patting and look up.

"All of my friends are." Their faces break open in broad grins, pink gums and white teeth flashing.

"What about drugs? They got like X, those club drugs?" I already miss the sing-song Southern accent. They drawl out the vowels: *cluuub dru-uugs.*

"Sure. But mostly hashish, a little coke."

"What kind of drugs you do?"

"Well, I—" You fool, I think. You're speaking with agents of the federal government. "I don't touch drugs."

"You don't?" They sound disappointed.

"Nope. Don't even take aspirin." They eye me up and down, as if indeed I am a suspicious character.

One of the kids makes another attempt to size up Spain. "They got big wide streets over there like Canal Street where everybody go?"

"Why, yes. Madrid has a wide avenue that people walk up and down day and night."

"Bet they don't call it Canal Street, do they?" The kid shakes his head as if that were the unlikeliest thing he could imagine: someplace without Canal Street.

I stand there beaming, surrounded by droopy-eyed passengers revving up baggage carts.

Even in the middle of nowhere, I'm still somewhere.

I'm home.

ONE YEAR AND A DAY
A Recipe for Gumbo and Mourning

Gumbo takes three days to make, if you do it right, although in a kitchen piled with greasy pots and smelling of shrimp heads, it may appear more like a year. According to Hebrew law, a body takes one year and a day to decompose inside a casket. In many cultures, the mourning period corresponds to this biblical measure. Here in New Orleans, a corpse buried in an above-ground tomb may not be "disturbed," as undertakers call it, or shifted below to make room for another burial for one year and a day after it has been sealed inside. Making gumbo and the decomposition of a body have little in common except that, like grief, both take time.

In Louisiana we have plenty of time, time to make a twenty-minute roux, to simmer a soup stock, to peel shrimp, and time to rock and chat, to chop and mourn, to stir and sway over cauldrons of memories. A Creole goodbye may take hours, as inching toward the door we kiss goodbye then talk some more, kiss again then come back to add what we forgot to say all evening, then kiss goodbye again, and so on.

Making gumbo can be a Creole goodbye for the dead.

Here we don't talk about dying but passing, a euphemism that reflects our superstitious cosmology. People who emphasize passing to the other side, rather than dying to this one, treat death as a celebration. And people who believe in passing also believe in ghosts and haunting, and in the dead supervising the affairs of the living. We live with the dead as vertical neighbors, not those on either side but those down there, where the bones go, and those up there, where the spirit resides. We say the dead look down, although I'm not sure from where. Perhaps this voyeuristic perch is an atavistic memory from when our ancestors lived in trees. All I know is that from somewhere on high, my mother directed the vigil that marked the one-year anniversary of her passing.

I had been trying to come up with some way to commemorate the occasion, which signaled the end of the traditional mourning period. When I was a child, powdery great-aunts with flowery French names still observed mourning by wearing dark clothes during the year and by not playing the Victrola or Motorola, as they called the phonograph and TV. From an earlier era, I have a brooch mounted with a tinted photograph of my great-great-grandfather Numa Landry that contains a lock of his hair soldered inside, and was probably pinned to my great-great-grandmother's dress during the year his family spent shuttered inside their house on rue Bourbon. At one time in New Orleans wearing ornate jewelry fashioned from the hair of the deceased was a common mourning practice, as were black armbands, black wreaths hung on the front door, black-bordered calling cards, special novenas, and votive candles lit at Mass and on bedroom prie-dieus.

All of this seemed hopelessly fuddy-duddy to my mother, a modern career woman who sported a pink pantsuit to my father's wake. The only mourning custom she maintained were cemetery visits to place flowers on the family tomb in St. Louis Cemetery every All Saints Day, Christmas, Easter, and on dead family members' birthdays. So after her passing I was cut adrift as to how to mourn, when and for how long. The dead linger with us for awhile, then move away. In a recurring dream, I am astounded to come across my long-deceased grandparents living in a crumbling cottage in some lost neighborhood of the city. Perhaps their dilapidated house reflects my own neglect of their memory, and they've become what the Chinese call "hungry ghosts," wandering spirits begging for morsels of food and attention.

Recently I ran into a friend who was on her way to Australia carrying half of her mother and a sixth of her grandfather in Ziploc sandwich bags. Not body parts, of course, but ashes. People die the way they live, and Americans are a rootless people. But the paucity of grieving rituals in the United States strikes me as part of a deeper denial, a childish refusal to acknowledge death that often masquerades either as hard-boiled pragmatism or New Age pantheism. The pattern now is a sensible

cremation, the memorial "life celebration"—you know, brie and anec-
dotes—democratically divided ashes, a check to charity in lieu of flowers,
releasing pastel balloons, holding hands in a circle, a little sentimental
Kumbaya borrowed from scouting jamborees, then chin up, back to
work, as though nothing had happened. This is followed months later
by sudden paralysis, depression, medication to get you "back on track,"
as if grief, that most ancient of emotions, the inspiration for so many of
the heartrending laments of world literature, were nothing more than
a chemical imbalance. Yes, sadness does follow death, as it must. But
depression is something else: a numbness, an inability to grieve, to experience that sadness. Deep feeling, like a river, needs banks, channels,
levees, and locks, or the water will not flow but dam up and stagnate, or
overflow and destroy.

How to mourn is something I worked out on my own, with candles,
cemetery visits, flowers, solitary strolls through familiar places, going
through papers and photographs. But you can walk only so far with the
dead, then you must let them go. Here some of us sing and holler and
dance our grief second-lining during a jazz funeral. As the year-and-a-
day marker approached, I decided to cook my grief, to end mourning by
making gumbo—that togetherness dish—and by inviting the friends and
family who had supported me during my sadness to gather once again
and—I don't know what to call it—suck crab claws to glory.

S tart with a carcass, if you have one.
     In this case, I used the remains of the Thanksgiving turkey roasted
at my cousin Karen's house, where we had gathered for a large family-
cooked meal a few months earlier. The dinner was the sort of warm,
woozy affair the dead hunger for: children watching cartoons on TV
while adults sip wine in the kitchen, arguing about whether the giblets
go in the dressing or the gravy, old folks reminiscing on a couch, card
tables added at the last minute, a dish forgotten, a missing chair. All of
this ended up in my mother's gumbo. Karen lives in the attic apartment
of a refurbished orphanage, where you can sense the spirits of orphans
in bloomers and knickers skipping along the wide wraparound veran-
das, presided over by nuns in starched sailboat wimples. How fitting, I
thought, to spend my first Thanksgiving as a fifty-something-year-old
orphan at an orphanage.

The frozen turkey carcass goes into a covered stock pot of boiling water along with bay leaves, several halves of peeled onions, a few carrots and stalks of celery, salt, thyme, crushed garlic, and red peppers. As the rich-smelling steam rises, lower the heat to a simmer, and leave the pot there for about three hours. Like mourning, cooking is the art of transforming the dead into the living, of wringing out a present from the past, constructing what is from what used to be. That Thanksgiving turkey, last picked over by children looking for leftovers, was still gobbling in a bubbling soup stock, memories swirling with the pungent holiday smell.

I had baked the turkey for our last Christmas together at my new apartment in the French Quarter crammed with packing crates, to which my mother brought not only a portable oxygen tank on wheels but a bedside potty. The winding staircase to my second-floor bathroom would have been too much for her to climb.

"I feel like a walking hospital," she complained, trying to untangle the yards of clear tubing that snaked into her nostrils. Should the need arise, my sister and niece had volunteered to hold a sheet around the potty, stashed in the living room next to the nativity crèche. "That stable is where the Virgin Mary would have to go to the bathroom," I reminded my mother. She was stoic but humiliated by the paraphernalia, the immobility imposed by the final stages of congestive heart failure. She wouldn't be here long, so I'd hung spruce garlands and put on her beloved, scratchy LP of Handel's *Messiah* that skipped. We sang along to the Hallelujah Chorus, which I conducted with a wooden spoon from the kitchen. As usual, her eyes watered at the solo "I Know That My Redeemer Liveth" as I was bringing in the caramelized yams. "That's my favorite part," she said. The next week she turned seventy-nine, and two weeks later was gone.

She had refused hospice care. "It makes me feel so . . . I can't think of the word." Five minutes later she called me back. "Doomed," she blurted into the phone just as I picked up the receiver. She needed that precise word, its thump of Faulknerian finality. So rather than at home, as I'd hoped, she died in an I.C.U. ward connected to beeping monitors, besieged by white coats with clipboards and name tags.

"My name Dr. Goo," said one in faltering English. "How long been sick?"

"Look it up on her chart, if you can lift it," I thundered, and ordered Dr. Goo from the room.

In the reptilian cortex of the brain, our bodies scamper to survive against all odds, in spite of any mammalian concerns with comfort or lofty ideals of dignity. Survival is like walking a Great Dane on a leash, dragging us down the grimmest of streets, especially that last one where we thought we'd never venture.

Doomed *is* the word.

"At least I'm here," I told my mother, taking her boney hand in mine, "and not in Timbuktu." That was where she always swore I'd be at this moment. A few months earlier I had moved back to New Orleans from Madrid after my mother had been rushed to the hospital for the third time in two weeks. Whole pages in her address book were devoted to my exotic whereabouts "away at sea," each neatly scratched out.

"Like you say, we all have to die sometime." The Great Dane's leash had broken, and she looked up at me, apparently amazed at where she was.

I broke down. "When you get to the other side, send me a sign, a purple flower. . . ."

"Even if it's from hell?" she rasped, a smile playing across her face.

"Just know that I love you."

"Have you always?" She cocked an eyebrow.

As members of a Southern family well rehearsed in historic denial, she and I had never discussed for one moment her committing me to the mental hospital in 1968, my ambiguous sexuality, or why I left New Orleans for thirty years. Beyond mother and son, what we'd become over the years was friends, there to support, not to disturb each other. And so despite our torturous history, I told her the truth, speaking not only as myself but as her resurrected brother, her father with his diamond question mark, and the man she'd helped me to become.

"Always."

She squeezed my hand, as if she understood all that was said and left unsaid: the unspoken.

Meanwhile my stormy sister was speed-walking the corridors, grilling everybody in a uniform she could buttonhole about our mother's prognosis. Dying must be somebody's fault, and my sister was going to get to the bottom of it. Occasionally she would burst red-faced into the room, ranting about upping the doses or lowering the doses because this stupid doctor says this and that stupid doctor says that.

Mother would just turn her face and sigh.

"Honey, I'm just not up to all this commotion," she confided to me, barely audible. Graciousness has its limits, and the deathbed may be one of them.

"Look," I said, "they're going to kick us off the ward at nine. I'm going home, and your dutiful daughter says she'll get a room in the hospital hotel to be near you."

"Tell her I won't pay for it." Mother pursed her lips. They call it Creole thrift, and hers was intact until the end.

And those were the last words my mother ever spoke to me, except for a mysterious comment she made as I was leaving the room. "It's so crowded in here," she marveled in a little girl's voice. Nobody else was in the room. What she saw were spirits coming to take her home, her own mother, perhaps, holding out a tiny lavender windbreaker: *Hurry up, Helen Alice, it's time to go.*

She passed that morning at six. My sister, who spent the night on a sofa in the hospital lobby, claims she was with her, but I'm afraid her presence was less palpable than the soothing shapes my mother witnessed filling her room like vapor.

It's time, Helen Alice.

Death does leave a carcass, and all you can do with it is to make soup. Don't waste your grief: use it to add flavor to your living. And after three hours, the turkey stock should be ready. Let it cool, then pour the contents from one pot into another through a colander, draining out bones, bits of flesh, vegetables, and spices, those earthly remains. The pure, milky broth is the essence, separated by fire from the residue: what continues, and what does not. Throw the boney, melted mash away, and place the stock in the refrigerator overnight.

Try to get some rest. You'll need it for the wake.

On the second day, gather the ingredients around you like old friends: onions, green bell peppers, and peeled celery, diced; a bunch of parsley and a few cloves of garlic, minced; some seasoning ham, cubed; two pounds of okra, sliced; sautéed andouille sausage (any smoked sausage will do); three pounds of chicken thighs and drumsticks, skinned;

a large can of tomatoes; flour and oil. This is a long process, so you had best put on some gospel or blues, and have a beer or glass of wine first, before you start dicing, cubing, mincing, slicing, sautéing, and skinning. Kick up a few dance moves around the kitchen to get started.

My friend Kim Sunée and I thought we would be the first to arrive at Schoen Funeral Home on Canal Street an hour before my mother's wake was to begin. Preparations were in order, and we were burdened with trays of sandwiches and tins of cookies from Winn-Dixie, as well as bottles of wine, liquor, and soft drinks. I was also lugging envelopes of family photographs to display on bulletin boards mounted on pedestals around the rooms, and photo albums to leave open on coffee tables. Soon scores of people would gather not only to mourn a death but to celebrate a life, and if they couldn't remember the stages of that life, I meant to remind them.

Crossed by early evening shadows, the plush parlors were already brimming with purple, lavender, and violet flowers, not only the ones I'd ordered but those sent by friends and family. Anyone who knew my mother knows she loved purple, so the color scheme was a given. Balancing a tray of sandwiches in one hand and a bag of clanking bottles in the other, I was steeling myself for the shock of seeing my mother's body in a casket, for that gut-level acknowledgment both of her fate and my own mortal flight risk. From this I came, to this I shall return, I thought, stepping forward through the gauzy light.

Only I couldn't see past my sister standing in front of the coffin, screaming.

"Look how they botched the job," she screeched without preamble, arms flailing above her head like Medea. "They're just going to have come back down here and embalm her again. And I mean *now*. She didn't look like that."

Of course she didn't, I thought, bracing myself to peer at the rouged, parchment face above the ruffled violet blouse, an old-lady doll tucked inside its box. But now she's dead. Once again, this was somebody's fault, and my sister was going to get to the bottom of it.

A parent's death dredges up whatever lurks in the profundities of our murky souls. Looking around, I was amazed to discover that at the depths of my mine were ham sandwiches and bottles of Beaujolais, old photographs and floral wreaths. And at the core of my Vesuvian sister was what I had recognized years ago as a boiling rage, the intractable kind that you give up trying to understand and just want to get away from.

Send her to a therapist? Sorry, but she *is* a therapist.

So I did the only thing I knew how to do. I sicced my sister on the undertaker—a mousey man with a stutter who launched into a rambling monologue about fluids—and started to redecorate. I shifted flowers, arranged bulletin boards, positioned the harpist, set up a bar, and spread out the food in a separate room with a Mr. Coffee that the morticians called "the kitchen," far out of earshot of my sister.

Speaking of things that boil and turn red, let me mention crabs, the only ingredient you may have to kill yourself. The shrimp and oysters are best bought the morning of the third day, when the gumbo is served, and added at the last minute. But one of the first ingredients to be thrown into the simmering stock is the crabs, broken in half. I use two pounds of gumbo crabs, those small Gulf crabs that are pre-cleaned and sold either frozen or submerged in icy vats at seafood shacks. I was raised never to buy a dead crab, and I'm not sure why gumbo crabs merit a special dispensation to this writ of Creole catechism, but they do. If they aren't available where you live, you will have to boil half a dozen live crabs, remove the shells, clean them, break them in two, and just pretend you're in New Orleans.

When you take the turkey stock from the refrigerator, skim off the thick yellow fat congealed on top. When the stock begins to simmer, toss in bay leaves, salt, and a few pinches of cayenne. At this point, you may add the skinned chicken parts to the pot. Remove them when the meat is cooked, cool, debone, chop into chunks, and reserve in the refrigerator for the third day, adding them to the gumbo along with the shrimp and oysters. Chicken cooked too long in gumbo turns stringy, ruining the velvety texture.

Now add the crabs, bring to a boil, and let the pot simmer. Meanwhile, heat cooking oil in a huge skillet, wok, or paella pan, to sauté the garlic with what we call the Holy Trinity: onions, bell pepper, and celery, adding them in that order. Pour yourself another glass of wine or beer, change the music to Aretha or B.B. King, and get ready to work it.

When the onions have cooked clear, add the okra and seasoning ham, stirring, stirring, stirring until the okra becomes gummy. Add three teaspoons of Chef Paul Prudhomme's Seafood Magic or Tony Chachere's

Original Creole Seasoning ("Good on Everything"). Authentic Creole seasoning is a delicate blend, like an Indian curry or Mexican molé, and there's no need to reinvent the wheel, especially when it's already rolling around town.

Into this gooey mixture go several heaping tablespoons of flour, stirring until it turns brown and smells toasty, like a roux. To this add a large can of peeled tomatoes chopped in strips, juice and all, and stir some more, until the mixture begins to bubble. Then scoop out every last bit of this sticky goulash into the simmering pot of turkey broth and crabs. Add slices of smoked sausage, after the sausages first have been pierced with a fork, fried for a few minutes, and drained on paper towels. Bring to a boil, and simmer for several hours, until most of the vegetables have disappeared into the primordial funk of the gumbo.

The mourners have begun to mingle, and the wake is under way.

Before the advent of funeral parlors, the dead used to be laid out on their dining-room tables the night before they were buried, and family, friends, and neighbors gathered around to eat, drink, and mourn. This cannibalistic detail of the dining-room table as the last resting place before the tomb shouldn't be missed. Like food, death draws people together. Dying constantly feeds living so that it produces yet more life, although this may not be the most appealing way to think of a lost loved one or a chicken-salad sandwich. In their ritual preparations of flesh, morticians have much in common with cooks.

Once mortuaries replaced private homes as the site of the wake, New Orleans funeral parlors had bedrooms upstairs where bereaved families camped out all night, stumbling up and down the stairs to tearfully greet visitors. These days few families spend the whole night, although the funeral director invited us to use the facilities as we wanted, noting some families even bring in Cajun bands. But now families seldom even have wakes but only spooky-sounding visitations the morning before the funeral. I made the undertaker scratch out the word "visitation" and insert "wake" in the obituary he was preparing for the *Times-Picayune*. My mother had prepaid her funeral, insisting on a real wake with food, booze, music, and lots of people. She'd also given me the model number of the lavender-lined oak coffin she picked out so that the funeral home didn't pull a fast one on her.

"Sometimes they substitute one of those cheap ones," she complained, "that look like they're made out of drier lint." The day she went to pick out her coffin, a friend dropped her off and, not wanting to waste money on a taxi, she bummed a ride home in the hearse. "Might as well know what it feels like," she said, "since I won't be around to see what I paid for."

She got her money's worth. Even though we have scant family left in town, my mother's many friends attended, and droves of my own, and it turned out they all knew each other. We say there is only one degree of separation between people in New Orleans, and all evening I was surprised by the unlikeliest combinations. My uptown Jewish writing student greeted my sister's Catholic ex-husband from Cajun country like an old friend: they had worked together in the same law office. At one point, I was standing in a circle of women, some my mother's friends, some mine, who had all acted in the same production of *The Women* at the Gallery Circle Theater in the French Quarter in 1964. My friend Lynn's boyfriend knew my cousin Roy from painting circles across the lake. Marta, the close friend who traveled with my mother in Spain, recognized Antonio, the husband of Mother's housekeeper, from their childhood in Nicaragua.

And those who didn't already know each other soon got to, rather quickly. I realized the wake was a success when I came upon my half-Choctaw uncle from Mississippi, married to my mother's sister, drunkenly pawing Karen, the cousin from the Thanksgiving dinner in the old orphanage, to whom I'm related on my father's side. My uncle then swiveled his gallant attentions and thick black bifocals toward my Korean friend Kim's aunt, an imposing, elderly actress in a mink coat. "One little detail I need to find out," he drawled, taking me aside in the kitchen. "I know she's one of your friends and don't get me wrong, hear. But is she really a woman?"

My mother had visited me only once during the many years I lived in San Francisco, and wasn't familiar with the term "multicultural." But one friend looked around and commented, "She sure had a wide variety of people in her life, know what I mean?" Dressed to the nines, several black staff members from her assisted-living home were perched on settees with their daughters and the Central American interpreters from her hospital job were chatting in Spanish while the drunk half-Choctaw uncle was chasing an actress in a mink coat and my beret-wearing bohemian friends were scarfing down all the sandwiches. The harpist was playing celestial strains of Mozart but all I could think of was Harpo.

During the past year I've heard people refer to each other as "someone I met at your mother's wake." Which brings me back to that aromatic pot of gumbo simmering on the back burner in the kitchen, crab blending with sausage, tomato with okra, turkey with ham. Gumbo began as a poor man's dish: you threw in what you had. Gumbo is the African cook's improvisation on French shellfish bouillabaisse, cooked with Native American seasonings. Out of the death and suffering of whipped slaves, massacred Indians, and French and Spanish settlers, who dropped by the thousands during cholera and yellow-fever epidemics, comes this regal concoction, this creolized tribute to a mixture of bloodlines, languages, and cultures, this culinary wake, thick and dark as the swamps we spring from.

The final touch of the second-day preparation is to make a roux the shade of bayou mud, the color gumbo should resemble. While the gumbo simmers, you must stir it every fifteen minutes to keep the ingredients from sinking and charring at the bottom of the pot. Meanwhile, heat a cup of cooking oil in a cast-iron skillet until it begins to bubble, then slowly blend in two cups of flour over a medium flame. With a wooden spoon stir and stir and stir this mixture in a counterclockwise direction for about twenty minutes, until it has turned thick and dark. You must give your undivided attention to making a roux; involve your whole body and soul. If the telephone rings, let it. While stirring I sway to blues or gospel, often tipsy, lost in reveries, weeping or chuckling at memories, as the rich nut-brown aroma of sautéed flour rises to fill the kitchen. But mourning is never finished: when the mixture turns bayou-colored, turn off the heat, then stir and sway a few minutes more, to keep the hot skillet from scorching the flour.

Then standing back, throw in a bunch of minced parsley. The roux will sizzle and sputter to a standstill, braking at the moment of its perfection. Ladle in broth from the simmering gumbo until you have a paste, then scrape it all into the gumbo pot. Bring to a boil then simmer another half hour or so, stirring regularly and checking the spices.

Cool.

The wake is over. Refrigerate overnight.

After great pain," writes Emily Dickinson, "a formal feeling comes— /
The nerves sit ceremonious, like Tombs—." This is the best description I've ever read of the benumbed formality of a funeral. I recalled these
lines the next day as my "Feet, mechanical" went round, greeting guests,
organizing pallbearers, choosing music, making sure the organist, singer,
and minister were cued and positioned, that everyone sat in the right pew
and stepped into the right limousine, that certain flower arrangements
were taken, or not taken, to the cemetery, that everyone received prayer
cards and signed the guestbook and found the bathroom. The minister
intoned his canned homily and we squirmed; the singer belted out "May
the Circle Be Unbroken" and we wept. At some point somebody slipped
me my mother's glasses in their frayed purple case, which I carried in
my pocket all day, and the last photograph ever taken of her, which I lost.

> This is the Hour of Lead—
> Remembered, if outlived,
> As Freezing persons, recollect
> the snow—
> First—Chill—then Stupor—
> then the letting go.

Mourning is the thawing of everything that must be frozen inside to
lumber with any degree of grace through the intricate waltz steps of a
formal goodbye.

Two hours before your guests are to arrive, slowly reheat the pot of
chilled gumbo over a low flame, stirring frequently to keep the heavy
mixture from sticking. Simmer an hour, until the very woodwork is im-
pregnated with its smell. Then just before the gumbo is to be served,
throw in several dozen raw oysters, the chicken chunks, and three pounds
of shrimp, which your first guests can help to peel, rolling up their sleeves
to tell you about who fell down at their own mamas' wakes. Bring to a
boil, then simmer for five minutes. Ladle the gumbo steaming hot into
bowls over small scoops of white rice.

Death makes everybody hungry, so after my mother's burial I gathered with friends for the repast at Mandina's, a classic neighborhood
restaurant across Canal Street from Schoen Funeral Home. My mother

had instructed me not to eat there after her funeral, as we had after my father's and my grandparents'. "It's too noisy," she admonished, "and the string beans are canned."

We didn't order the string beans, and I don't think she minded.

Seated at three tables pulled together, we spooned dark, pungent turtle soup laced with sherry into our mouths, teary-eyed, weary, but oh so alive. The memories of everyone's death we had ever loved melted into that one moment. Mandina's was crowded that afternoon, jam-packed like my mother's hospital room with spirits. But we fed those "hungry ghosts" through spoons rising to our lips, swaying together for a while, until the fried oysters and soft-shelled crabs arrived, then we dug in to feed the living.

Like a well-placed punctuation mark, death further unites those already close, or forever separates those who are not. Several days after the burial, my sister and I were to meet with the lawyer at my mother's assisted-living apartment to sign the succession papers. I arrived early with a few cardboard boxes, planning to begin organizing my mother's belongings. I opened the door to find my sister already in full cry, heaving everything within reach into a supermarket shopping cart parked in the middle of the room. My mother labeled hatboxes, sorted clothes by the season, and alphabetized her files, and for the rest of my life I will wheel around a vision of this tidy lady's possessions being tossed in a roiling heap into a metal shopping cart, as if she were being sent homeless into the universe. I quickly filled a few boxes with what I planned to take, then disappeared down the corridor. My sister came charging after. Finally she had gotten to the bottom of dying and death. No stupid doctors or undertakers were left to blame for her loss: now it was my fault. "I hate your guts," she screamed, doubling over and pumping her fists like a three-year-old in a tantrum.

"After I'm gone you're going to have one heck of a time with that sister of yours," my mother would tell me with a rueful chuckle. She pictured our fate as a common scenario from her downtown childhood: the aging siblings connected at the pocketbook like Siamese twins, living in either side of a shotgun-double, infirm, alone, and cranky, not having spoken a single word to each other in over thirty years. To avoid broken crockery,

I didn't invite my sister to the one-year vigil, although in many families a feud begun during one funeral often ends at another.

At the vigil I placed a framed photograph of my mother behind a votive candle next to where the gumbo was being dished out. I thought of poet Louis Simpson's line about "setting tables for death," the destiny of those of us who don't sail on toward the next horizon, following the sun with mad Columbus, forever "away at sea." Wondering if this were now my fate, to the memorial table I added three Bartlett pears as an offering, unsure if spirits liked fooling with gumbo. Guests brought lavender tulips and purple orchids to fill vases around the photograph, and from this perch Mother presided as the guest of honor, finally more out of the tomb than in it.

In New Orleans the whitewashed tombs are designed like little brick houses with steps, porches, alcoves, and slanted roofs, and cemeteries are laid out like cities of the dead. Newborns with just-opened eyes are photographed in their beaming mother's arms in front of the family's little houses, just so the babies know where they come from, and where they're headed. A marble tablet bolted in place, inscribed with names and dates, serves as a door to the shelves on which the coffins rest. As a boy, I was fascinated by our dollhouse of the dead, and in tracing the weathered lineage of names, engraved with dates preceded by *né* and *décédé*, back to the immigrant French great-great-grandfather who purchased the tomb in the 1880s. Although I'm the last in the family to still speak Creole or what I call "kitchen French" (which is where I learned it), I've continued the *né* and *décédé* tradition with the inscriptions. To my ear, my mother is not exactly deceased. She is *décédée*, which, like an honorary degree, confers many more privileges.

To complicate the matter, through marriage many families have several such tombs. I'm not sure why, but these tombs inevitably pop up in conversation when we're eating boiled seafood. Whenever a pile of crab shells, shrimp peels, and crawfish heads began to mount on top of newspaper obituary pages spread across our kitchen table, that was when our family hashed out "who wanted to be with who," swilling beer and gesturing our allegiances with sticky, seafood-smelling fingers. My mother wanted to be with her family in the French tomb, my father with his in the Irish tomb. "Does this separate tomb arrangement mean you two will be divorced in heaven?" I once wondered out loud. I wanted to be with my mother, usually because I'd just argued with my father about some explosive topic such as who really owns the Panama Canal. My grandfather insisted he didn't want to be in the French tomb if his sister-in-law Mercedez were buried there. "The way that woman yaks," he'd say, "I'll never have any peace."

Tombs are not engraved immediately after a burial. The dead are not quite gone yet but still linger on the tomb's shallow marble porch, putting on their jackets and saying their Creole goodbyes. The last image I have of my mother comes in a dream, eight months after her death. She has moved to a ramshackle shed on a barrier island off the Pacific Coast, facing west. Isolated on the windy rim of the world, the one-room cabin is painted a dull red. She is seated in an aluminum patio chair on the wooden back porch overlooking the pounding surf, the pink plastic kerchief she wore to protect her hairdo knotted fifties-style under her chin, her tiny body calm and accepting as she stares straight ahead into the tremendous force of sunlight and sea spray surrounding her. Then in a flash, she has passed, every hair in place.

On an overcast January afternoon the day after the gumbo vigil, I brought the lavender tulips and the purple orchids to the tomb where my mother's names and dates had been inscribed since All Saints Day. After placing the flowers on the tomb, I joined my friend Joanna Côté at nearby Café Degas for a cup of coffee. I felt a year of obligations sliding from my shoulders, as if I'd been pallbearing the weight of that oaken coffin all year. I was ready to put it down. Suddenly a friend of Joanna's burst through the café doors and exclaimed, "I just buried my mama. And you know something? She directed the whole thing."

"I don't know your name," I told the woman, "but sit down. We've got to talk. I just left the cemetery, and today is one year and a day since I buried mine."

We locked eyes and exchanged stories, both convinced that our mothers, looking down, had been in charge of their wakes and funerals. Joanna's friend liked my idea of the gumbo vigil, and promised to try it for her mother's one-year anniversary.

"Did you use your mother's recipe?" she asked me.

"No, my grandmother's."

"Bet your mama is jealous." She flashed me a wink, sure of a set-to inside our tomb.

"You know, my mother never really made gumbo. She always said it was too much trouble." I stared down at fingers still redolent of garlic, shrimp, and cayenne. That familiar kitchen smell, almost impossible to scrub away, was all I had left of the year my mother passed.

ACKNOWLEDGMENTS

I would like to acknowledge the encouragement and support of Richard Burgin, editor of *Boulevard* magazine, in which fourteen of these memoirs were originally published. I also would like to thank artist Steven Kenny, several of whose works graced the covers of the *Boulevard* issues in which these chapters first appeared, for permission to use his painting *Perch III* as a cover image for this book. I appreciate the collaboration of several friends who worked with me on various aspects of the book's production: Kathleen Grieshaber and Becky Betancourt in technical graphic assistance; lawyer Maurice Ruffin in legal counsel regarding permissions; and Carolyn Perry in proofreading.

I owe many thanks to Craig Gill, my efficient editor at the University Press of Mississippi, for his careful attentions to my manuscript during the stages of its consideration and growth into a book; to copy editor Will Rigby for his expert corrections and revisions; to book designer Pete Halverson for the beautiful cover image and text design; to managing editor Shane Gong Stewart for shepherding this book through the publication process; and to marketing director Steve Yates, who is spearheading its promotion. In short, kudos to the publishing team in Jackson.

Grateful acknowledgment is made to the following magazines, newspapers, and anthologies in which these chapters were previously published:

Boulevard: Sixty-Eight; A Fanatic Heart; The Diamond Question Mark; Stairway to Paradise; The Garden of Eden; What Was Behind the Green Door; Scene of the Crime: A Love Story; First Morning; I'll Be Watching You; Cinderella Sweeping Up on Desolation Row; Black and White, with

Brown Water All Over; Hope Chest; Alone in the Urban Museum; The Middle of Nowhere

The Gastronomica Reader, ed. Darra Goldstein (University of California Press, 2010): One Year and a Day: A Recipe for Gumbo and Mourning

North American Review: Parchment and Laptop

St. Petersburg Times: The Open Road

Washington Post: Our Hell in High Water

The following chapters appeared in the collection *Fumadores en manos de un dios enfurecido: Ensayos a caballo entre varios mundos*, translated into Spanish by María Gomis, prologue by Eduardo Lago (Madrid: Enigma Editores, 2005): The Open Road; First Morning; Hope Chest; Alone in the Urban Museum; Parchment and Laptop.